D1551515

RURAL AND SMALL PUBLIC LIBRARIES: CHALLENGES AND OPPORTUNITIES

ADVANCES IN LIBRARIANSHIP

RURAL AND SMALL PUBLIC LIBRARIES: CHALLENGES AND OPPORTUNITIES

Edited by: Brian Real

Advances in Librarianship Volume 43

Advances in Librarianship Editors

Paul T. Jaeger, University of Maryland, Series Editor
Caitlin Hesser, University of Maryland, Series Managing Editor

Advances in Librarianship Editorial Board
Denise E. Agosto, Drexel University
Wade Bishop, University of Tennessee, Knoxville
John Buschman, Seton Hall University
Michelle Caswell, University of California, Los Angeles
Sandra Hughes-Hassell, University of North Carolina, Chapel Hill
R. David Lankes, University of South Carolina
Don Latham, Florida State University
Ricardo L. Punzalan, University of Maryland
Lynn Westbrook, University of Texas

ADVANCES IN LIBRARIANSHIP   VOLUME 43

RURAL AND SMALL PUBLIC LIBRARIES: CHALLENGES AND OPPORTUNITIES

EDITED BY

BRIAN REAL

Public Services Librarian, Calvert Library,
Prince Frederick, MD, USA

United Kingdom – North America – Japan
India – Malaysia – China

Emerald Publishing Limited
Howard House, Wagon Lane, Bingley BD16 1WA, UK

First edition 2018

British Library Cataloguing in Publication Data
A catalogue record for this book is available from the British Library

ISBN: 978-1-78743-112-6 (Print)
ISBN: 978-1-78743-111-9 (Online)
ISBN: 978-1-78743-253-6 (Epub)

ISSN: 0065-2830 (Series)

ISOQAR certified
Management System,
awarded to Emerald
for adherence to
Environmental
standard
ISO 14001:2004.

Certificate Number 1985
ISO 14001

INVESTOR IN PEOPLE

EDITOR'S DEDICATION

I have learned basically everything I know about public libraries through two major parts of my life: my work as a Public Services Librarian with the Calvert Library, a rural public library system in southern Maryland, and my work as a research associate on the Digital Inclusion Survey at the Information Policy and Access Center (iPAC) at the University of Maryland's iSchool. This book is dedicated to my colleagues at both organizations—and especially Professor John Carlo Bertot of iPAC—as I would not have the knowledge or skills needed to oversee this volume without them.

I would also like to acknowledge my wife, Dr. Sarah Cantor, whose love and support has been essential in guiding me through writer's block and other crises, both major and minor.

CONTENTS

ABOUT THE CONTRIBUTORS

Bobbie Bischoff <starnebj@email.sc.edu>, University of South Carolina, is a doctoral student in the School of Library and Information Science at the University of South Carolina. Bobbie has earned an AGS in history from Brazosport College (TX), a bachelor's in interdisciplinary studies from the USC–Lancaster, and an MLIS from USC–Columbia. She has extensive experience as a teacher-librarian in Charleston County and has also worked as a mechanical engineering technician in the Nuclear Power Industry and as an aquatics director at Leroy Springs Recreation Complex. Her research interests are at the intersection of archives (as a memory institution), management of the record, the cultural pursuit of knowledge to facilitate memory, and the transmission of memory within the material culture. In addition to her work as an aquatics instructor, she developed and taught numerous professional development courses in Charleston County School District and was an adjunct instructor at Charleston Southern University, where she developed and taught the first Web-based technology course.

Bradley Wade Bishop <bbisho13@utk.edu>, University of Tennessee, is an associate professor in the School of Information Sciences at the University of Tennessee. Bishop's research focus is on geographic information (GI) organization, access, and use, and his educational focus is on bolstering the curation, preservation, and metadata creation of GI. He has published several articles utilizing GI systems as a tool in the analysis of public libraries. He has published works related to public libraries in *Library and Information Science Research*, *Public Libraries*, *Public Library Quarterly*, *Government Information Quarterly*, *Library Quarterly*, *Library Trends*, *Journal of the American Society for Information Science and Technology*, *Journal of Education for Library and Information Science*, *College and Research Libraries*, and *Portal: Libraries and the Academy*.

Natasha Hollenbach <nhollenb@utk.edu>, University of Tennessee, is a recent graduate from the master's program in the School of Information Sciences at the University of Tennessee. Hollenbach was a student assistant hired to conduct action research with rural libraries in the Southern and Central Appalachian region.

ix

Jennifer L. Jenkins <jenkinsj@email.arizona.edu>, University of Arizona, is a professor of English at the University of Arizona. Jenkins teaches film history and theory, literature, and archival practice at the University of Arizona. She is the founder of Home Movie Day Tucson and regularly lays student hands on film of many gauges. She is the outgoing director of the Northeast Historic Film Summer Symposium. Since 2011, she has been Curator of the American Indian Film Gallery, a digital humanities project that seeks inclusive repurposing of mid-century films about Native peoples of the Americas. In a process termed "tribesourcing," we invite Native narrators to record new audio files for the films in indigenous or/and European languages to provide culturally competent counter-narratives to the films, thereby expanding access and enriching the collection's information base. In 2017, this project was awarded funding by the National Endowment for the Humanities.

Bharat Mehra <bmehra@utk.edu>, University of Tennessee, is an associate professor in the School of Information Sciences at the University of Tennessee. Mehra's research examines diversity and intercultural communication, social justice in library and information science, critical and cross-cultural studies, and community informatics or the use of information and communication technologies to empower minority and underserved populations to make meaningful changes in their everyday lives. Mehra has collaborated with racial/ethnic groups, international communities, sexual minorities, rural librarians, and small businesses to represent their experiences and perspectives in shaping the design and development of community-based information systems and services. He primarily teaches courses on public library management, collection development, resources and services for adults, diversity services in libraries, and grant development for information professionals.

Karen Miller <millerk8@email.sc.edu>, University of South Carolina, is a doctoral candidate in the School of Library and Information Science at the University of South Carolina. Karen's work as a graduate assistant for the IMLS-funded Assessing the Economic Value of Public Library Collections and Services: A Review of the Literature and Meta-Analysis project led to her research interest in the assets of rural public libraries and their potential investment in community development initiatives. A doctoral candidate with a cognate in statistical analysis, Karen is currently writing her dissertation. In addition to her MLIS degree from the University of South Carolina, Karen also holds a JD from the University of South Carolina School of Law and an MBA from a joint Furman University/Clemson University program.

Robert P. Partee II <rpartee12@utk.edu>, University of Tennessee, is a recent graduate from the master's program in the School of Information Sciences at the University of Tennessee. Partee II was a student assistant hired to conduct action research with rural libraries in Tennessee. He completed his bachelor's degree in chemistry with a minor in biology and a pre-medicine focus. While working on his graduate degree at the University of Tennessee, Partee II focused on team science and participated in collaborative efforts to address scientific challenges that leveraged the expertise of professionals trained in different fields. Partee II has plans to pursue a career in medicine either as a scientist or a practicing physician.

Herman A. Peterson <hpeterson@dinecollege.edu>, Diné College, is college librarian at Diné College, the tribal college for the Navajo Nation, where he supervises three libraries in two different states. Formerly he worked as the Head of Reference and Instruction and Associate Professor at Morris Library of Southern Illinois University in Carbondale, IL. Dr. Peterson is the author of *The Trail of Tears: An Annotated Bibliography of Southeastern Indian Removal* as well as several articles, conference presentations, and over 50 book reviews.

Claire Petri <clairepetri@gmail.com>, York County Libraries, is the coordinator of the Salem Square Library, York County Libraries, York, PA. She coordinates services and programming for children and adults, including one-on-one computer and Internet assistance to the many local residents who have limited technology access at home. She also coordinates partnerships with local agencies and nonprofits to offer workforce development opportunities, job search support, and ESL classes. Claire's career and education have focused on the power of libraries and librarians to connect people of all backgrounds with resources that will empower them to transform their lives and communities. She holds a master's degree in Library and Information Science from the University of Maryland, where she specialized in Diversity and Inclusion.

Kari Quiballo <Kariqui@email.arizona.edu>, University of Arizona, is a doctoral candidate in the American Indian Studies program at the University of Arizona. She is currently working as a Research Assistant in the UA James E. Rogers College of Law and at the Native Nations Institute (NNI) on the U.S. Indigenous Data Sovereignty Network (USIDSN). Quiballo's research examines epistemic injustice in nontribal archives, libraries, and museums (ALM), resulting from a lack of knowledge American Indian law and policy and legal identity within U.S. law of ALM professionals. Quiballo's master's degree is from the UA School of Information. She is a Knowledge River Scholar (KR), which is a singular scholarship program at UA focusing on American Indigenous information issues. While a KR scholar, her research focused on the commodification of information and the resulting privatization and commercialization in ALM. Her work has also concentrated on the control non-Native-run institutions have over Indigenous cultural information and identity.

Guillermo Quiroga <opmuseum@icloud.com>, Old Pascua Museum and Yaqui Culture Center, is the director of the Old Pascua Museum and Yaqui Culture Center and Pascua Yaqui Tribal member. He has over 25 years of executive administration experience in the educational, nonprofit, and profit sectors. He is a graduate of the University of California with a degree in sociology and earned a Master of Business Administration from the University of Arizona, where he is an Alumni Achievement awardee. He has over 15 years of experience as an entrepreneur with a focus on Nation Building while President and CEO of Native American Botanics, Inc. He has lectured, mentored, and taught other start-ups, as well as executive-level entrepreneurs. He created problem-solving curriculum for elementary, middle, high school, and community college educators while directing programs at the UA Eller College McGuire Entrepreneurship program. He successfully authored several small business innovations research (SBIR) grants and other federal, state, local, and private grants totaling over $8 million.

Brian Real <breal@umd.edu>, Calvert Library, is a public services librarian for the Calvert Library, a public library system in rural southern Maryland. He holds a Master of Library Science (2011) and PhD in Information Studies (2015) from the University of Maryland, where he currently teaches graduate courses in public libraries and reference services. During his graduate studies, Brian worked under Dr. John Carlo Bertot on several cycles of the Digital Inclusion Survey, a national-level study of how public libraries use information and communication technologies to benefit their local communities. He is the author of numerous academic journal articles on public libraries and film archives for venues including *Library Quarterly*, *Public Library Quarterly*, and *The Moving Image*. Brian served as the lead author of the report *Rural Libraries in the United States: Recent Strides, Future Possibilities, and Meeting Community Needs*, which was published by the American Library Association in summer 2017.

R. Norman Rose <norman.rose@gmail.com>, Wagner School of Public Service, is a graduate of NYU's Wagner School of Public Service. He is a veteran of wrangling messy data sets, planning and managing surveys, conducting data visualization, and writing. He has worked for the City of New York and for the American Library Association on the Public Library Funding and Technology Access Study and Digital Inclusion Survey. He also founded and continues to manage the popular SB Nation sports site Rumble in the Garden. Currently in New York State, he develops professional development workshops for public service workers.

Vandana Singh <vandana@utk.edu>, University of Tennessee, is an associate professor in the School of Information Sciences at the University of Tennessee. Singh's research interest areas are the use of information technology for learning in work places as well in distance education, computer supported cooperative work, human computer interaction, and information systems. Singh has received multiple research grants from federal agencies, including the National Science Foundation, Institute of Museum and Library Services, and United States Geological Society. Her work has been published and recognized in several national and international conferences and journals.

Rhiannon Sorrell <rsorrell@dinecollege.edu>, Diné College, is an instructor and digital services librarian at Diné College in Tsaile, Arizona, on the Navajo Nation. Born to Kinłichíí'nii (Red House People) and Ta'neezahnii (Tangle People) Clans, Rhiannon has an interdisciplinary background in English and Information Literacy instruction, creative nonfiction, special collections and archival services, and Web and user experience design. Rhiannon's current research interests include incorporating traditional knowledge systems in information literacy, STEM in the Tribal College Library, and alternative forms of Native nonfiction.

Travis L. Wagner <wagnertl@email.sc.edu>, University of South Carolina, is a doctoral student in the School of Library and Information Sciences at the University of South Carolina. Travis also received a Graduate Certificate in Women's and Gender Studies from USC's Department of Women's and Gender Studies, where they continue to serve as a lecturer. Their major research area focuses on the role socially constructed identities play within the information organization practices of visual image catalogers, with particular focus on representations of diverse gender identities. Some other research areas for Travis include a re-examination of and advocacy for overlooked visual media, incorporating service learning into SLIS classrooms, and the deployment of queer theoretical interventions into knowledge management practices. Travis also spends time working closely with multiple community archives within Columbia, South Carolina, helping organizations create cost-effective strategies for the digital preservation of archival content.

EDITORS' INTRODUCTION TO THE *ADVANCES IN LIBRARIANSHIP* SERIES

Through a combination of economic changes, political forces, and technological changes, libraries now find themselves in a position of meeting ever-increasing community needs and filling roles that otherwise would go unmet in key areas of economic and workforce development, health and wellness, education, civic engagement, and fostering and supporting open governments, among much else. Despite often decreasing financial support, the growing political pressures to reduce support for public goods such as libraries, and the voices claiming that Google has made libraries obsolete, libraries of all types—public, school, academic, and special—have never been more innovative, more community focused, and more in demand than they are now.

Libraries play significant roles in digital literacy and digital inclusion, online education, provision of social services, employment skills, and even emergency response. They are creating partnerships with local government agencies and nonprofits to address local needs. They adopt and innovate with new technologies and expand their services and materials through new channels provided by emerging technologies, from online reference to the curation and management of digital resources. At the same time, libraries serve as a primary support structure for social justice and human rights by fostering and promoting inclusion, access, and equity for individuals, for their communities, and for society as a whole.

The *Advances in Librarianship* book series offers a completely unique avenue through which these major issues can be discussed. By devoting each volume—often in the range of 100,000 words—to a single topic of librarianship, the series volumes devote a great amount of consideration to a single topic. By including contributors who are library professionals, administrators, researchers, and educators from many different places, the series volumes bring an unparalleled range of voices to these topics of librarianship. And by exploring these topics as broad issues with a wide range of societal impacts, these volumes not only inform those within the library profession, they inform community members, policymakers, educators, employers, health information professionals, and others outside of libraries who are interested in the impacts of libraries.

The ability to address current and future issues from both practice and research perspectives at great depth makes this series uniquely positioned to disseminate new ideas in libraries and to advocate for their essential roles in communities. To ensure the most current and future utility, each volume includes contributions in three areas: (1) current best practices and innovative ideas, (2) future issues and ways in which they might be prepared for and addressed, and (3) the large-scale societal implications and the way in which the focus of the volume impacts libraries as a social institution.

This volume of *Advances in Librarianship* focuses on the importance of rural libraries and community archives to their communities. The majority of communities in the United States are rural, and they frequently have greatly reduced access to many services—from healthcare to broadband—available to urban and suburban communities. Many rural communities do have a library, and these libraries provide innumerable services and contributions to their communities. Yet, in the library and information science professional and academic discourse, rural libraries receive far less attention than seems appropriate given how numerous they are and how central they are to their communities. This volume is intended to help fill that gap, presenting a range of perspectives demonstrating the unique value and impact of rural libraries and community archives in their communities.

Ultimately, volumes in this series share innovative ideas and practices to improve overall library service and to help libraries better articulate their vital and myriad contributions to their communities. The range of library impacts can be seen in the recent volumes in the series, which have explored such important topics as library services to people with disabilities, libraries as institutions of human rights and social justice, and efforts to promote diversity and inclusion in the field. Forthcoming volumes will be devoted to socially innovative programs in libraries, library services for LBGTQ populations, the pedagogical roles of academic libraries, and new approaches to MLIS education. As fewer venues publish materials related to library practice, education, and research and many of the journals formerly devoted to library research have shifted their focus more to information issues, the *Advances in Librarianship* book series is an unwavering venue devoted to documenting, examining, exchanging, and advancing library practice, education, and research.

Paul T. Jaeger, *Advances in Librarianship* Series Editor
Caitlin Hesser, *Advances in Librarianship* Managing Editor
University of Maryland

INTRODUCTION: RURAL PUBLIC LIBRARIES IN ACADEMIC AND POLITICAL CONTEXTS

Brian Real

Perhaps the most famous public library building in the United States is the main location of the New York Public Library (NYPL), which has expanded to nearly 650,000 square feet since its opening in 1911. Its iconic marble lion statues were re-christened Patience and Fortitude during the Great Depression by Mayor Fiorello La Guardia (New York Public Library, 2011). As iconic as the NYPL may be, 6,408 of the United States' 16,695 public library buildings serve areas with populations of 2,500 or fewer people and possess a median of 1.9 full-time equivalent employees (Real & Rose, 2017). Rural library buildings average just 2,592 square feet, which is slightly smaller than a typical single-family home built within the United States (Perry, 2016). However, while not as physically imposing as the NYPL, the positive influences that these rural libraries have on the lives of their patrons each year are just as impressive.

Rural libraries offer free broadband access, inclusive of computer terminals and staff assistance in using the Internet, in parts of the country that have the lowest broadband adoption rates (Federal Communications Commission, 2016). The availability of these technology resources is invaluable, as rural areas continue to face employment stagnation, many companies

Rural and Small Public Libraries: Challenges and Opportunities
Advances in Librarianship, Volume 43, 1–11
Copyright © 2018 by Emerald Publishing Limited
All rights of reproduction in any form reserved
ISSN: 0065-2830/doi:10.1108/S0065-283020170000043001

now only allow job applications to be filled out online, and employers are increasingly searching for candidates with at least basic computer skills. These libraries act as a free educational resource as rural America continues to have the lowest educational attainment rates (United States Department of Agriculture, 2017). Rural parts of the country have the fewest physicians per capita (Weigel, Ullrich, Shane, & Mueller, 2016), but rural libraries can at least help patrons search for health information. Any list of the challenges that rural America faces can be met with a discussion of how rural public libraries and librarians actively work to mitigate these issues.

This volume, *Rural Public Libraries: Challenges and Opportunities*, presents data that show just how much rural public libraries do for their communities. As most of the authors of the chapters that follow are academics, I first address the historic and current relationship between academia and rural libraries. This is followed by a brief overview of each chapter, including how they relate to each other and their practical implications for rural librarians. Finally, I conclude by acknowledging the modern political climate that currently surrounds rural America and rural libraries. The current state of affairs presents an opportunity for rural libraries to show their value and obtain greater support, as more attention is being paid now than in recent decades to the challenges those in rural parts of the country face. Rural public librarians are already going above and beyond to benefit their communities, and any additional support will allow them to go even further.

I. THE RECENT STATE OF SCHOLARSHIP ON RURAL PUBLIC LIBRARIES

Excellent scholarship is being conducted on rural libraries by scholars in the library and information science (LIS) field. Of particular note are the efforts of Dr. Bharat Mehra of the School of Information at the University of Tennessee–Knoxville, who in recent years has used his research as a means to meet the practical needs of rural libraries and librarians. Two chapters in this book document his and his colleagues' work in this area, and anyone wishing to learn more about how academics can do more to help rural and small libraries would be well served by delving further into his published research.

Likewise, the recently published book *Small Libraries, Big Impact: How to Better Serve Your Community in the Digital Age*, by Dr. Yunfei Du (2016) of the University of North Texas, provides a broad overview of the specific needs of rural libraries. The book includes a particularly good chapter at the end on library assessment, including how librarians can assess the needs of their communities and measure the impacts of their libraries. While outside of the direct scope of the public library literature, a book published in 2016 called *The Small and Rural Academic Library: Leveraging Resources and Overcoming Limitations* should be of value to any librarian working in areas that face geographic and economic challenges. The volume is tightly edited by two academic librarians, Kaetrena Davis Kendrick and Deborah Tritt, and features a wealth of practical and actionable advice to overcome resource limitations from their colleagues throughout the field (Kendrick & Tritt, 2016).

This is only a sampling of recent research on rural libraries, and considerably more is cited and discussed throughout the chapters that follow. Any oversights leading to the exclusion of significant portions of the research in this area should be considered the fault of the editor of this volume. Despite the good work already being published, however, there is much more that can and should be done in this area. Academics need to take a leadership role in conducting research that can be used to positive effect by rural librarians, their funders, and their allies. We also need to work with rural library practitioners to help them share information that can be used by their peers in other locations, regardless of whether this is through publication or other means.

When compared to a decade ago, the library and information science corner of academia has fallen behind where we were in terms of advocating for rural librarianship. Much of the most important work in this area was overseen by Dr. Bernard Vavrek of Clarion University, who was a faculty member from 1971 through 2008. He founded the Center for the Study of Rural Librarianship (CSRL) in 1978, which continued operation until shortly after his retirement. Despite Vavrek's departure and the closure of CSRL, Clarion does still make a serious effort to reach out to librarians in less populous areas and regularly offers a course on rural librarianship.

Vavrek and CSRL were responsible for a wealth of activities that were supported by partnerships between scholars and rural librarians, including numerous research projects, conferences, and symposia (Glotfelty, 2017). Perhaps their most significant contribution to the field, however, was providing organizational support that led to the founding of both the Association for Rural and Small Libraries (ARSL) and the Association of Bookmobile and Outreach Services. Both highly active organizations continue to operate as the primary professional organizations for their respective, but related, fields. CSRL also published the academic journals *Rural Libraries* from 1980 through 2008 and *Bookmobile and Outreach Services* from 1998 through 2008.

At present, however, academics in the LIS field are not doing enough to show librarians—in rural areas or otherwise—that we actually care about their work and their needs. This is perhaps too broad of a statement, but one of the key indicators of a disconnect is ARSL's 2016 call for presentations for its annual conference, which stated that it "is not the proper venue for post-graduate dissertations or marketing products" (Association for Rural and Small Libraries, 2016). The fact that an organization that was started with the support of an academic research center and that previously co-published an academic journal is now lumping academics together with people who are trying to sell them something is a problem. Knowing some of the people from ARSL personally, I can confidently say that this should not be taken as a blanket statement without nuance, but there is hesitancy to trust some academics to produce work that has practical implications for rural librarians. LIS academic programs do not have a right to a constituency, and rural librarians are not required to see value in research activities or graduate education programs. The burden of proof for this rests solely on those of us in the academic community, and the authors in this volume have made an earnest effort to meet this.

The chapters that follow include rigorous academic research, including in-depth and complex statistical analysis. However, the authors have attempted to make their work accessible, never losing track of the practical implications of our research. Our intention is for these findings to be useful for those working in the field, whether for direct application in libraries or for broader advocacy purposes. None of the chapters should be the final word on what they present, but should instead act as a foundation for further scholarship that can show the practical value of LIS research.

II. CHAPTER LAYOUT AND CONTENTS

The first chapter of this volume, Claire Petri's "Rural Libraries and the Human Right to Internet Access," argues that access to certain forms of information to which people are considered to have a right, including government information that allows one to fully engage in a democracy, can only be fully and efficiently accessed through the Internet. If the Internet is essential to exercising one's rights, then it can be said that the Internet, in itself, is a right. Considering that rights are only meaningful if they are extended to all people in a society, government intervention to diminish the impacts of geographic and economic barriers to broadband deployment and Internet access in rural areas is not just a means to increase rural residents' quality of life, but is also an act of social justice.

This is followed by a chapter I co-wrote with Norman Rose, "Rural Public Libraries in America: Continuing and Impending Challenges," on broad national trends for rural public libraries. The first half of the chapter uses data from both the Institute of Museum and Library Services' (IMLS) Public Libraries in the United States Survey and the Digital Inclusion Survey, the latter of which I worked on under Dr. John Carlo Bertot at the University of Maryland's Information Policy and Access Center. Norman and I split the data from these studies in a manner that shows a more nuanced understanding of rurality, delineating how trends across libraries change as they are farther from population centers. What we found was that rural libraries near the fringes of population centers have more resources than those that can be described as "distant" or "remote." This three-tier breakdown provides a better understanding of what types of libraries must be targeted to address the needs of rural residents than previous statistical analyses, which have most often grouped all rural libraries together.

While the first half of this analysis primarily focuses on technological issues, the second half moves on to look at obstacles that are caused by organization structures that do not facilitate resource sharing, as well as small and aging buildings. These long-term problems will be exacerbated as it becomes more cost prohibitive to purchase increasingly in-demand digital resources without consortia in place and as the public library field's increased focus on public programming leaves behind locations without adequate physical infrastructure. Statistical data for the analysis of these issues are combined with information gathered from conversations with Becky Heil and Andrea Berstler, library professionals in Iowa and Maryland, respectively, who are both past presidents of ARSL. The end result does not lead to a simple, silver bullet solution to some of the primary challenges rural public libraries will face in the coming years, but we define the problems and begin the discussion about next steps.

This leads into "Exploring Rural Public Library Assets for Asset-Based Community Development (ABCD)," by Karen Miller of the University of South Carolina. The first portion of this text includes a discussion of the ABCD framework developed by John Kretzmann and John McKnight of the Center for Urban Affairs and Policy Research at Northwestern University. Under this model, communities can improve the quality of life for local residents by first focusing on what assets they already possess and then combining these with other local assets to allow for a multiplier effect in terms of positive impact. Miller argues that computer terminals, well-trained and helpful staff, information resources, and other library offerings constitute such assets.

Miller follows this with some of the most in-depth statistical analysis of the state of rural libraries available. Using the fringe, distant, and remote coding, she looks at significant factors that determine what assets libraries have to offer their communities. This includes considering government funding assistance and how it allows libraries in some parts of the country to do more for their patrons, regional trends in the number of librarians who hold a Master of Library Science (MLIS), average numbers of computer terminals and how these meet patron needs, and more. Miller combines her statistical analysis with discussions of the practical implications of her findings, making suggestions as to what librarians, governments and other funding bodies, and those of us in the academic community can do to help close service gaps between libraries in different parts of the United States.

"A Gap Analysis of the Perspectives of Small Businesses and Rural Librarians in Tennessee: Developments Towards a Blueprint for a Public Library Small Business Toolkit" by Dr. Bharat Mehra, Dr. Bradley Wade Bishop, and Robert P. Partee II of the University of Tennessee–Knoxville acts as an appropriate follow-up to Miller's research by analyzing library resources as potential assets for small businesses. Through short interviews with librarians and small business operators throughout the Appalachian region, the research team found that there is a significant amount of crosstalk between these two groups. Rural librarians have certain expectations of what types of information small business owners need. The actual information needs of small business operators often differs from these expectations, and business operators are often unaware of the library as a potential source for informational guidance in general. The practical implications of this research are clear, not only providing a framework that the authors intend to use in development of a small business toolkit and suggested outreach actions for rural public libraries, but also putting forth a research model that can be emulated to better understand relationships between libraries and other potential user groups.

Research from the University of Tennessee–Knoxville's School of Information Sciences continues in the next chapter, "Rural Librarians as Change Agents in the 21st Century: Applying Community Informatics in the Southern and Central Appalachian Region to Further ICT Literacy Training," by Dr. Bharat Mehra, Dr. Vandana Singh, Natasha Hollenbach, and Robert P. Partee II. Using federal grant funding from IMLS, Mehra and his team developed an MLIS program that specifically targeted professionals already working in rural Appalachian libraries. As discussed at various points in this volume, the majority of rural librarians do not hold a MLIS, so targeting individuals already working in the field allowed persons who had already shown their dedication to the profession to expand their skill sets and better serve their communities. The research team worked with an advisory board of professionals in the field to initially shape the curriculum, and students were expected to complete projects in their courses that could then be used in their own libraries. As the full findings discussed in the chapter demonstrate, the end result is a highly practical MLIS program that can serve as a model for academics in the field. This is the case regardless of whether some of the concepts are adopted into MLIS programs or integrated into non-credit-bearing continuing education programs.

This is followed by research on the preservation and promotion of rural cultural heritage in "Defining Community Archives within Rural South Carolina," by Travis L. Wagner and Bobbie Bischoff of the University of South Carolina. Through interviews with representatives from nine different cultural heritage organizations throughout rural South Carolina, the authors show how local culture is often preserved and promoted in informal ways that often do not fully align with proper archival and museological practices. Rather than suggesting that these practices need to be changed or improved, Wagner and Bischoff probe the reasons for these variations from rigorous professional norms and find that they are often rooted from necessity and a desire to better connect with local communities. This is followed by discussions of outside resources that are available to small organizations for the care, preservation, and digitization of their materials, as well as suggestions for how more resources of these types can be developed in the future. This exploration of the archives space is not, by any means, a deviation from this volume's primary focus on rural libraries. Instead, the authors note that several of the collecting institutions they analyzed were founded by being spun off from the activities of rural public libraries and that many of the tools detailed can be used to preserve and promote rural library collections. As public libraries in general move toward a greater focus on public programming, an understanding of how local cultural heritage collections are formed and used will be invaluable for rural librarians who wish to design events that build on the history of their communities.

Jennifer L. Jenkins of the University of Arizona continues to look at cross-over between the archives and rural public libraries in her chapter, "Exhibiting America: Moving Image Archives and Rural or Small Libraries." She begins with a historical analysis of how rural libraries historically used small-gauge motion picture films to educate and entertain their publics. This included circulating these materials via bookmobiles and setting up makeshift screenings in remote areas that lacked access to theatres and other forms of visual entertainment. While the advent of video and other distribution means led to the end of these practices and declines in the popularity of small-gauge film, Jenkins argues that there is much that rural public libraries can still do with historic motion pictures. Several regional film archives have begun collecting home movies, amateur productions, educational works, and other materials that document and reflect neglected and forgotten elements of local culture. Jenkins discusses how some of these archives have successfully partnered with rural public libraries to present programs that reinforce the value of local culture and details potential resources that have not yet been tapped by the library community.

This volume then concludes with "Rural and Small Libraries: The Tribal Experience" by Jennifer L. Jenkins, Guillermo Quiroga (Yaqui), Kari Quiballo (Sioux), Dr. Herman A. Peterson (Diné), and Rhiannon Sorrell (Diné). This chapter begins with a brief literature review of research on tribal libraries, followed by interviews with Quiroga, Peterson, and Sorrell about their work in cultural heritage organizations for their respective tribes. The authors argue that tribal libraries and other cultural organizations have traditionally faced geographic and economic restraints that have created barriers to service in ways that parallel challenges faced by rural public libraries throughout the United States, as well as substandard broadband deployment that has hindered digital inclusion. These findings make it clear that as the rural public library community develops advocacy and action plans to overcome these problems, tribal librarians need to be included in the discussion. Likewise, the work of these institutions in preserving and promoting the cultural identities of their communities—even with limited resources—can provide invaluable lessons to rural librarians who wish to develop or expand their own community heritage activities.

III. CONCLUSION: THE STATE OF THE FIELD, CURRENT DISCUSSIONS, AND LOOMING THREATS

To conclude this preface and frame this volume, it seems necessary to acknowledge two recent, major developments in the modern political landscape. The first is that, in the wake of the 2016 presidential election, rural America is getting more press attention. To say that this rhetoric has some questionable elements would be something of an understatement, and fully parsing this out is beyond the scope of this volume. Key among these issues is that the phrase "white working class" has become synonymous in many cases with "rural" (Ehrenfreund & Guo, 2016), although rural America is most certainly not racially homogenous and the working class is not solely the domain of white persons. Perhaps, a less loaded concept is the idea of rural Americans being "forgotten," as repeated by campaigns and various news outlets (Przybyla, 2017). It is in this climate of the election that the book *Hillbilly Elegy*, on the lives of rural Americans in the Rust Belt and Appalachian regions, became a bestseller (Rothman, 2016). Put simply, people across the political spectrum are paying attention to rural problems. This is a difficult political situation to navigate, with serious potential for cynicism and empty promises from both major parties, but at least policymakers will not risk ignoring rural America and the challenges it faces during the coming years.

The second is that public libraries, and especially rural libraries, are once again at risk of serious funding reductions. In the years following the 2008 recession, public libraries saw significant budget cuts and staffing decreases, along with a loss of funding to state libraries and other support organizations (Lyons & Lance, 2011). We have seen these trends reverse as the economy has recovered and strengthened, but even after a return to stability, the President's recently proposed budget has asserted that the federal government does not need to support public libraries. This proposal called for the complete elimination of IMLS (Bullard, 2017).

Stating a desire to fix the problems of rural America and cutting support to public libraries—and doing so through the elimination of IMLS specifically—is a contradiction. I do not say this out of partisan alignment. I say this as a person who grew up in a rural area, as a public librarian for a rural system, and a researcher with years of experience analyzing what rural libraries actually do. The authors in this volume provide clear documentation as to how rural libraries assist their local residents with finding job information, developing skill sets that lead to employment, locating health information, applying for government benefits, interpreting information that allows for greater participation in our democracy, and other activities that improve people's quality of life. Several chapters in this volume also discuss how libraries can engage in cultural heritage activities in a manner that increases rural residents' pride in and sense of personal connection to their communities, which can make these areas more appealing to current and potential residents.

IMLS has been one of the staunchest advocates for rural public libraries, most notably dedicating millions of dollars from their budget each year to specifically benefit these communities by supporting broadband development, technology training, and other efforts (Bullard, 2017). Several of the authors in this volume have, as discussed throughout the following chapters, worked on IMLS-funded research projects that have directly benefited rural libraries and librarians. ARSL has condemned the elimination of the agency in no uncertain terms, noting its unassailable value to the operations of rural public libraries (Calhoun, 2017).

If both major parties are now determined to win over the hearts and minds of rural residents, allowing for any reduction in support for rural libraries should be a political dead end. This is a difficult line to walk, as tipping in too partisan of a direction can in itself be an attack on public libraries' relative neutrality or their strength as places that welcome persons of all backgrounds and beliefs. Instead, the response to any assault on public library support should be a clear and firm assertion of how every dollar spent on libraries is paid back in the form of various community benefits. Considering the budget restraints that most rural libraries face, we need to remind people that we have not yet seen the upward limit on how these institutions can make their communities stronger. As rural librarians and their allies argue that they should not accept less but instead deserve more support, I hope that the documentation in the following chapters of how rural libraries help their communities will be useful.

REFERENCES

Association for Rural and Small Libraries. (2016). ARSL 2016 call for proposals. Retrieved from http://arsl.info/proposals-for-presentations-2016-arsl/.

Bullard, G. (2017, March 16). Institute of Museum and Library Services issues statement on the President's proposed FY18 budget. Retrieved from https://www.imls.gov/news-events/news-releases/institute-museum-and-library-services-issues-statement-presidents-proposed.

Calhoun, J. (2017, March 20). ARSL position on IMLS funding. Retrieved from http://arsl.info/arsl-position-on-imls-funding/.

Du, Y. (2016). *Small libraries, big impact: How to better serve your community in the digital age.* Santa Barbara, CA: Libraries Unlimited.

Ehrenfreund, M., & Guo, J. (2016, November 23). If you've ever described people as "white working class," read this. *Washington Post.* Retrieved from https://www.washingtonpost.com/news/wonk/wp/2016/11/22/who-exactly-is-the-white-working-class-and-what-do-they-believe-good-questions.

Federal Communications Commission. (2016). *2016 Broadband progress report.* Retrieved from https://www.fcc.gov/reports-research/reports/broadband-progress-reports/2016-broadband-progress-report.

Glotfelty, C. (2017). Finding aid: Center for the Study of Rural Librarianship Records, 1978–2008. Retrieved from http://www.clarion.edu/libraries/archives-documents/CenterForStudyOfRuralLibrarianship.pdf.

Kendrick, K. D., & Tritt, D. (Eds.). (2016). *The small and rural academic library: Leveraging resources and overcoming limitations*. Chicago, IL: Association of College and Research Libraries.

Lyons, R., & Lance, K. C. (2011). The recession's effects. *Library Journal*. Retrieved from http://lj.libraryjournal.com/2011/11/managing-libraries/lj-index/class-of-2011/the-recessions-effects.

New York Public Library. (2011). Fun facts about the library. Retrieved from http://exhibitions.nypl.org/100/learn/fun_facts.

Perry, M. J. (2016, June 5). New U.S. homes today are 1,000 square feet larger than in 1973 and living space per person has nearly doubled. *American Enterprise Institute*. Retrieved from http://www.aei.org/publication/new-us-homes-today-are-1000-square-feet-larger-than-in-1973-and-living-space-per-person-has-nearly-doubled.

Przybyla, H. M. (2017, May 23). Trump budget hard on "forgotten" rural American supporters. *USA Today*. Retrieved from https://www.usatoday.com/story/news/politics/2017/05/23/trump-budget-hard-forgotten-rural-american-supporters/102065680.

Rothman, J. (2016, September 12). The lives of poor white people. *New Yorker*. Retrieved from http://www.newyorker.com/culture/cultural-comment/the-lives-of-poor-white-people.

United States Department of Agriculture. (2017). Rural education at a glance, 2017 edition. Retrieved from http://www.ers.usda.gov/topics/rural-economy-population/employment-education/rural-education.aspx.

Weigel, P. A., Ullrich, F., Shane, D. M., & Mueller, K. J. (2016). Variation in primary care service patterns by rural–urban location. *Journal of Rural Health*, *32*(2), 196–203.

RURAL LIBRARIES AND THE HUMAN RIGHT TO INTERNET ACCESS

Claire Petri

ABSTRACT

This chapter analyzes the ways national, international, and library professional policies address Internet access as a human right. This includes documenting the ways rural libraries fulfill their patrons' human right to the Internet and demonstrating how Mathiesen's (2014) framework can be used by library professionals and policymakers to ensure that people have physical, intellectual, and social access to the Web. The author's intention is to help facilitate a more meaningful definition of access that goes beyond just providing hardware access to bridge the digital divide, but instead asserts the need for librarian assistance and technology training if we wish to allow all members of a society, without exception, to fully enjoy their human rights.

The author analyzes existing national and international policies pertaining to providing information and Internet access in rural and otherwise under-served areas, as well as precedents involving the deployment of previous information and communication technologies (ICTs) in rural areas. This

Rural and Small Public Libraries: Challenges and Opportunities
Advances in Librarianship, Volume 43, 13–35
ISSN: 0065-2830/doi:10.1108/S0065-283020170000043002

segues into an analysis of barriers to rural Internet access using facets and determinants developed by Mathiesen, leading to the argument that rural librarians' ability to help underserved populations use the Internet is essential to making Web access meaningful.

- *The United Nations (UN) has supported arguments that people have a right to information access and the technologies that support this, suggesting that Internet access is a human right.*
- *The U.S. government has a history of facilitating access to ICTs in rural areas that dates back to 1934 and continues through the present.*
- *Funding mechanisms that facilitate Web access in the United States focus primarily on making broadband connections, hardware, and software accessible, leaving out the essential training and assistance components that are essential to making many rural residents and other underserved persons able to actually use the Internet.*

Scholarship on rural libraries, including some of the research in this volume, has argued that rural public libraries provide an invaluable service by offering both access to and guidance in using the Internet. While these publications commonly discuss the socioeconomic benefits of providing this access, they often treat the motivation for providing such services as self-evident. This chapter analyzes policies and legal precedents to argue that Internet access for rural residents, through public libraries and other means, is not merely a privilege that will benefit people if funded, but instead a human right that cannot be ignored.

Keywords: Human rights; United Nations; unfunded mandate; universal service; rural libraries

I. INTRODUCTION

Internet access is inextricably linked with human rights. At the most basic level, it makes information more accessible to those who may not know what their rights are or how to seek redress if their rights are being violated. The Internet is also a tool for exercising specific rights. The rights to free speech, education, a free press, and assembly are all facilitated by Internet access in ways that differ from and exceed the capacity of previous ICTs. For people living in remote and rural areas, geographic constraints limit access to community spaces, government services, legal assistance, and many other resources. Being able to use the Internet can give rural residents access to information and services they would otherwise have difficulty reaching.

Because of the Internet's ability to enable or enhance fundamental human rights, legal scholars, and policymakers have proposed that Internet access itself is a human right. One of the most notable persons to promote this stance is Frank LaRue, who previously served as the special rapporteur on the promotion and protection of the right to freedom of opinion and expression for the United Nations (UN). In his 2011 report to the UN, he asserts that Internet access is a human right under the Universal Declaration of Human Rights (UDHR):

> By explicitly providing that everyone has the right to express him or herself through any media, the Special Rapporteur underscores that article 19 of the Universal Declaration of Human Rights and the Covenant was drafted with foresight to include and to accommodate future technological developments through which individuals can exercise their right to freedom of expression. Hence, the framework of international human rights law remains relevant today and equally applicable to new communication technologies such as the Internet (LaRue & United Nations Human Rights Council, 2011, no. 21).

A section of the text of Article 19 reads, "Everyone has the right to ... seek, receive and impart information and ideas through any media and regardless of frontiers." Although there are no international declarations or U.S. statutes that specifically call Internet access a human right, there are several statements that include some variation of "through any media" in their discussions of certain communication rights. There are also several United Nations documents, U.S. programs, and professional organizations that treat Internet access as both a negative and a positive right, a need that governments and other organizations have an obligation to fulfill. Essentially, even though no one explicitly says, "Internet access is a human right," there are numerous policies from international, national, and library professional organizations that describe it as a vital need and aim to make Internet access universal. Some of these simply address access for all people, while others recognize that within that universality the specific needs of rural areas must be addressed.

This chapter focuses on Internet access as a positive right and illustrates that, although it is described as a tool, in practice this access is approached as a right. Often, physical access is addressed while intellectual and social factors are ignored. I will argue that the "tool" or means-to-an-end rhetoric can be used to the advantage of those who are looking to expand the definition of access beyond the physical access to the technology. Building on this foundation, I will discuss a few of the barriers to Internet access for rural populations in the United States by examining those barriers using the framework proposed by Mathiesen—a synthesis of the standard threat analysis and the physical, intellectual, and social (PhIS) definition of access that I will call the Facets and Determinants framework (Mathiesen, 2014). I will conclude by looking at how rural libraries are equipped to address those barriers in their communities and how public policy, academia, and professional organizations can support them in doing so.

II. IS INTERNET ACCESS A HUMAN RIGHT?

Throughout this chapter, I argue that there is a precedent for treating access to the Internet and the resources it contains as a human right, rather than a mere luxury. This perspective is informed by the historical reaction to new ICTs that have altered how people connect to each other and find information, including the notable example of the United States supporting rural telephone deployment in the early twentieth century. What follows is a brief overview of how the international community, the U.S. federal government, and the library community have reacted in ways that treat Web access as a necessity for persons who wish to engage in and enjoy their human rights to the fullest extent.

A. An International Perspective

Article 19 of the UDHR, discussed in LaRue's (2011) report above, is just one instance where the UN indirectly addresses Internet access as a right. Several more recent UN declarations have highlighted the necessity of access to ICTs for the realization of widely recognized human rights, including one from the World Summit on the Information Society (WSIS).

In 2003, the WSIS, a UN-sponsored conference, met in Geneva and produced a Declaration of Principles. Section 9 explicitly states, "We are aware that ICTs should be regarded as tools and not as an end in themselves." However, several subsequent sections express a resolve to vastly improve access to ICTs. For example, Section 21 states, "universal, ubiquitous, equitable and affordable access to ICT infrastructure and services ... should be an objective of all stakeholders involved in building [the Information Society]" (World Summit on the Information Society, 2003).

When defining access, the Geneva Declaration does not focus purely on equipment and infrastructure. Section 29 affirms that all people should have "the opportunity to acquire the necessary skills and knowledge in order to understand, participate actively in, and benefit fully from, the Information Society and the knowledge economy." In reference to remote and rural residents, the Declaration says, "we are resolute to empower the poor, particularly those living in remote, rural and marginalized urban areas, to access information and to use ICTs as a tool to support their efforts to lift themselves out of poverty" (Section 14).

Although it stops short of declaring Internet access a fundamental right, the Declaration puts forth a strong mandate for universal ICT access. Because of its instrumental role in the realization of many rights, including freedom of expression, education, economic advancement, and political involvement, the Declaration urges all governments to take serious steps toward providing that access.

More recently, in 2016, the UN's Human Rights Council passed a non-binding resolution called *The Promotion, Protection and Enjoyment of Human Rights on the Internet.* Unlike the Geneva Declaration, the resolution focuses explicitly on Internet access. In this resolution, the Council "affirms ... the importance of applying a human rights-based approach in providing and in expanding access to Internet," and "calls upon all States to consider formulating ... and adopting national Internet-related public policies that have the objective of universal access and enjoyment of human rights at their core."

The resolution also demonstrates an understanding of access that goes beyond a simple network connection. It focuses on the need to bridge digital divides, particularly those relating to gender, disability, and other factors. It also mentions an often-overlooked aspect of access: "the importance of building confidence and trust in the Internet," which is viewed as a barrier to making use of the Internet for development, innovation, cooperation, and education. The resolution makes no explicit mention of special considerations for rural and insular areas, but the specific mention of persons who have traditionally faced barriers to enjoying the full benefits of modern society makes this implicit.

B. The United States Perspective

In the United States, there is similarly no explicitly stated right to Internet access. However, the U.S. does have legally mandated national programs aimed at expanding access. Many of the current broadband access plans have grown out of the long history of universal service programs. In the United States, the Communications Act of 1934 established the Telecommunications Development Fund, which was to be used in part "to support universal service and promote delivery of telecommunications services to underserved rural and urban areas" (§614). The Act also established that telecommunications services must be affordable, that people in rural and insular areas should be charged rates comparable to those in urban areas, and that libraries and educational institutions should receive services at a discounted rate (§254).

The relevance of the Communications Act of 1934 and the USF to discussions of modern ICT access, especially rural access, should not be understated. The precedent of the U.S. government stepping in and using a carrot-or-stick approach to correct market failures and ensure that rural residents have more equitable access to ICTs goes back more than 80 years.

The advent of the Internet as a new ICT prompted Congress to update the Communications Act of 1934 into the Telecommunications Act of 1996. The Federal Communications Commission (FCC) built on this by establishing the Universal Service Fund (USF), which addressed the need to provide rural residents with Internet and eventually broadband access in much the same way as previous legislation ensured rural access to telephonic communications. The USF provides subsidies to lower the costs of ICT services in order "to advance [their] availability … to all consumers" (FCC, n.d., para. 7) in areas or institutions where cost would otherwise be a barrier, particularly focusing on "rural and insular areas" (FCC, n.d., para. 2). The High Cost Areas program supports the expansion of ICT services into rural and other areas that were not financially lucrative for private companies because they could not achieve economies of scale that come with larger population service bases. The USF's subsidies allow these companies to provide their services at a cost similar to urban areas. Meanwhile, the USF's support for schools and libraries, known as "e-rate," provides ICT access to libraries and educational institutions. Another recently developed program makes ICT access more affordable for rural healthcare providers.

A notable piece of the USF is the Lifeline program, which began subsidizing landline phone connections for low-income citizens in 1985 and later expanded to include cell phone service. The goals of the program, which began in 1985, include "being able to connect to jobs, family, and emergency services." Thirty years later, Internet access has become indispensable for achieving those same goals. The FCC acknowledged this fact in March 2016 when it approved the Lifeline Modernization Order, expanding the program to include subsidies for broadband access (FCC, 2017, para. 3).

More recently, the 2009 American Recovery and Reinvestment Act (ARRA, commonly known as the Stimulus bill) included about $7 billion in grants to expand broadband access into unserved and underserved areas of the United States. The fact that this funding comes from the stimulus bill is an indication that the programs see Internet access as a tool for economic recovery, and not as a human right. The goal was to fund projects that would provide access to a greater number of consumers, institutions, small businesses, and public safety agencies by providing both technology and training ("Broadband Expansion Programs in the Recovery Act," 2013). The mention of training indicates an understanding that access goes beyond connectivity.

In response to the requirements in the ARRA, the FCC has several initiatives targeting universal Internet access. For example, the National Broadband Plan's third long-term goal specifically aims for universal access for individuals: "Every American should have affordable access to robust broadband service, and *the means and skills* to subscribe if they so choose" (FCC, 2010, Goal No. 3, emphasis added). Almost all of the plan's programs focused on technology and connectivity, but the intention was to create a National Digital Literacy Corps (FCC, 2010, Goal No. 3) to provide skills as mentioned above. However, the Corps never actually received funding (Castañeda, Fuentes-Bautista, & Baruch, 2015, p. 152). While plans for the Corps did not initially include public libraries, the FCC altered this in recognition of the fact that public librarians had already acted in this role through an unfunded mandate for years before the FCC proposed the program—and continue to do so today (Bittner, 2012).

C. A Library Professional Perspective

There are also professional organizations that place a high value on Internet access. For example, the International Federation of Library Associations and Institutions published a document called the Lyon Declaration (2014) to encourage the UN to recognize the centrality of information access to human rights and sustainable development. The Declaration is adamant that people need access to information to better their lives, and it explicitly refers to information as a right. In contrast, ICTs offer "support" (para. 2) and are "a means of implementation" (Section 6b). Like in the UDHR and WSIS documents, the directly stated right is the access to information, but could be interpreted to include the right to the means of that access.

The Lyon Declaration does specifically mention the urgency of ICT access in remote areas (Section 5) and points out that libraries can contribute by "offering training and skills to help people access and understand the information and services most helpful to them" (Section 4f).

The American Library Association's statements on access are similarly open to interpretation in terms of whether Internet access is itself a human right. Equity of access is one of the organization's key action areas. Their page states that all people should have access to information "in a variety of formats—electronic, as well as print" (ALA, 2007, "Why Equity"). Also, as quoted on their Professional Ethics page, the Intellectual Freedom Manual refers to "the right of unrestricted access to information and ideas regardless of the communication medium used" (ALA, 2008b, para. 1) as a necessary element of intellectual freedom.

When it comes to access for rural populations and the scope of the definition of access, the ALA's Equity of Access statement is much more explicit. It acknowledges that people in rural areas are less likely to use the Internet than those in urban or suburban areas and then continues, "the barrier is not only access to computers. Many people lack the basic literacy and computer skills needed to navigate the Web" (ALA, 2007, "Why Equity").

Interestingly, the Association for Rural and Small Libraries does not have any statements of values or express a mission beyond their commitment to their member libraries and librarians. However, other specialized organizations include sentiments similar to the ALA's in their statements of values, although none use the word "rights." The Reference and User Services Association's Statement on Access says they value libraries' function of providing people with access to information "in all formats" (ALA, 2008a) but makes no mention of either the Internet or rural areas.

At a state level, results are similarly uneven. Using an example from the author's home state, part of the Maryland Library Association's mission statement is to promote equal access to information, but it does not address Internet access or rural issues at all (Maryland Library Association, n.d.). In fact, a keyword search of the word "rural" on their website yields zero results, as does the word "urban," even though Maryland has many communities that are distinctly one or the other. With this said, in their chapter in this volume, Real and Rose discuss how state-level support for rural libraries in Maryland implies that even if residents of the state do not have a right to information and Web access, they are entitled to something very close to it.

These are a sampling of the international, national, and professional stances on Internet access as a human right. Many refer to a right to access information, while none directly state, "Everyone has a right to Internet access." Considering that the ability to access and use the Internet is now often a prerequisite to many other services that are considered part of basic human rights, Web access is at least an element of people's ability to exercise and enjoy their rights.

D. A Right in Practice

In a controversial 2012 New York Times editorial, Vinton G. Cerf, a vice president at Google, expressed concern about enshrining a specific technology alongside other fundamental rights. Perhaps the creators of the documents discussed above share his hesitancy. But the more ubiquitous the Internet becomes, the more difficult it is for people without access to fully participate in society. Does it make sense to say something is not a right if it is the only way to access other rights? In the United States, many government forms are now available only online, and in a rural area, government offices can be many miles away. If someone does not have access to the Internet to apply for unemployment benefits, what good is it to say they have a "right to security in the event of unemployment" (UN, 1948, Article 25)? Now that the majority of job applications in the United States must be completed online, what good is "the right to work, to free choice of employment" (UN, 1948, Article 23) without Internet access?

Whether any official laws or agreements explicitly say the Internet is a right, the UN and the United States, along with many other countries around the world and many information-related professional organizations, are treating it as if it is by releasing statements and passing laws that aim to provide universal access.

III. BROADENING OUR PERSPECTIVE ON ACCESS

Regardless of how we label it, Internet access is becoming increasingly necessary to survive and to live a full life. The next question is whether someone can be said to truly have access just because they have a device that is hooked up to Internet service. The way we define access is essential to ensuring that the Internet is useful in achieving all of the goals we have set out for it. Does a person really have Internet access if they have a connected computer but they do not know how to operate a mouse or a keyboard? Does a person really have Internet access if they are afraid to use it because they have been taught that Web browsing is unsafe, or that there is no trustworthy information available online? Despite the answer to these questions being an obvious and emphatic "no," federal funding in the United States has primarily focused on technology and infrastructure, while the one piece of the National Broadband Plan that would have helped people learn how to make use of the technology never received any funding. The fact that libraries receive only a small amount of their support from the federal government, yet have become essential in facilitating citizen actions that the federal government deems essential among people in the nation, constitutes what Jaeger and Bertot (2011) of the University of Maryland's Information Policy and Access Center have, in this precise context, called an unfunded mandate.

In this respect, the government seeing Internet access as a tool provides an advantage to advocates for a broader definition of access. When policymakers conceive these programs to help increase access, they do not see hardware connected to the Internet as an achievement on its own. The goal is for people to be able to *make use* of this infrastructure to improve the economy, to find and share information that is relevant to their lives, and to bring people together. When we view Internet access as a tool rather than an end in itself, we understand that if we want to meet our goals, our definition of access needs to be broader than just physical access to technology. We need to create content relevant to the people we are trying to reach. We need to teach people how to use the technology effectively and in a way that is relevant to their needs and interests. We need to show people the value that connectedness can have for themselves and their community. While this "we" needs to include government organizations at all levels and society as a whole, in reality the one American institution that has consistently made practical efforts to actually achieve this is our nation's public libraries.

Existing statements and policies vary in the breadth of their definitions of Internet access. Most statements, particularly those from the UN and U.S. government, focus almost exclusively on physical access to technology, only making passing reference to any type of training or skills. The American Library Association specifically cites computers, computer skills, and reading skills as necessities for equity of access. A more systematic approach to thinking about access can help to achieve these necessities, ensuring that essential factors are not overlooked.

IV. FACETS AND DETERMINANTS

One reason that the focus is generally on access to technology and infrastructure may be that these types of access are easier to conceptualize and quantify. However, looking at access as a big picture can help governments and information professionals better achieve their goals. Mathiesen's (2014) synthesis of

Shue's standard threats analysis with Burnett, Jaeger, and Thompson's PhIS account of access provides us with a powerful framework for conceptualizing the "facets of access" that are often left out of the conversation. Her article suggests that the best way to study information access is using the five components of the standard threats analysis: availability, reachability, findability, comprehensibility, and usability, looking at each of those in terms of PhIS factors (which she called determinants, the PhIS). I refer to this method as the Facets and Determinants approach, after the way Mathiesen describes the two systems she combines.

As we can see from the international, national, and professional perspectives above, one of the difficulties with discussing Internet access is that the Internet could potentially refer simply to connectivity to the global network, but could also mean the information that is on that network. For the purpose of this framework, we can base our definition of Internet access on Mathiesen's definition of access to information: a person has access to the Internet when they have the freedom or opportunity to connect to, make use of, and benefit from the Internet and the information available on it (see Mathiesen, 2014, p. 607).

Issues dealing with the "connect to" element primarily focus on physical access to the network itself, while "make use of" and "benefit from" center on access to both the network and the information on it. Additionally, in order to understand the Facets and Determinants framework, it is important to understand that this definition describes a relationship between a person and the Internet and that it does not make sense to talk about access without talking about both of those elements.

A. Facets: The Standard Threats Analysis

The goal of the standard threats analysis "is to provide an account of access to answer a particular question, i.e., what conditions would need to be fulfilled so that someone's human right to information access is satisfied?" (Mathiesen, 2014, p. 607). If we look at the question of Internet access through the standard threats analysis, we will ask the following questions:

1. Is the Internet available? For example, has an Internet provider installed the appropriate infrastructure in the area?
2. Is the Internet (or the connection) findable? For example, do people know that the service is available?
3. Is the Internet reachable? For example, does the person have a device that can connect to the Internet?

4. Is the Internet comprehensible? For example, does the person understand how to navigate websites?
5. Is the Internet usable? For example, is the connection fast enough to browse the desired website?

B. Determinants: The PhIS Analysis

These facets are then combined with the three PhIS determinants from Burnett et al. (2008). This leads us to ask questions like the following:

1. What are the physical determinants of whether the Internet is available?
2. What are the intellectual determinants of whether the Internet is available?
3. What are the social determinants of whether the Internet is available?

These three determinants would then be discussed for each of the remaining four facets.

Physical access to the Internet involves simply getting to the Internet. Infrastructure, geographical location, and home network connectivity are some examples. It would also involve knowing that the Internet was available in your area, knowing how to set up a connection, and being able to afford the service (Burnett et al., 2008, p. 57). Although this is not the only category we need to consider when we talk about access, it is the first step to any type of access. Without physical access, intellectual and social access are meaningless, and it is worth emphasizing that affordability is one of the primary barriers to physical access.

Intellectual access to the Internet means knowing how to use the Internet and understanding the information found there. This involves things like cognitive ability; understanding the language, dialect, or jargon; knowing where to look for the needed information and how to navigate the Internet; and knowing how to use a computer (Burnett et al., 2008, p. 57). It also involves being able to evaluate sources, judge the reliability and accuracy of the information, and find and evaluate opposing points of view (Burnett et al., 2008, p. 57).

Social access has to do with the groups that one identifies with and the values and norms those groups hold. These groups could be based on religion, politics, profession, neighborhood, family, or other factors. Burnett et al. explain, "Within specific social contexts, information behaviors—like other day-to-day activities—must be seen as normative.... The value of information is not universal; it is rooted within the norms and the attitudes of a particular social world" (2008, p. 58)

Burnett et al. outline several concepts that comprise social access. The first is the idea of social norms, which have to do with social appearances and what is proper with regard to those appearances (2008, p. 58). This could limit someone's access to the Internet if it is not presented in a way that is socially acceptable.

Second is worldview, which is the group's view of what is important and what is inconsequential. As Burnett et al. point out, "Members of a small world will tend to view information that does not mesh with their community's worldview as lacking, trivial, or as something they can safely ignore ... world-view can lead a community to limit access to some information simply because it defines that information as having little importance" (2008, pp. 58–59).

The third aspect of social access is the concept of social types. This has to do with a person's role within the group. If a person's type is considered trust-worthy or "desirable," then information from that individual is more likely to be taken seriously (2008, p. 59). However, if a person's type is considered untrustworthy or undesirable, information that otherwise might be seen as good or relevant is less likely to be accepted, no matter how urgently the information is needed (2008, p. 59).

The final aspect of social access is information behavior, which relates to whether a person will act on the information, or how that information will be used (Burnett et al., 2008, p. 59). It is the end result of the above three aspects, which deal with whether information will be accepted. Information behavior asks, once the information is accepted, what will the person or group do with it?

C. Internet as Information

The scholarly debate about whether there is a human right to the Internet is really about whether the human right is exclusively to information itself or if it encompasses the tool that, in today's times, is the way most information is most easily (and often exclusively) available. Thus, it does not make sense to talk about a right to the Internet without also talking about a right to information.

Similarly, when the people making these international, national, and profes-sional policies and programs talk about the benefits of Internet access, they are really talking about access to information. The problem is that when they come up with ways to give people access, they often only think about or fund the elements dealing with physical access and availability. The fact that the FCC could not get funding for the National Digital Literacy Corps—the only piece of the Broadband Expansion Plan that was not focused on physical access—is telling. There seems to be an attitude that Internet availability *is* information access, or else just a lack of consideration of any other aspects of access.

Instead, when planning how to provide universal access, lawmakers need to go back to the reason they decided access was important in the first place and figure out what is preventing that underlying goal from becoming a reality. Did they want to encourage economic growth? The people working in small businesses in the area will need to know how to use the Internet to promote their business. Did they want to improve education? Potential students will need to know how to use the computer to take online classes. Did they want to help jobseekers look for work? People will need to know how to search and apply for jobs online and create and upload resumes.

Trying to think of all the possible barriers to access requires some type of strategy, and this is where the Facets and Determinants come in. A full analysis of access would ask five main questions with six sub-questions each. This chapter will use one of the main questions as an example of further work that can be done to more fully explore the concept of Internet access. Mathiesen's fifth facet is usability or quality, as in, can the user make use of it? And did the provider make it well? I also consider relevance—did the provider make a quality service that is relevant to the user? This is an important question in addressing barriers to Internet access, because a Pew study found that "32% of non-internet users cite reasons tied to their sense that the Internet is not very easy to use" (Zickuhr, 2013, p. 2).

Understanding access as a relationship means that there are two ways to create access where it does not already exist (Mathiesen, 2014, p. 607). When we think of Internet access, our choices are either to change something about the Internet and the system that delivers it or to change something about the person trying to access the Internet. For example, a person may not be able to do much on the Internet because they have a very low literacy level. Improving access may mean making more information available in ways that do not require reading, or it may mean helping that person improve their reading skills. Taking into account the facets, the determinants, and the relationship between the Internet and the user, a Facets and Determinants analysis of the usability of the Internet looks like this:

- Is the Internet usable?
  - Physical barriers on the side of the patron—physical or visual disabilities make the equipment difficult to use.
  - Physical barriers on the side of the service—some digital content is not optimized for use on mobile devices.

- ○ Intellectual barriers on the side of the patron—patron does not know how to navigate the Web.
- ○ Intellectual barriers on the side of the service—poor instructions or guidance for use are offered. Websites are difficult to navigate.
- ○ Social barriers on the side of the patron—patron does not believe that information found on the Internet is trustworthy or that web browsing is safe.
- ○ Social barriers on the side of the service—few resources relevant to rural life are available online.

V. HOW RURAL LIBRARIES HELP

Now we can look at how a rural library may be able to address some of these barriers, trying to take into consideration that rural financial resources are limited, although there are a number of federal and private grant opportunities that are available if rural librarians are able to obtain them. The federal programs discussed earlier often focus on underserved areas. Some, such as the e-rate program from the USF, are specifically designed to benefit libraries, and others focus on rural areas generally.

Physical barriers on the side of the patron—physical or visual disabilities make the equipment difficult to use. Affordability is a major factor in physical access, and adaptive technologies may be prohibitively expensive for many individuals with disabilities, especially considering the high poverty rates in many rural areas. In a 2009 survey, the FCC found that adults with disabilities had a broadband adoption rate that was two-thirds the national average (Horrigan, 2010, p. 3). By providing accessible workstations, rural libraries can make the Internet available to those who are unable to afford the equipment for themselves. Although these technologies can also be expensive on a small library's budget, special funding is often available (e.g., Institute of Museum and Library Services, n.d., para. 4; Texas State Library and Archives Commission, 2015).

Libraries can also provide resources for individuals who want to get their own adaptive technology. Many nonprofit organizations offer funding to individuals to cover some or all of the cost of this type of equipment (Assistive Technology Industry Association, n.d.), but it can be difficult to find information about these offerings, especially for a person who cannot use the Internet to search for it. Librarians have the skills necessary to help their patrons find the type of support that may ultimately allow them to have access to the Internet at the library or at home.

Physical barriers on the side of the service—some digital content is not optimized for use on mobile devices. Eleven percent of rural Americans own a smartphone but do not have any other form of high-speed Internet access at home (Pew Research Center, 2015, p. 18). Smartphone users often encounter difficulties with online content, meaning that their devices are acting as a barrier to that online access: "49% of smartphone owners experience content that they are trying to access not displaying properly on their phone at least on occasion, with 10% saying that this happens to them 'frequently'" (Pew Research Center, 2015, p. 15).

Simply by providing public access computers, libraries are already addressing this issue. Rural libraries are excelling at this, considering that on an average day only 18.4% of rural libraries experience at least some patron wait times for public access computers—far below the national average of 30.7% (Bertot, Real, Lee, McDermott, & Jaeger, 2015, p. 8).

Intellectual barriers on the side of the patron—patron does not know how to navigate the web. Teaching people basic Internet skills is another area where libraries are already doing good work, although rural libraries do not offer as many learning opportunities as libraries in urban and suburban areas. A large majority of libraries in the United States offer introductory Internet training, including 86.6% of rural libraries. However, a smaller percentage of rural libraries offer training than the national average (Bertot et al., 2015, p. 20).

In order to offer Internet training, some libraries partner with volunteers or other community organizations. Rural libraries are more likely than the national average to do so (Bertot et al., 2015, p. 26), and this is one of their strengths. Limited staff and funding make it difficult for librarians to offer all of these services on their own, but partnering with other individuals and organizations in the community who specialize in Internet and technology can provide new training to patrons without putting as much of an additional burden on the library staff.

Intellectual barriers on the side of the service—poor instructions or guidance for use are offered. Websites are difficult to navigate. These are certainly problems with many aspects of Internet service. For their own part, libraries can make sure their websites are straightforward and offer clear instructions and in-person assistance for any of their digital offerings. As far as these types of difficulties from the content provider, librarians can choose databases and other digital materials that are easier to navigate and can communicate to vendors that this is a priority when choosing which resources to purchase for the library. Otherwise, libraries do not have control over most Web content, so this is a case where making changes on the patron's side of the equation makes more sense. 24.5% of rural libraries offer formal basic Internet classes and 78.8% offer informal point-of-use assistance, both of which can strengthen patrons' skills in this area (Bertot et al., 2015, p. 25).

Social barriers on the side of the patron—patron does not believe that information found on the Internet is trustworthy or that Web browsing is safe. One way some libraries are already addressing these issues is through the training they offer. 55.2% of rural libraries offer training specifically on Internet safety and privacy (Bertot et al., 2015, p. 20). Similar to the need for support in teaching people basic Internet skills, libraries also need support in offering Internet safety training. If the community recognizes the librarian as a positive and trustworthy social type, then this training offered by the librarian should help patrons feel confident and safe on the Internet. If the library chooses to partner with a community member or community organization for this training, they should be sure that partner is also seen as a desirable type by the population they are trying to reach.

Social barriers on the side of the service—few resources geared specifically toward rural life are available online. The FCC found that 14% of people who do not use the Internet cited reasons related to a lack of relevance (Horrigan, 2010, p. 27). Libraries are already developing both physical and digital collections that are customized to the specific needs of their communities. Librarians have the skills necessary to seek and provide access to digital content that is relevant to their patrons' lives. While these resources may be difficult for individuals to find, librarians adding them to the library's collection will be gathering them in one place, significantly increasing access for their patrons.

Another way libraries are helping overcome this barrier is by teaching their community members how to create their own content. For example, 49.7% of rural libraries offer social media training, 5.3% offer training on website development, and 5.2% offer training on digital content creation such as mobile app development or digital photography tools (Bertot et al., 2015, p. 20). Even though complex content creation or web development is beyond the skills of most new Internet users, offering this training to community members who already have moderate computer skills can benefit the community as a whole, as content from within the community may be more socially accessible. Rural libraries may also be able to share content created by people in other rural communities when it deals with issues common to rural life.

VI. HOW SOCIETY CAN HELP RURAL LIBRARIES

As discussed throughout this volume, rural public libraries are often doing the best they can with the limited resources available to them. With their resources stretched to—and even beyond—their limits, the question should not be how rural librarians can do more, but how key stakeholder groups and allies can expand their resources to allow these librarians to have greater impacts on their communities.

A. Professional Organizations, Education, and Advocacy

There is a lot of talk in the field and in society at large about how libraries can stay relevant in a digital world, but the truth is that libraries already are relevant. The fact that they are doing such crucial information access work is evidence of this. The work of serving the community and ensuring people's human rights is never going to become irrelevant, and it is time for the profession to begin understanding itself in these terms.

If we are asking whether print books or desktop computers are still going to be relevant in 10 years, we are asking the wrong question. Libraries do not need to be about specific information or specific technologies—they are about serving, educating, and transforming. None of those things are ever going to become irrelevant. In fact, the more privatized and profit-driven our society becomes, the more relevant and crucial a role the library's mission plays. This is the narrative through which our professional organizations and library science programs need to advocate for our profession: no matter how much the technology changes or how the information is accessed, libraries are here to empower their patrons and serve their communities.

Master of Library and Information Science (MLIS) programs also need to emphasize the breadth of what access encompasses and what information rights mean. From physical access to technology for people with disabilities, to social access to health information for LGBT individuals in a conservative small town, at present the Internet is often the most effective way of accessing information. MLIS students need to be thinking about the complex issues of access for diverse populations throughout the course of their studies. Some of these graduate programs have developed concentrations focusing on these needs, and the author of this chapter is a graduate of the University of Maryland's Diversity and Inclusion track. As Real discusses in his introduction to this volume, recent political rhetoric has framed white rural residents—and especially white men—as a distinctly disadvantaged social group in rural America. However, what has been lost in this rhetoric is that it is not just white "working class" men who feel the challenges of rural life, but that these factors instead act as a multiplier on the disadvantages felt by persons who already face adversity due to race, gender identity, sexual orientation, or ability. As academic programs in the library and information science field move forward, they need to find ways to help rural librarians reach out to, gain the trust of, and support persons who face these multifaceted challenges, regardless of whether this entails credit-bearing courses, accessible and practical written guides, or continuing education programming.

Additionally, both MLIS classes and continuing education classes from professional organizations should include offerings on user technology instruction to help librarians offer more effective training. If academics did more research on specifically what types of Internet training saw the best results in rural libraries, this could provide valuable guidance to rural librarians as they develop classes for their patrons. As the Alliance for Affordable Internet (2016) explains, Internet accessibility research needs to "get more granular on measuring affordability and uptake across different population groups. Universal access requires targeted strategies."

B. The Private Sector

The private sector has made significant contributions to increasing Internet connectivity throughout the developing world. Programs like Google's Project Link and Facebook's Internet.org have made strides in many poor countries toward helping people use the Internet to connect with, learn from, and do business with the rest of the world. These companies recognize that Internet access is indispensable in less-developed nations. They can expand on that to recognize that it plays a similar role in less-developed parts of the United States. The access challenges in rural areas in both developed and developing nations often overlap, particularly a lack of relevant information and a lack of profitability for Internet providers, and many of the benefits overlap as well. Private-sector support through grants, equipment donations, or further subsidies has the potential to improve libraries' abilities to expand access to their communities.

C. Public Policy and Funding

It is worth reiterating the importance of affordability, which falls at the intersection of reachability and physical accessibility. Obviously, libraries address affordability for individuals in their community by providing their services for free. However, rural libraries operating with small budgets can struggle to afford higher-speed connections and new technologies. Simply put, libraries need more money if they are going to effectively build on the information rights work they are already doing. As Sin's 2011 study of library funding sources noted, "If a society is truly concerned with equal opportunity for every individual to access and use information, fundamental and systematic improvement in the library funding mechanism is most needed" (p. 51).

Basic Internet training is an area where national policy needs significant improvement. For example, the DigitalLiteracy.gov website may be well intentioned, but there is little logic to requiring someone to use a computer on their own in order to learn how to use a computer. For both intellectual and social reasons, this type of introductory training requires human interaction. For patrons who find computers frustrating to use, it is unreasonable to expect they will be willing to independently use a computer for training. For patrons who do not trust the Internet, a website is not a desirable "type" to learn from, but a librarian or other community member can be a trustworthy source to provide training. For patrons who do not believe the Internet has anything relevant to add to their lives, librarians are able to tailor training to the needs and interests of the community in the way a national website could never do.

Had it been funded, the National Digital Literacy Corps could have at least provided direct federal support for person-to-person interaction. Instead, as Susan Hildreth pointed out, "U.S. libraries are the nation's de facto digital literacy corps," ("IMLS Announces Digital Literacy Grant," 2012, para. 2) and policymakers who talk about universal Internet access need to take that into account when allocating funding for their programs. The National Digital Literacy Corps would have been a step toward overcoming the intellectual barriers, but it could never provide the personalized and socially relevant service that librarians, as trusted and knowledgeable members of their communities, are able to provide.

As it continues to implement its National Broadband Plan, instead of seeking money for a whole new digital literacy corps, the FCC should instead provide more money for the Library Services and Technology Act grants, a system that is already in place. That money could be earmarked specifically for Internet training programs and could be used by libraries to expand their current offerings themselves or in partnership with other community organizations.

Funding can also make a huge difference in libraries' ability to offer more Internet training beyond the basics. Community-generated content could go a long way in making the Internet more relevant to residents of rural communities, but comparatively few libraries offer classes in Web development, digital content creation, or even social media.

The American Library Association (2015) notes that 84.4% of public library funding nationwide comes from local sources, declining to 6.9%

coming from state support and 0.5% being federal funding. When libraries are doing such important work to advance the literacy and human rights goals our national and state lawmakers have laid out, surely those lawmakers can provide more extensive funding.

As far as physical accessibility for people with disabilities, there is already legislation in place that, while imperfect, has the capacity to do a lot of good. Section 508 of the Rehabilitation Act of 1973 was passed with the intention of making information technologies accessible to people with disabilities. However, a 2011 article by Lazar and Jaeger summarized the problems Section 508 has faced in practice:

> Compliance with and enforcement of these laws have not been very effective. A recent study found that more than 90% of federal home pages were not in compliance with Section 508. Although the Justice Department has responsibility for collecting data from federal agencies on compliance every two years, it has not collected any data since 2003. The section508.gov Web site, which is managed by the General Services Administration, was redesigned in the summer of 2010, but the new version is not in compliance with Section 508. For instance, the feedback form has form fields that are not labeled properly, so that although the form looks normal to a user who can see, a user who is blind cannot determine what each form field is supposed to represent. (p. 76)

If the federal government would actually enforce these rules, it would resolve some accessibility issues that libraries simply are not equipped to address. Pairing Section 508 enforcement with additional funding for libraries to obtain or upgrade adaptive technologies would go a long way in helping libraries fulfill the information rights of people with disabilities. It is important to emphasize that if information and access to it can be construed as a human right, as various international bodies and library organizations have argued or implied, then no person is exempt from this. Special attention needs to be paid to rural residents due to the barriers to access they face, but rural librarians and their allies must also reach out to and meet the needs of diverse populations in rural communities.

VII. CONCLUSION

This is just a small example of the power that Mathiesen's Facets and Determinants framework has to help us conceptualize the complex issues surrounding Internet and information access. Rural libraries are already fairly well situated in overcoming some of these barriers. Using this information, the next step is to convince policymakers to draw the connection between the services the libraries are providing and the goals of their universal Internet access policies. Rural libraries are making the goals of governments and advocacy groups happen and can do a better job of it if they receive the support needed to expand their offerings. Library professional organizations and academic institutions need to be part of this process, helping make these connections by advocating for libraries' role in society as institutions of justice and human rights.

ACKNOWLEDGMENTS

I would like to thank Dr. Paul Jaeger and Fiona Jardine of the University of Maryland's iSchool for their guidance and feedback in developing this chapter.

REFERENCES

Alliance for Affordable Internet. (2016). *The 2015–16 affordability report*. Retrieved http://a4ai.org/affordability-report/report/2015

American Library Association. (2007). Equity brochure HTML. Available: http://www.ala.org/aboutala/missionhistory/keyactionareas/equityaction/equitybrochure

American Library Association. (2008a). About RUSA. Retrieved September 25, 2015, from http://www.ala.org/rusa/about

American Library Association. (2008b). Professional ethics. Retrieved September 25, 2015, from http://www.ala.org/advocacy/proethics

American Library Association. (2015). Library operating expenditures: A selected annotated bibliography. Retrieved from http://www.ala.org/tools/libfactsheets/alalibraryfactsheet04.

Assistive Technology Industry Association. (n.d.). ATIA Funding Resources Guide. Retrieved November 30, 2015, from http://www.atia.org/i4a/pages/index.cfm?pageid=4219

Bertot, J. C., Real, B., Lee, J., McDermott, A. J., & Jaeger, P. T. (2015, October 1). 2014 digital inclusion survey: Findings and results. Retrieved http://ipac.umd.edu/

Bittner, M. (2012). IMLS announces grant to support libraries' roles in national broadband adoption efforts. Retrieved from https://www.imls.gov/news-events/news-releases/imls-announces-grant-support-libraries%E2%80%99-roles-national-broadband-adoption

Broadband expansion programs in the Recovery Act: Economic stimulus funding for federal broadband infrastructure. (2013). *Congressional Digest*, *92*(4), 6–7, 10–11, 32. Available: http://www.congressionaldigest.com

Burnett, G., Jaeger, P. T., & Thompson, K. M. (2008). Normative behavior and information: The social aspects of information access. *Library & Information Science Research*, *30*(1), 56–66.

Castañeda, M., Fuentes-Bautista, M., & Baruch, F. (2015). Racial and ethnic inclusion in the digital era: Shifting discourses in communications public policy. *Journal of Social Issues*, *71*(1), 139–154. doi:10.1111/josi.12101

Cerf, V. G. (2012, January 4). Internet access is not a human right. Retrieved from http://www.nytimes.com/2012/01/05/opinion/internet-access-is-not-a-human-right.html?_r=0

Communications Act of 1934, 47 U.S. Code §§ 151-614. Available http://transition.fcc.gov/Reports/1934new.pdf

Federal Communications Commission. (2017, June 30). Lifeline program for low-income consumers. Retrieved July 11, 2017, from https://www.fcc.gov/general/lifeline-program-low-income-consumers

Federal Communications Commission. (2010). National broadband plan – Executive summary. Retrieved September 26, 2015, from http://www.broadband.gov/plan/executive-summary/

Federal Communications Commission. (2016). Rural health care program. Retrieved July 15, 2016, from https://www.fcc.gov/es/general/rural-health-care-program

Federal Communications Commission. (n.d.). Universal service. Retrieved September 28, 2015, from https://www.fcc.gov/encyclopedia/universal-service

Horrigan, J. B. (2010, February). *Broadband adoption and use in America* (Working paper). Retrieved https://apps.fcc.gov/edocs_public/attachmatch/DOC-296442A1.pdf

IMLS announces digital literacy grant. (2012). Retrieved from http://www.webjunction.org/news/webjunction/Digital_Literacy_Grant.html

International Federation of Library Associations and Institutions. (2014). The Lyon declaration. Available: http://www.lyondeclaration.org/

Institute of Museum and Library Services. (n.d.). Grants to states. Retrieved November 29, 2015, from https://www.imls.gov/grants/grants-states

Jaeger, P. T., & Bertot, J. C. (2011). Responsibility rolls down: Public libraries and the social and policy obligations of ensuring access to e-government and government information. *Public Library Quarterly*, *30*(2), 91–116.

LaRue, F., & United Nations Human Rights Council. (2011, May 16). Report of the Special Rapporteur on the promotion and protection of the right to freedom of opinion and expression, Frank La Rue. Geneva: United Nations.

Lazar, J., & Jaeger, P. (2011). Reducing barriers to online access for people with disabilities. *Issues in Science and Technology*, *27*(2), 69–82.

Maryland Library Association. (n.d.). Mission and vision statements. Retrieved November 26, 2015, from http://www.mdlib.org/content.asp?contentid=146

Mathiesen, K. (2014). Facets of access: A conceptual and standard threats analysis. *IConference 2014 Proceedings*, 605–611. doi:10.9776/14265

Pew Research Center. (2015, April 1). U.S. smartphone use in 2015. Retrieved from http://www.pewinternet.org/files/2015/03/PI_Smartphones_0401151.pdf

Sin, S.-C. J. (2011). Neighborhood disparities in access to information resources: Measuring and mapping U.S. public libraries' funding and service landscapes. *Library & Information Science Research*, *33*(1), 41–53. doi:10.1016/j.lisr.2010.06.002

Texas State Library and Archives Commission. (2015). Assistive technology funding guide. Retrieved from https://www.tsl.texas.gov/sites/default/files/public/tslac/tbp/dirc/AT%20Funding%20Guide%20OCT2015.pdf

United Nations. (1948). Universal Declaration of Human Rights. Available: http://www.un.org/en/documents/udhr/

United Nations Human Rights Council. (2016, June 27). *The promotion, protection and enjoyment of human rights on the Internet* (United Nations, Human Rights Council). Retrieved from https://documents-dds-ny.un.org/doc/UNDOC/LTD/G16/131/89/PDF/G1613189.pdf

World Summit on the Information Society. (2003, December 12). Declaration of principles. Available: http://www.itu.int/net/wsis/docs/geneva/official/dop.html

Zickuhr, K. (2013, September 25). Who's not online and why. Retrieved http://www.pewinternet.org/files/old-media//Files/Reports/2013/PIP_Offline%20adults_092513_PDF.pdf

RURAL PUBLIC LIBRARIES IN AMERICA: CONTINUING AND IMPENDING CHALLENGES

Brian Real and R. Norman Rose

ABSTRACT

This chapter analyzes major trends in rural public libraries, beginning with a discussion of changes in service offerings since the advent of the Internet. These outlets are now better able to help patrons with their employment, education, and civic engagement needs than they have been at any point in the past. However, rural public libraries still lag behind their peers in broadband speeds, technological infrastructure, and various forms of service and training offerings that use these technologies. The difference in public offerings is not only due to problems of technology, but also limited funding for staff, aging and small buildings, and a lack of state and regional support to allow these libraries to achieve economies of scale. As libraries nationwide shift to focus more on public programming and digital offerings, these factors will be barriers to rural outlets keeping up with modern trends in the field.

This study uses Institute of Museum and Library Services (IMLS) and Digital Inclusion Survey data to analyze trends among rural public

Rural and Small Public Libraries: Challenges and Opportunities
Advances in Librarianship, Volume 43, 37–59
Copyright © 2018 by Emerald Publishing Limited
All rights of reproduction in any form reserved
ISSN: 0065-2830/doi:10.1108/S0065-283020170000043003

libraries. The authors returned to the original data sets from these studies to find nuance between types of rural outlets, primarily dividing this information based on libraries' distances from more densely populated areas. These statistical data are supplemented through qualitative interviews with professionals in the rural library field. Key findings include:

- *Rural public libraries have made major strides in improving broadband quality and increasing related service offerings since the advent of the Internet in the mid-1990s.*
- *Rural libraries still lag behind those in more populated areas in terms of technical infrastructure and training offerings, and this becomes more acute among those located farther from population centers.*
- *As the public library field places a greater emphasis on public programs, rural libraries' small and aging buildings will likely be a barrier to them keeping up with their peers.*
- *The lack of regional consortia and strong state libraries in some parts of the country limits rural libraries' abilities to achieve economies of scale and negatively impacts the range of services they can offer their patrons.*

Rural libraries have often been combined together in statistical analyses of their service offerings. This chapter shows nuance between these outlets, demonstrating that libraries that are distant and remote from population centers face more difficulties than those on the fringes of cities and suburbs. Likewise, while much of the advocacy surrounding rural libraries has focused on the need for improved broadband and technological infrastructure, this study moves on to study how building infrastructure, low staff funding, and a lack of mechanisms for collaboration will hinder libraries' abilities to keep up with modern changes in the field.

Keywords: Rural libraries; geographic distance; library consortia; state libraries

The original research from this chapter was supported by an Institute of Museum and Library Services (IMLS) grant administered by the American Library Association (ALA). This includes further parsing of data from the IMLS Public Libraries in the United States Survey and the Digital Inclusion Survey and interviews with Becky Heil and Andrea Berstler. Portions of this text and most of the data points have been taken from the report "Rural Libraries in the United States: Recent Strides, Future Possibilities, and Meeting Community Needs," published by ALA in summer 2017. Any differences of interpretation from the report and this chapter should be attributed to the lead author of this piece rather than ALA or IMLS.

Rural public libraries in the United States use Internet-enabled computing for the benefit of their communities. The general trend that can be observed from national-level survey data on public libraries is that rural outlets have lagged behind their peer institutions in more populated areas in terms of offering technology access and training, but this gap has considerably narrowed over the past two decades. Rural librarians routinely use Web-based resources to assist the public with employment, community and government engagement, and educational needs. These service offerings are a testament to the dedication of rural librarians, but there is enough room for improvement that further advocacy is still needed to ensure that these libraries are fully capable of serving their publics.

However, although many advocates for rural libraries have argued that improved broadband and other technology infrastructure are these libraries' greatest needs, librarians will require far more to respond to shifts in our culture and changing public expectations of libraries. As the Internet becomes more available and accessible, a new generation of digital natives needs less guidance in basic computing skills, and circulation of physical materials sees declines in response to competition from commercially available digital services, libraries have begun to reconsider their service roles to their publics in ways that represent almost as much change as the addition of Internet-enabled computers two decades ago. Larger and improved physical spaces are needed to host increasingly popular face-to-face public programs, librarians need training to guide customers in using more advanced technologies, and solutions must be found to allow small and rural libraries to afford access to digital content platforms for patrons as both the cost and popularity of these resources increase.

This chapter begins with an analysis of how far rural public libraries have come in terms of technological capacity as well as how they have improved in terms of librarians offering guidance in various forms of computer usage. These strides have been impressive, but there is still much room for improvement. Supporting rural public libraries' broadband and technological infrastructure needs to remain a priority for the foreseeable future, and any plan to help these institutions must include this as a substantial element. The authors move on from this, though, to discuss how low levels of staffing, limited open hours, small and aging spaces, inabilities to reach economies of scale, and other factors impact rural librarians' abilities to strengthen their communities. These factors must be overcome, especially if rural public libraries plan to keep up in recently expanding service areas such as public programming. Advocacy plans must be developed and action must be taken to help rural libraries improve their physical plants, increase staff training, and develop more meaningful collaboration between each other and with other institutions.

I. METHODOLOGY

As noted above, the statistical data for this report come primarily from two related sources. IMLS's Public Libraries in the United States Survey is a study of approximately 17,000 public library outlets that has been conducted annually since 1988. This census of public libraries collects a range of data essential for understanding public library operations. It may be examined through the use of geographic locale codes, described in more detail below.

The second major data source is the Digital Inclusion Survey, the most recent cycle of which was concluded in 2014 by the Information Policy and Access Center (iPAC) at the University of Maryland in partnership with the American Library Association, the International City/County Management Association, and Community Attributes International. Funding was provided by IMLS through a National Leadership Grant. This survey and its predecessors, the Public Libraries and the Internet Study (1994–2009) and the Public Library Funding and Technology Access Study (2010–2012), have each been built off IMLS's Public Libraries in the United States Survey data, asking a wide range of questions pertaining to the impact of Internet-enabled computing technologies on libraries and their publics.

Unless otherwise noted, the statistical data presented in this report come from the 2014 Digital Inclusion Survey and the fiscal year (FY) 2011 Public Libraries in the United States Survey. Although the FY2012 through FY2014 Public Libraries in the United States Survey reports are now available, the 2014 Digital Inclusion Survey was constructed using the most recent IMLS data then available at that time, which were from 2011. Primarily relying on the 2011 IMLS data and the 2014 Digital Inclusion Survey allows for more valid comparisons between these two data sets. Any deviation from these two iterations of these surveys is noted in the text of this chapter.[1]

The lead author supplemented these data through qualitative interviews with Andrea Berstler, executive director at Wicomico Public Libraries (Wicomico County, MD) and Becky Heil, library consultant for the State Library of Iowa. Berstler was president of the Association for Rural and

Small Libraries in the period 2013 to 2014, and Heil was a founding board member of the organization and its president for the period 2012 to 2013. The interviews were conducted in summer 2016. These contributors provided comments based on their local and national-level expertise.

II. DIFFERENT TYPES OF RURAL LOCALES: FRINGE, DISTANT, AND REMOTE

According to the 2010 Census, 19.3% of the population of the United States lives in rural areas (with a population of 2,500 or less). While rural communities are often juxtaposed with their more populous counterparts, there is significant nuance within the Census category of "rural" that is meaningful. The U.S. Department of Education's National Center for Educational Statistics (NCES, 2006) breaks down city, suburban, town, and rural designations to show differences within these types of locales. The subdivisions for the rural category are:

- Rural, Fringe: Census-defined rural territory that is less than or equal to 5 miles from an urbanized area (a city or densely populated suburb), as well as rural territory that is less than or equal to 2.5 miles from an urban cluster (a town).
- Rural, Distant: Census-defined rural territory that is more than 5 miles but less than or equal to 25 miles from an urbanized area, as well as rural territory that is more than 2.5 miles but less than or equal to 10 miles from an urban cluster.
- Rural, Remote: Census-defined rural territory that is more than 25 miles from an urbanized area and is also more than 10 miles from an urban cluster.

As both IMLS and the Digital Inclusion Survey use the NCES standards for defining rural areas, this will be the primary framework for presenting data throughout this study.[2] It is also important to note that the data for the 2014 Digital Inclusion Survey report were weighted within the four main locales—city, suburb, town, and rural—to ensure that the survey sample more closely resembled libraries across the United States (Bertot et al., 2014). Weighting factors included proximity to population center or cluster, geographic region, and physical size. These processed data are used for the primary locales throughout this report, including when the authors note a trend for "rural" libraries without mentioning one of the subdivisions. However, data for rural fringe, distant, and remote libraries have been left unweighted, using all available responses for libraries within these categories.

III. LIBRARIES, RURAL LIBRARIES, AND THE INTERNET

It is easy to forget just how significantly technology has advanced since the Internet became more commonly available just over two decades ago. The 1996 cycle of the Digital Inclusion Survey's predecessor, the Public Libraries and the Internet Survey, repeatedly referred to the "graphical" Internet. This meant the availability of computers that could access and display images through HTML and other visual means, rather than text-only systems like Gopher, FTP, and subscription reference databases. Likewise, respondents were asked if they foresaw themselves offering the Internet to the public or if they assumed only librarians would have access for reference questions and other services. In 1998, 10.5% of the 85.8% of public libraries that had some form of Web access did not offer this to the public, often because connection speeds were not robust enough to split between staff and patrons.

To say that the situation changed in the ensuing decades would be an understatement. Libraries in more populated areas were better equipped, both in terms of geography and funding, to respond to what was a rapid and costly change in how public libraries, and society more broadly, operated. Rural libraries initially lagged behind considerably, but have narrowed the gap between their outlets and those in more populated areas in recent years. Even if rural libraries still have considerably slower connection speeds and weaker technological infrastructure than city, suburban, and town libraries, the fact that they also have smaller service populations has made it so that these divides have relatively limited impact.

IV. BROADBAND AND TECHNOLOGICAL CAPACITY

Libraries in communities of all sizes have improved their technological capacity in recent years. In 2014, for instance, 14.9% of rural libraries had subscribed Internet download speeds of 1.5 Mbps or less, compared with 43% in 2010. Libraries overall have a median subscribed download speed of approximately 16 Mbps, with a high of 40 Mbps for city libraries, 25 Mbps for suburban outlets, and 15 Mbps for town locations. Rural libraries have the weakest capacity, at a median of just 10 Mbps, falling well below the FCC's broadband standard of 25 Mbps for home (not library or school) access, where bandwidth is divided by members of a single household rather than staff and patrons of an entire library. Furthermore, this is a fraction of the 100 Mbps goal set by the Federal Communications Commission (2014) for all libraries serving 50,000 people or fewer. Rural fringe libraries have the best broadband capacity, at a median of 13 Mbps for downloads and 8.6 Mbps for uploads, showing that these libraries' proximities to population centers make them more likely to be able to take advantage of local infrastructure. Rural distant libraries stand at a median of 7.7 Mbps for downloads and 2.2 Mbps for uploads, while rural remote outlets stand at 6.7 Mbps and 1.0 Mbps, respectively.

Another measure of library broadband quality is adequacy of connections for patron use, as reported by librarians. In 2008, only 42% of libraries reported their Internet connection speed was adequate to meet patron demand most of the time. In 2014, this improved to 60.8% of libraries across all locale types, but rural libraries were the least likely to report speeds adequate to meet demand most of the time. One in 10 rural libraries report that Internet speeds rarely meet patron needs.

Rural libraries still have room for improvement in terms of broadband capacity, and this becomes far more striking as one moves farther from major population centers. A significant mitigating factor is that rural libraries have lower population density and, as a result, broadband capacity is commonly split among fewer people. However, as new applications continue to develop that require greater broadband capacity, more will need to be done to ensure that rural libraries and households are able to keep up.

V. BASIC TECHNOLOGY SKILLS

Rural libraries (84%) are quite comparable with their peers (87%) with regard to basic computer training. The gap in training offered in using basic office productivity software is similarly small (84.4% overall and 80.7% for rural libraries). Differences become greater in relation to more specialized training, such as social media and introducing patrons to new technologies, as illustrated in Table 1.

Training or technology assistance may be offered through formal classes, individual help by appointment, informal point-of-use training, and through online training materials. Libraries commonly offer training through multiple means, but ad-hoc assistance through informal point-of-use training is the most common form of assistance. Offerings of formal classes tend to decrease

Table 1.   Percentage of Libraries Offering Basic Technology
Assistance, by Locale.

	Overall	City	Suburb	Town	Rural	Rural Fringe	Rural Distant	Rural Remote
General Internet use (e.g., set up e-mail)	89.9	89.2	93.3	92.3	86.6	89.2	87.9	82.4
Social media (e.g., blogging, Twitter)	55.9	62.2	58.6	59.6	49.7	57.1	50.3	47.9
General familiarity with new technologies	61.8	68.5	73.0	63.4	50.6	62.1	52.0	48.0

with population density. As an example of this trend, 78.3% of libraries that offer training in general Internet use do so through informal point-of-use training, while 43.4% offer formal classes in this area. City libraries are the most likely to offer training in both formats, with 80.4% doing so on an ad-hoc basis and 60.6% providing classes. By comparison, 76.5% of rural libraries that assist patrons with general Internet use do so through informal point-of-use interactions, while only 31.5% provide such offerings in a class. This is likely due to the simple reason that, with smaller population sizes in rural areas, it is not possible to gather together enough people with the same training request on a regular enough basis to meet patron needs through a group format. This practical decision to primarily use ad-hoc training sessions and limit reliance on formal classes has limited impact on types of services offered. For a broad range of computer skills, rural patrons are almost as likely as those in more populated areas to be able to find such services at their local public library.

VI. EMPLOYMENT AND ECONOMIC DEVELOPMENT

Rural population growth has been stagnant for years, actually declining 0.3% between 2010 and 2014 before becoming simply flat in 2015 (United States Department of Agriculture, 2016). Job growth was also flat prior to the recession, with smaller losses during this period but also smaller gains in recovery years. With negative population growth and a relative lack of new industries, including technology-oriented businesses, many rural communities do not have a path toward economic growth. Libraries can be part of the solution in terms of building job skills and supporting new businesses.

As shown in Table 2, 73.1% of all libraries help patrons develop skills needed to advance a career. This is achieved through training in developing

Table 2. Percentage of Libraries Offering Local Economic Development Programs, by Locale.

	Overall	City	Suburb	Town	Rural	Rural fringe	Rural distant	Rural remote
Applying for jobs (e.g., interviewing skills, resume development)	73.1	81.1	77.7	79.8	63.4	71.7	69.1	61.4
Accessing and using job opportunity resources	68.3	78.6	76.0	69.5	58.3	69.7	62.7	50.0
Providing work space(s) for mobile workers	36.1	34.8	37.6	38.3	34.5	33.8	32.1	34.8
Supporting small business development	32.2	43.0	41.0	30.3	22.8	29.2	22.3	20.1
Accessing and using online business information resources	47.9	67.0	63.7	43.3	31.9	48.4	31.6	26.3

resumes, assisting patrons with completing online applications, and mock interviews or other interviewing training. A majority of rural libraries provide employment-related programming, and close to one-quarter are engaged with small business development activities.

National trends show that public libraries can make contributions to the development of small businesses (American Library Association, 2016a) and provide other services that allow workers to thrive, but limited resources have led rural libraries to be less likely than their peers on average to provide services that directly address these matters. Considering that the United States Department of Agriculture (USDA, 2017) has found that economic growth and non-recessionary employment gains in communities are positively correlated with educational attainment, the fact that nonmetro areas fall behind metro regions in high school and college completion is a hurdle that must be overcome. Libraries cannot support local economic growth without also supporting local education.

VII. EDUCATIONAL ASSISTANCE

Educational attainment in rural and other nonmetro parts of the United States has improved significantly in recent years. About 15% of residents in nonmetro areas did not have a high school degree or equivalent as of 2015, which represents a significant improvement from 24% in 2000 (USDA, 2017).

Metro areas fare only slightly better, with 13% of residents having not completed high school degrees or equivalencies. However, differences become more dramatic in relationship to postsecondary education, with only 19% of rural residents having obtained a bachelor's degree or higher, compared with 33% of metro residents. Considering the potential impact of geography on allowing rural residents access to colleges and universities, as well as access to specific majors and courses of interest, distance education can be part of the solution in bridging this divide. As such, responses to the Digital Inclusion Survey showed that rural libraries are the most likely to provide assistance in accessing online degree courses (e.g., virtual high school, university, college, community college, technical school, and online certification programs). About 70.4% of libraries overall offer such services, ranging from a high of 74.7% for rural outlets to a low of 61.2% for city locations.

Table 3, however, shows that rural libraries are less likely to offer formal after-school programs, such as learning labs or the Let's Move! program. Just over one-quarter of rural libraries report offering these services. Rural fringe libraries outpace their peers at 37.9%, dropping to 28.4% for rural distant outlets and 25.9% for rural remote locations. It is worth noting that this does not include standard reference help with homework and school projects, nor does it include providing the library as a safe after-school space without any activities specifically planned for this age group.

More research is needed to understand why planned after-school programs decline with population density, but this likely relates to limited open hours, staff time and availability, adequacy of facilities, and the ability of students to reach their local library. On this last point, public transportation quality and the ability to walk to nearby libraries decreases as one moves away from urban centers. In a recent study of after-school programs in rural

Table 3.   Libraries Offering Educational Assistance, by Percent.

	Overall	City	Suburb	Town	Rural	Rural fringe	Rural distant	Rural remote
After-school programs (e.g., homework help)	36.3	51.4	44.1	33.2	26.5	37.9	28.4	25.9
Science, technology, engineering, arts, math (STEAM) events (e.g., maker spaces)	34.2	48.9	47.7	32.8	19.7	36.4	20.9	14.4
GED or equivalent education	34.9	48.4	35.2	40.0	26.6	28.0	26.6	26.3
ESL/ESOL/ELL	24.9	42.5	35.5	21.4	12.6	17.5	10.8	8.0

communities, the Afterschool Alliance found that these distances and the transportation issues they entailed prevented many schools from seeing after-school programs as being cost effective, while students and parents were often unable to easily access extant programs due to these barriers (Afterschool Alliance, 2016).

Rural libraries also lag in STEAM offerings, preparation for GED exami-nations, and providing English as a Second Language (ESL) training. Staff availability and expertise are probable reasons for the unavailability of such services, corresponding with population declines and distance from popula-tion centers. Additionally, ESL, GED, and other more specialized education training that requires staff expertise and greater time commitments make them less practical offerings in rural areas where formal classes for small numbers may not be considered cost-effective.

VIII. COMMUNITY ENGAGEMENT AND GROUP EVENTS

Rural libraries provide civic and social engagement services to patrons. As shown in Table 4, 61.1% of all public libraries offer book discussions and other social events for adults. This is true for roughly 50% of rural locations. Rural fringe outlets outpace other rural locations at 62.9%, however. About

Table 4. Percentage of Libraries Offering Community and Civic Engagement Programs, by Locale.

	Overall	City	Suburb	Town	Rural	Rural fringe	Rural distant	Rural remote
Hosting social connection events for adults (e.g., book discussion groups)	61.1	69.7	70.3	64.0	49.8	62.9	52.8	44.3
Hosting social connection events for young adults (e.g., gaming)	59.8	78.9	76.6	56.3	42.6	56.6	45.2	32.4
Hosting community engagement events (e.g., candidate forums)	40.2	49.1	47.8	42.6	30.2	33.8	32.1	26.3
Assisting patrons with access and use of online government programs and services	75.6	82.9	77.1	79.7	69.4	72.0	72.0	65.8

43% of rural libraries offer events for young adults, with a low of 32.4% of rural remote locations and a high of 56.6% for rural fringe. Finally, about 30% of rural libraries offer civic engagement events like candidate forums and community conversations, with remote libraries the least likely to do so.

A strong majority of rural libraries offer core services that bridge the digital divide and ensure that a lack of access to or high costs of broadband services do not need to result in the local population being excluded from changing elements of society. More specialized services targeting specific community needs are less commonly available through many of these rural outlets than their counterparts in more populated areas, but this is often due to practical considerations involving demand. However, there are real problems of achieving economies of scale that prevent rural libraries from having as robust offerings as towns, suburbs, and cities. Some of these barriers are described in the following sections.

IX. MOVING BEYOND TECHNOLOGY: NEXT STEPS TOWARD SERVICE EXPANSION

Overcoming the challenges that rural public libraries face would be a relatively simple matter if the only obstacle were technological infrastructure. Broadband access and speeds continue to improve in rural America while the prices of computers and other technological infrastructure continue to decline. Considering these market trends, combined with federal support that has mitigated the impact of market failures that would normally prevent broadband providers from reaching rural areas, there are plans in place to close the technology gap between rural public libraries and their peers in more populated areas. However, technology is only one problem that affects rural libraries' service impacts. The elephant in the room is rural libraries' budgets and how relatively limited funding negatively impacts staffing, open hours, and more costly infrastructure problems like the size, design, and age of libraries' physical plants.

About 84.4% of library budgets nationwide come from local governments, followed by 6.8% from state governments and just 0.5% from federal investments (American Library Association, 2016b). This has a clear impact on rural libraries' salaries and staffing. Rural areas tend to have less local tax revenues as a result of lower average salaries, lower land values, and a higher proportion of retired individuals. This has only become worse as rural population growth has declined in recent years, in turn limiting the amount of new revenue that has been made available.

What follows is a discussion of how the high level of dependency on local funding limits how much rural libraries and librarians can do. Rural libraries will need to overcome these considerable challenges and rethink their structures if they wish to keep pace with national trends in evolving service offerings.

X. STAFFING AND HOURS OPEN

As libraries are located farther from urban centers and serve smaller population bases, it makes sense that there is a corresponding decrease in the number of full-time equivalent (FTE) employees per location. Rural fringe libraries have a median of 4.2 FTEs per location, versus 2.0 for rural distant locations, and declining further to just 1.3 for rural remote outlets. However, declines in available staff can only go so far before also having a logical impact on the number of hours libraries are open to the public. An average rural fringe library is open 1,747 hours per year, versus 1,444 for rural distant outlets and 1,367 hours annually for rural remote locations. As a result of this, a barrier to libraries serving their communities is the ability to keep the doors open enough hours to meet patrons' needs and schedules. Even if the library is open at times that are compatible with patrons' schedules, the staff may not have enough time to directly assist with their information needs.

Libraries in more remote areas are also less likely to have a librarian with a Master of Library and Information Science (MLIS) on staff. About 66.2% of rural fringe libraries employ at least one librarian with an MLIS, declining to 29.5% for rural distant locations and 13.8% for public libraries in rural remote locales. Another problem that comes with lower levels of staffing and the fact that most rural libraries are part of small systems, including many systems that are comprised of a single library outlet, is the lack of specialized staff. In the next chapter of this volume, Miller goes further into depth discussing rates of rural public librarians holding MLIS degrees and what this means for general services. Likewise, in their chapter "Rural Librarians as Change Agents in the 21st Century," Mehra et al. detail their IMLS-funded efforts to provide rural librarians with MLIS degrees that build students skill sets according to the needs of their communities. There are practical solutions to problems of lack of training for rural librarians, and with online teaching improving with advances in the technology that supports it. The academic community has a responsibility to be part of this, regardless of whether the end result is continuing education units or a terminal graduate degree.

Meanwhile, the median librarian salary for rural libraries is $28,508, with a high of $32,856 for rural fringe locations, declining to $27,370 for rural distant libraries and further to $25,950 for rural remote outlets. By comparison, city public librarians have a mean salary of $37,853, and suburban librarians see an insignificant drop to $37,762. Town librarians lag behind those closer to major urban centers, and only slightly outpace rural librarians, with a median salary of $28,914. A decline in salaries in correlation with distance from urban centers is not surprising, as salaries are generally set according to the local cost of living.

An important disclaimer on the data above is that this does not suggest that librarians in rural areas are less dedicated or competent than those in more populated areas. The lack of an MLIS may result in newly hired rural librarians taking more time to acclimate to their positions, but a 2007 survey of American rural libraries by Robert Flatley and Andrea Wyman (2009) found that 47% of responding librarians had been in their career for a decade or more, and an additional 22% had been librarians for 6 to 10 years. Furthermore, 66% of respondents to Flatley and Wyman's survey noted that they planned to remain in the library profession until retirement, and 97% reported that they were satisfied or very satisfied with their careers, suggesting that these individuals are dedicated to their careers and assisting with the needs of their patrons. Considering this enthusiasm, the most logical barrier to librarians offering particular services is the problem of resources, and a lack of funds can result in various forms of infrastructural limitations.

XI. AGING AND INADEQUATE LIBRARY BUILDINGS

Broadly speaking, rural libraries are small and their buildings are less up to date. The median physical size for rural libraries is 2,592 square feet, versus a median of 12,680 for city libraries, 12,578 for suburban outlets, and 9,300 for town locations. This ranges from a median of 4,276 square feet for rural fringe outlets, 2,500 for rural distant, and 2,380 for rural remote. These medians cover the entirety of these library outlets, including staff offices and other areas that are not accessible to the public, shelves for circulating and reference collections, and public access computers (PACs). Although these are luxuries that many rural libraries do not have space to accommodate, in some cases this includes designated children's areas, private meeting and study rooms for patron use, and other general-use spaces.

More research needs to be conducted into the exact limits having smaller physical plants places on rural libraries, but a problem that is readily apparent is that it is difficult to accommodate new, increasingly popular public programs with a building that is aging and not easily reconfigured, due to space and other problems. As discussed in IMLS' 2013 Public Libraries in the United States report, annual circulation of materials held by public libraries hit a peak high in 2010, with the corresponding peak impact of the recession leading patrons to see the public library as an alternative to buying or renting entertainment and other informational materials. However, circulation has been gradually declining since, dropping 3.6% between 2010 and 2013, even though this still includes a 25.4% increase since 2003. Similarly, general PAC usage has been a relatively new way for libraries to show their community impact since the mid-1990s, but overall PAC sessions have decreased 9.2% for all public libraries between 2010 and 2013. Circulation and PAC usage are still highly important means of libraries showing their value to communities, but these metrics will not be an effective means for libraries to show growth or argue for higher funding.

The greatest area of recent growth for public libraries, and thus the best means to argue for increased funding, is through public programs. For libraries overall, public program attendance has increased 28.6% between 2006, when this was first measured, and 2013 (Institute of Museum and Library Services, 2016a). Programs targeting young adults have brought in 15.2% more patrons in 2013 than just two years before, in 2011. These are promising developments, as national, state, and local-level publicity that shift patrons' perceptions of libraries in a way that puts greater—but not exclusive—emphasis on public programs will frame libraries in a way that will correspond with growth and innovation for many outlets. However, considering that many rural libraries lack the physical space and staff time to plan and execute these activities, a shift in public perceptions of libraries that includes a positive focus on programs would leave many smaller outlets behind.

Beyond physical space, the age of facilities is an issue. The average year for American public library buildings having opened is 1970, with rural libraries falling behind this with an average opening year of 1969 but still having newer buildings overall than town libraries, which have an average opening year of 1965. City and suburban libraries have the newest buildings on average, with respective opening years of 1975 and 1974. Furthermore, 21.3% of public libraries have been renovated or newly constructed in the past five years. City libraries have been the most likely to be renovated or newly built, at 33.4%; suburban and town libraries have fared about equally, at 22.4% and 23.0%, respectively; and rural libraries are the least likely to have been constructed or updated, at 14.8%. How recently the facility has been brought up to date is no small matter. To point out just a few differences, 57.6% and 58.1% of libraries that have not been updated in the past five years offer social connection programs for adults and young adults, respectively, versus 75.6% and 68.4% for those that have. About 34.1% of libraries that have not been renovated offer space for mobile workers, falling behind the 43.7% of those that have more up-to-date facilities. About 33.2% of older library facilities provide after school programs, while 51.7% of outlets that have been renovated or newly constructed in the past year do so.

To be clear, the figures above denoting differences between libraries that have been updated in the past five years and those that have not are for American public libraries broadly, not just rural outlets. Likewise, in this instance, evidence shows a definite correlation between how up to date libraries are and the programs they offer, but not quite causation. More research needs to be conducted to fully understand the impact of physical building quality on rural libraries' abilities to serve the public, including controlling for staffing differences and other factors. There is the obvious question of whether the newness of a library's facilities allows it to do more programming or if a higher preexisting budget that allowed for new construction or upgrades had already allowed for more expansive service offerings. However, considering the dramatic differences in programming for more and less up-to-date buildings, the question is likely not if building quality affects the variety of services to which patrons have access, but how much of an impact this has. Ranking the priorities that should be given to certain library improvements is beyond the scope of this report, but facility size and meeting rooms or other flexible spaces that can be configured for a range of activities should be considered alongside technological capacity, staff time and training, and other factors when considering how to expand the scope of rural public libraries' service offerings.

In short, rural libraries face staffing shortages and physical limitations that limit the diversity of services they can offer. The most obvious and effective solution to these problems would be a general increase in public library funding, especially from the state and federal level. Advocating for this is an important long-term goal, but in the short term it is necessary to consider how to allocate limited resources in ways that allow rural libraries to have the greatest possible positive impacts on their communities. What follows is a discussion of solutions that have been enacted in some areas, as well as ideas for new courses of actions that can increase rural libraries' effectiveness.

XII. STATEWIDE AND REGIONAL SOLUTIONS

Rural libraries are often geographically isolated from their peer libraries and other resources, but this does not mean that they need to be institutionally isolated from other libraries and other support agencies. Such connections at the local, regional, and state levels can help overcome the resource avail-ability and allocation problems that many rural libraries face on a daily basis. The following section details how such collaborations can work using the state of Maryland as a specific example, followed by thoughts on what is lost when such connections are not present and reasons why libraries and their funding agencies are reluctant to promote and support formalized col-laboration.

XIII. MULTI-TIERED COOPERATION AT STATE, REGIONAL, AND LOCAL LEVELS

The state of Maryland has specifically enacted organizational solutions intended to address resource gaps between rural regions and more populated areas. The public libraries throughout the state are primarily organized as county-level systems, rather than operating as smaller units like towns or municipalities, with the Enoch Pratt Free Library (EPFL) system serving the independent city of Baltimore. Eighteen of the state's 23 counties have pri-marily rural land masses and, while none of these counties have a library system that is constituted by a single branch, system sizes range from two to five outlets, thus limiting resource sharing and economies of scale compared with more populated counties.

Maryland has two primary solutions for this problem. First, the state has funded three regional library systems to facilitate cooperation between librar-ies in 14 of the 15 least populated counties: the Eastern Shore Regional Library (ERSL) with eight member systems, and the Western Maryland Regional Library (WMRL) and Southern Maryland Regional Library Association (SMRLA), with three member counties each. Services provided by these mul-ticounty associations include cataloging, maintaining online catalog systems for staff and patron use, providing training programs for employees through-out constituent counties, and overseeing inter-library loan between counties, allowing patrons access to far more materials than they would find in just their home counties. They also negotiate with vendors to purchase databases, often receiving rates that are considerably lower than what each county sys-tem could negotiate alone.

Recognizing the difficulty that rural areas face in supporting their librar-ies through local tax funding, the state of Maryland is the primary funder of the three regional library consortia, providing approximately $6.4 million in 2015, which constituted about 75% or ERSL's budget (with virtually all of the remainder coming from federal sources) and almost 95% of WMRL and SMRLA's support (Maryland Division of Library Development and Services, 2016). Most funding for the individual county library systems still comes from the local level, but removing a majority of the responsibility for technical services, interlibrary loan, and other operations from each member library system's budget allows these local funds to be used to maintain and enhance patron-oriented services.

Meanwhile, the second major support structure for rural libraries throughout the state of Maryland is the State Library Resource Center (SLRC), housed in the central location of Baltimore's EPFL. SLRC provides services to all state libraries that are similar to—but not redundant with—those offered by the state's regional libraries, including coordinating statewide interlibrary loans, implementing training programs that include Maryland state librarian certification, and negotiating the purchase of certain databases. SLRC also oversees specialized reference and collections, assisting librarians throughout the state when their patrons' needs go beyond the resources of the local library.

Andrea Berstler, executive director of the ESRL-member Wicomico Public Libraries, sees these county, local, and state support mechanisms as invaluable to expanding the scope of what her libraries can do. In particular, Wicomico's smaller branches do not have staffing budgets that justify hiring subject specialists, with most librarians acting as generalists who can do a bit of everything. Being able to rely on both the staff expertise and specialized reference materials available through SLRC and the affiliated EPFL through a formalized, state-level connection ensures that this does not diminish customer service quality. Likewise, when discussing the value of having state and regional-level staff negotiate for databases, using a large number of library outlets as leverage for obtaining favorable financial terms, Berstler notes that "We all know that negotiating is a skill and librarians are not necessarily good negotiators. We're too helpful. We all want to help the process along, and the best negotiating tool is the threat of walking away from the table." Similarly, smaller outlets throughout the ESRL cooperative do not have enough technological needs to justify dedicated IT staff, so having the regional system split dedicated employees' services between multiple libraries allows for considerable savings while not compromising technology quality.

Perhaps most importantly, Berstler notes that the collegial support provided by the county, regional, and state structures is invaluable for her, her staff, and her colleagues. For Berstler specifically, these cooperative systems encourage her to discuss ideas with the directors of other county systems or to "pick up the phone and bounce some ideas off the administrator" at

ESRL. For library administrators specifically, this provides them with assistance in thinking through major issues and avoiding a sense of isolation that can come with upper management.

While the average public library in the United States receives 6.9% of its support from state funding, 15.7% of the overall budget for Maryland's public libraries comes from this level (Maryland Division of Library Development and Services, 2016). It is possible for libraries in other states to emulate some of Maryland's collaborative library mechanisms without this level of state funding by pooling part of the funding provided by local governments, but even initial steps toward this are difficult or impossible in many parts of the country.

XIV. LACK OF COOPERATION AND CONCERNS ABOUT AUTONOMY

In Berstler's experience, branches in her system do not lose significant autonomy or their own identity by being part of their county, regional, or state systems. Instead, removing a wide range of responsibilities inclusive of—but not limited to—more advanced information technology management, maintenance, payroll, grant writing, and database acquisition from library outlets allows librarians to spend more time focusing on their patrons' needs and enhancing services. Or, as Berstler puts it, each library can "pay attention to just being a library." The end result of support from higher levels is not that the branches below become copies of the libraries and other bureaucratic offices above them, but instead that the staff has more time to focus on its public programs, training activities, and collection development in ways that meet the needs and desires of their nearest constituents.

Despite this, in Berstler's experience working for several libraries in another state, most of the libraries were not part of local systems even at the county level, with single outlets serving a municipality or other small geographic area. The state government had relatively weak control over the libraries and limited funds to assist them, resulting in libraries spending more on resources for less service to patrons. Berstler observed that many of the libraries refused to join each other because of their staff and board members not wanting to sacrifice their authority and autonomy and local government officials not wanting to cede part of their control over institutions under their purview. As she puts it, "they're not willing to give up a little to gain a lot."

Becky Heil has seen similar issues in her current career as one of the six library consultants for the State Library of Iowa, each of whom oversees a section of the state and provides assistance to public libraries in those areas. In Iowa, the idea of home rule is ingrained into both the culture and the law, with power being ceded to local governments whenever possible. The end result of this is significant impacts on public library structures and service offerings. In Heil's experience, there is little interest on the part of local government officials to cede part of their control and change this status quo. Municipalities and other local governments each commonly having their own independent library, combined with sparse population density, has resulted in Iowa having the third highest number of libraries per capita, primarily comprised of small outlets designed to serve a limited legal or de facto service area. Of the 534 total outlets in the state, 63.5% have service populations of under 2,500, with more than half of those servicing less than 1,000 people (Institute of Museum and Library Services, 2016b). About 98.1% of the libraries are single direct service outlets rather than being part of a system organized under a legal basis.

Despite the State Library of Iowa having a limited budget, the organization and its library consultants provide invaluable services such as helping design websites for libraries that are not able to do so themselves, working with local staff to develop operational policies for individual libraries, and coordinating statewide interlibrary loan, although there is no real-time federated catalog for libraries throughout the state to facilitate the latter activity. Database acquisitions are not possible at the state level due to a lack of funds, and regional collaborations do not exist in a formalized manner, resulting in libraries fending for themselves in terms of acquiring digital resources. The state has coordinated and funded the purchase of a single database, Learning Express, through funding from Iowa's Workforce Development office rather than state library funding. In opposition to Berstler's thoughts on Maryland's public library structure facilitating cooperation and collegiality between library staff, Heil notes that the lack of formal connections between libraries limits librarians' abilities to connect with and learn from each other. Staff from libraries throughout individual counties or areas have attempted to meet with each other in some cases on a periodic basis, but funding is not commonly available for such activities, and it is often impossible to maintain regular meetings without closing libraries—due to the small number of employees per outlet—or otherwise conflicting with librarians' commitments. As a result, it is difficult to maintain viable support networks for librarians in these situations on an ongoing basis.

Further investigation into the positive impact of collaboration and multi-tiered library superstructures, as seen in Maryland, is needed to fully verify that advocacy for the advancement of such arrangements will significantly benefit rural public libraries. If this proves to be a valid direction, then more research will be needed to understand the nuances of why government officials and librarians in many rural areas throughout the country have been reluctant to cede local control to system-level operations that can allow rural libraries to operate more efficiently and effectively. Greater understanding of the reluctance in this area can lead to counter arguments and advocacy that can reverse these trends. The preliminary research presented in this report suggests that such advocacy and changes to the operational structure of many rural libraries can benefit librarians and their communities, making library services more impactful and cost effective.

XV. CONCLUSION

America's rural public libraries have advanced considerably in their ability to offer technology access and training to their publics. Although gaps between rural libraries and those in more populated areas still need to be addressed, they have become considerably less pronounced each year. These gaps are widest when comparing rural distant and especially rural remote outlets, showing that future analysis and resource distribution needs to take greater geographic barriers to resources into account rather than lumping all rural libraries together. These differences are discussed in the following chapter, in which Karen Miller analyzes how federal funding can mitigate the factors that lead to the most geographically disadvantaged libraries falling behind.

Despite these obstacles, rural libraries are now able to do more than ever before to connect their patrons to employment information and training, health information, government services, and educational opportunities. As encouraging as this is, considerable challenges are looming. For rural libraries to thrive, they will need more space and improved buildings, strong partnerships with nearby libraries and state organizations, and better funding structures. All of these things are possible with greater advocacy, provided that the academic community and national-level support organizations continue the research that will be needed to support these arguments.

ACKNOWLEDGEMENTS

The authors would like to thank Larra Clark, deputy director of the American Library Association's Office for Information Technology Policy and the Public Library Association, for guiding the original research report that led to this chapter.

NOTES

1. Reports from the IMLS Public Libraries in the United States Survey and the iPAC Digital Inclusion Survey are available, respectively, at https://www.imls.gov/research-evaluation/data-collection/public-libraries-united-states-survey and http://digitalinclusion.umd.edu/. Predecessor studies to the Digital Inclusion Survey are available at http://plinternetsurvey.org/. These websites include annual reports and other targeted white papers, issue briefs, and the statistical data sets for each survey cycle. More detailed information about each survey cycle's methodology is included in these annual reports.

2. Other conceptual models of urbanized versus nonurbanized areas appear throughout this report, such as those of the United States Department of Agriculture (USDA), which has its own systems of defining rurality. It would be impractical to reprocess the data from these other studies to make them compatible with the NCES standard, but leaving out information from other in-depth studies about rural areas would limit the analysis of uniquely rural problems in this report. To minimize confusion, the authors have attempted to note the original source as clearly as possible when data do not conform to NCES standards, allowing the reader to find the original study for more information.

REFERENCES

American Library Association. (2016a). One small business at a time: Building entrepreneurial opportunity in America's communities. Retrieved from http://www.ala.org/news/sites/ala.org.news/files/content/ALA-SmallBizEntrep-2016Nov10.pdf.

American Library Association. (2016b). Library Operating Expenditures: A Selected Annotated Bibliography. Retrieved from http://www.ala.org/tools/libfactsheets/alalibraryfactsheet04.

Afterschool Alliance. (2013). America after 3pm special report: The growing importance of afterschool in rural communities. Retrieved from http://www.afterschoolalliance.org/AA3PM/Afterschool_in_Rural_Communities.pdf.

Bertot, J. C., Real, B., Lee, J., McDermott, A. J., & Jaeger, P. T. (2014). 2014 Digital Inclusion Survey: Findings and results. Information Policy and Access Center. Retrieved from http://digitalinclusion.umd.edu/sites/default/files/uploads/2014DigitalInclusionSurveyFinalRelease.pdf.

Federal Communications Commission. (2014). Summary of the E-Rate modernization order. Retrieved from https://www.fcc.gov/general/summary-e-rate-modernization-order.

Flatley, R., & Wyman, A. (2009). Changes in rural libraries and librarianship: A comparative survey. *Public Library Quarterly*, *28*(1), 24–39.

Institute of Museum and Library Services. (2016a). Public libraries in the United States survey, fiscal year 2013. Retrieved from https://www.imls.gov/sites/default/files/publications/documents/plsfy2013.pdf.

Institute of Museum and Library Services. (2016b). Public libraries in the United States survey, fiscal year 2013: Supplemental tables 1–7a. Retrieved from https://www.imls.gov/sites/default/files/fy2013_pls_tables_1_thru_7a.pdf.

Maryland Division of Library Development and Services. (2016). Maryland public library annual report FY2014. Retrieved from http://dlslibrary.state.md.us/publications/Exec/MSDE/ED23-104(d)_2014.pdf.

National Center for Educational Statistics. (2006). Rural education in America: Definitions. Retrieved from http://nces.ed.gov/surveys/ruraled/definitions.asp.

United States Department of Agriculture. (2016). Rural America at a glance, 2016 edition. Retrieved from https://www.ers.usda.gov/webdocs/publications/80894/eib-162.pdf?v=42684.

United States Department of Agriculture. (2017). Rural education at a glance, 2017 edition. Retrieved from http://www.ers.usda.gov/topics/rural-economy-population/employment-education/rural-education.aspx.

EXPLORING RURAL PUBLIC LIBRARY ASSETS FOR ASSET-BASED COMMUNITY DEVELOPMENT

Karen Miller

ABSTRACT

This chapter explores differences in fringe, distant, and remote rural public library assets for asset-based community development (ABCD) and the relationships of those assets to geographic regions, governance structures, and demographics.

The author analyzes 2013 data from the Institute of Museum and Library Services (IMLS) and U.S. Department of Agriculture using nonparametric statistics and data mining random forest supervised classification algorithms.

There are statistically significant differences between fringe, distant, and remote library assets. Unexpectedly, median per capita outlets (along with service hours and staff) increase as distances from urban areas increase. The Southeast region ranks high in unemployment and poverty and low in median household income, which aligns with the Southeast's low median per capita library expenditures, staff, hours, inventory, and programs. However,

Rural and Small Public Libraries: Challenges and Opportunities
Advances in Librarianship, Volume 43, 61–96
ISSN: 0065-2830/doi:10.1108/S0065-283020170000043004

the Southeast's relatively high percentage of rural libraries with at least one staff member with a Master of Library and Information Science promises future asset growth in those libraries. State and federal contributions to Alaska libraries propelled the remote Far West to the number one ranking in median per capita staff, inventory, and programs.

This study is based on IMLS library system-wide data and does not include rural library branches operated by nonrural central libraries.

State and federal contributions to rural libraries increase economic, cultural, and social capital creation in the most remote communities. On a per capita basis, economic capital from state and federal agencies assists small, remote rural libraries in providing infrastructure and services that are more closely aligned with libraries in more populated areas and increases library assets available for ABCD initiatives in otherwise underserved communities.

Even the smallest rural library can contribute to ABCD initiatives by connecting their communities to outside resources and creating new economic, cultural, and social assets.

Analyzing rural public library assets within their geographic, political, and demographic contexts highlights their potential contributions to ABCD initiatives.

Keywords: Rural public libraries; asset-based community development; community development; data mining; supervised classification; random forest decision trees

I. INTRODUCTION

The Institute of Museum and Library Services (IMLS) defines "rural" libraries in terms of their distance from urbanized areas or urban clusters. Derived from World Geodetic System 1984 geocoding in partnership with the U.S. Census Bureau, the "Locale," or urban-centric, code in the annual IMLS Public Library Survey file enables researchers to identify rural libraries (IMLS, 2015a, pp. 17–18). Based on the Locale code in the IMLS 2013 Public Library Data file (IMLS, 2015b), 4,216, or 45%, of the 9,309 public library systems in the United States were classified as "rural." The Locale code also segments rural libraries into fringe, distant, and remote categories. Table 1 contains the distances from urbanized areas or urban clusters for each

Table 1. 2013 Rural Public Libraries by Locale (Urban-Centric) Code.

Locale	Description	Definition	Count	Percent
41	Fringe	≤5 miles from urbanized area, or ≤2.5 miles from urban cluster	512	12%
42	Distant	>5 miles but ≤25 miles from urbanized area, or >2.5 miles but ≤10 miles from urban cluster	2,069	49%
43	Remote	>25 miles from urbanized area and >10 miles from urban cluster	1,635	39%
Total			4,216	100%

category (IMLSa, 2015, p. 18) and shows that the majority (49%) of rural public libraries are in the "distant" rural category, followed by 39% in the "remote" rural category and 12% in the "fringe" rural category.

Whether located in a fringe, distant, or remote rural area, each rural library possesses a unique set of assets available for investment in asset-based community development (ABCD) initiatives like those described by Kretzmann and McKnight in *Building Communities from the Inside Out* (1993). ABCD initiatives build connections between local assets to create new assets that can be used to solve local issues. Working together to achieve shared goals, local individuals, associations, institutions, and businesses use their assets to overcome economic or other constraints while building and strengthening the community. Possessing "rich local institutional assets" (Hildreth, 2007, p. 9), rural public libraries can make important contributions to ABCD initiatives.

II. RESEARCH PROBLEM/QUESTIONS

While the Mehra, Bishop, and Partee study in this volume, "A Gap Analysis of the Perspectives of Small Businesses and Rural Librarians in Tennessee," adopts the ABCD perspective and a recent dissertation acknowledges the approach (Ginger, 2015), there are few recent studies of rural public libraries conducted from the ABCD perspective, intentionally or otherwise. Furthermore, quantitative studies of rural public library assets predicated on the Kretzmann–McKnight ABCD framework are lacking. To help fill that gap, this study explores the rural public library assets available for investment in ABCD initiatives using an IMLS data set enriched by demographic variables provided by the U.S. Department of Agriculture (USDA). This research seeks to answer the following questions:

> Q1: What are the differences in the asset holdings of fringe, distant, and remote rural libraries?
>
> Q2: What are the relationships between fringe, distant, and remote rural public library asset holdings and library service area population size, geographic regions, political (governance) structures, and community demographics?

Analyzing rural public library assets by distance from urbanized areas and clusters and considering those assets within their broader geographic, political, and demographic contexts provides broader insight into the potential contributions of these important local institutions to ABCD initiatives.

III. ASSET-BASED COMMUNITY DEVELOPMENT

The ABCD approach was developed by John Kretzmann and John McKnight of the Center of Urban Affairs and Policy Research at Northwestern University in the early 1990s. For communities struggling to solve crime, illiteracy, underemployment, and other social issues, the ABCD framework provides an "inside-out," "glass half full" alternative to "outside-in," needs-driven, "glass half empty" policies and institutional responses. While outside-in methods to solving community issues treat residents as clients, the inside-out ABCD approach respects and builds on the agency of individuals, local associations, and local institutions. Detailed in their groundbreaking work, *Building Communities from the Inside Out* (Kretzmann & McKnight, 1993), the ABCD approach has been adopted by a variety of domestic and international communities (see, e.g., Green, 2010, p. 4; Kretzmann & McKnight, 1993, p. 355; Mathie & Cunningham, 2008; Rans & Altman, 2002; Snow, 2001, pp. 72–75), is recognized as an effective community development model by philanthropic organizations (see, e.g., Russell & Nurture Development, 2009, Carnegie UK Trust; Snow, 2001, Blandin Foundation), and has influenced social work praxis (Scales, Streeter, & Cooper, 2014, pp. xvi–xvii). The Asset-Based Community Development Institute, founded at the Northwestern School of Education and Social Policy and now housed at DePaul University's Irwin W. Steans Center for Community-Based Service Learning & Community Service Studies (https://resources.depaul.edu/abcd-institute/Pages/default.aspx), continues to encourage ABCD initiatives through faculty speeches, workshops, consultations, and publications.

The ABCD framework arose from Kretzmann and McKnight's rejection of the "institutional" assumption that individual and community well-being derives from institutional systems such as welfare and the infrastructures supporting those institutions (McKnight, 2003, p. 2). In the institutional assumption, local residents are treated as clients whose well-being is determined by the consumption of institutional services. The agency and relationships of citizens and community associations are omitted from the social map of the community under the institutional assumption (p. 2). In contrast, Kretzmann and McKnight's ABCD approach centers on the agency of citizens and their established community associations in effecting social change. This requires a new map centered on and flowing outward from individuals—individuals and families take center stage in the new map, surrounded by *local* associations, institutions, and businesses resources (p. 3). Social systems driving the institutional assumption remain on the periphery of the new map, and consumption of institutional resources is directed by citizens rather than by clients (McKnight, 1996, p. 16). Grounded in the new map of social policy centering on the agency of individuals, families, local associations, and local institutions, ABCD initiatives mobilize, exchange, and create economic, cultural, and social capital assets within the community.

IV. ASSETS

In the ABCD paradigm, "Successful communities use the talents of people, the web of associations, the strength of institutions, and their available land, property, and economic power to create new opportunities for themselves. In short, they build on their assets" (Snow, 2001, p. 2; see also Green & Haines, 2012, p. 9). ABCD "is about identifying assets that can help, developing the leadership to mobilize residents, and building the capacity to act in the future" (Snow, 2001, p. 3). Therefore, an ABCD initiative begins with an inventory of all community assets, including individual, associational, and institutional economic, cultural, and social capital assets. Once inventoried, the community works to connect those assets "in ways that multiply their power and effectiveness," drawing in under- or nonutilized assets as community development projects grow and flourish (Kretzmann & McKnight, 1993, pp. 5–6). ABCD connections build outward from the skills, knowledge, tangible assets, and social networks of individuals to those of local volunteer associations and local institutions, including public libraries and librarians. Once assets are connected, actors build information pathways and identify shared goals.

The ABCD list of economic assets includes: individuals' skills and work experience, natural resources available for production or tourism, consumer economic power and spending patterns, and business opportunities (Green & Haines, 2012, p. 12); it also includes any abilities of citizens, local associations, and local institutions "to produce, not just consume" (Snow, 2001, p. 3) or to convert economic assets to other forms of capital that may be mobilized to strengthen communities. ABCD initiatives employing these economic assets often produce new economic assets through the cooperative efforts of community individuals, local associations, and local institutions that include businesses, libraries, and schools, among others.

Cultural assets are critical components of ABCD initiatives. Bourdieu (1985, p. 242) identified a tripartite typology of cultural capital assets:

1. Embodied—characterized by personal knowledge, tastes, social skills, and competence
2. Objectified—cultural objects, such as art or literature
3. Institutionalized—credentials, such as educational degrees

Embodied cultural assets in the form of individual skill or competence may be inherited or gained through investments in self-improvement (p. 242). Objectified cultural capital is obtained through the conversion of economic capital or other forms of capital and may exist in tangible or symbolic form. Institutionalized cultural assets in the form of academic qualifications or titles (p. 247) are related to symbolic power and are displayed as a competence or authority (p. 244, 255, n. 3). Phillips and Shockley (2010, p. 98) view cultural capital as a creative, innovative force holding "much potential to influence the broad sphere of community development" (p. 92). For example, ABCD initiatives to establish arts-based communities or colonies may generate broader economic development within the community (Blejwas, 2010; Phillips & Shockley, 2010, pp. 98–104).

The role of social capital assets in rural community development is well documented (Duncan, 2001; Khan, Rifaqat, & Kazmi, 2007; Scales, Streeter, & Cooper, 2014), and social capital comprises the third category of assets mobilized during ABCD initiatives. Bourdieu defined social capital as the "aggregate of the actual or potential resources which are linked to possession of a durable network of more or less institutionalized relationships of mutual acquaintance or recognition," as in group membership (Bourdieu, 1985, p. 248). Lin (2001) provides a less prolix definition: "investment in social relations with expected returns in the marketplace" (p. 19). Social relationships are maintained through the material and symbolic exchanges that take place within physical, economic, or social space. The amount of social capital possessed by an individual agent depends on two factors: (1) the size of the network (group) that can act in the interest of the individual, and (2) the aggregate capital (economic, cultural, and social) possessed by the individual and available to the individual through network connections. Analogous to an economic multiplier, the capital available through network connections exerts a multiplier effect on the social capital possessed individually (Bourdieu, 1985, p. 249). Or, put another way, communities gain more when local stakeholders work together than they do when these persons and organizations operate on their own. Maintenance of social capital requires a "continuous series of exchanges in which recognition is endlessly affirmed and reaffirmed," requiring investments of time, energy, and, often, economic capital (p. 250).

The social capital assets inventoried in ABCD initiatives are the relationships or connections between individuals, local associations, and local organizations. Those connections define the existing social networks within a community. As ABCD initiatives progress, new connections or links are formed within and between community networks, which mobilizes assets in ways that could not have been previously foreseen. This includes opportunities to take advantage of weak ties (Granovetter, 1973) or exploit structural holes (Burt, 1992) in social networks. ABCD descriptions of "connecting the dots" or "building bridges between assets" specifically describe efforts to extend existing social networks (see, e.g., Snow, 2001, pp. 78, 86; Dewar, 1997, p. 23). In Bourdieu's terms, an actor's new relationships within an ABCD initiative, or "field," comprise the social capital available to be mobilized in achieving ABCD goals. Green and Haines (2012) summarize the importance of social capital to ABCD initiatives: "Collective action ... is often built on social networks and trust, which are generated through social capital" (p. 151). Social relationships "enhance the ability of residents to act collectively to address local concerns" (p. 11) and provide "the basis for building other community assets, such as human and financial capital" that can be used in ABCD initiatives (p. 13).

Although developed in an urban setting, the ABCD approach to building communities is well suited to rural communities: "There's something very rural about ABCD.... rural areas have always had to 'use what we've got, to get what we want.' [ABCD is] a 'building from within' cycle that rural communities have always used and understood" (Snow, 2001, pp. 3–4). Snow's list of rural assets available for use in ABCD initiatives includes: (1) the talents and skills of individual citizens and their relationships; (2) local associations and their relationships; (3) local institutions (religious, business, and government) committed to locally directed, "from within," community development; (4) tangible physical assets (including buildings and natural resources); and (5) economic assets, including monetary assets, consumer spending power, and the experience, training, and skill of individuals (pp. 80–83).

In summary, grounded in a new map of social policy centering on individuals, families, local associations, and local institutions, ABCD initiatives mobilize economic, cultural, and social capital assets. ABCD initiatives promote purposive agency among individuals and organizations through the creation and exchange of economic, cultural, and social capital assets.

V. RURAL PUBLIC LIBRARIES AND ABCD

Rural public libraries are positioned to participate in ABCD initiatives from "a positive, strong position in their communities" (Hildreth, 2007, p. 8). As active ABCD agents, rural public libraries mobilize their economic, cultural, and social assets for community development activities. Their economic capital available for community development includes payroll and employee spending remaining in the community, library expenditures within the local economy, and funds attracted to the community from outside sources such as grants. Cultural capital in the form of books, videos, databases, technology access, and more are administered by public libraries in trust for the community. Public libraries and librarians build and expend social capital through interactions with community individuals and organizations; encouraging library use as public space; and providing personal, educational, and business skill development opportunities (Goulding, 2004; Johnson, 2012; Kretzmann & McKnight, 1993, pp. 191–205; Majekodunmi, 2011; Vårheim, 2007, pp. 425–426).

Examples of rural public library asset investment in community development activities appear in recent literature. The authors of the first IMLS-targeted analysis of rural public libraries comment that rural and small libraries are forming alliances with other educational, community, and economic development programs (Swan, Grimes, & Owens, 2013, p. 9). Heuertz (2009, pp. 104–106) noted the formation of community alliances and engagement in community-building work in her case studies of three rural libraries, while Majekodunmi (2011, p. 20) identified rural public libraries as "engines for social change and community development." Hancks' (2011) case studies of five rural Illinois public library adult education programming and community outreach efforts concludes that "the libraries had a role in community economic sustainability efforts" (pp. 9, 136). Smith (2014) discussed the role of the rural public library as a "community commons," noting that libraries are "one of the only public spaces open on a regular basis" (p. 85). Becker et al. (2010) identify public libraries as pivotal local institutions providing technology resources connecting residents with educational, career, health, and government services (pp. 9–10). By providing computer training and technical expertise and taking the lead in broadband infrastructure, Alemanne, Mandel, and McClure (2011) observe that "The public library is clearly playing a linchpin role in many rural communities" (p. 19).

Research collaborations also demonstrate the investment of library assets in community development projects. For example, the small business toolkit developed by Mehra, Bishop, and Partee, described in this volume in their chapter "A Gap Analysis of the Perspectives of Small Businesses and Rural Librarians in Tennessee," in partnership with Tennessee rural libraries will enable those libraries to participate more broadly in business development within their communities. Flaherty and Miller (2016) describe their project with a rural North Carolina library to increase health promotion in the community.

Kretzmann and McKnight (1993) state that libraries "can play an essential role in the process of community-building and should be seen as vital assets that exist at the very heart of community life" (p. 191). Their descriptions of library assets available for investment in community-building initiatives include personnel, building spaces, materials and equipment, expertise, and economic power (pp. 192–194). Kretzmann and Rans (2005) expand the inventory of library assets to include library constituents and networks of connections to other institutions, associations, and individuals (p. 40, Figure 3.1). Hildreth's (2007, p. 9) list of library assets for use in ABCD initiatives includes: (1) individual staff members, trustees, volunteers, supporters, and users; (2) library buildings that serve as community centers and public spaces as well as portals to government services; and (3) bookmobiles connecting libraries to citizens in more remote areas. Through investing their assets in community-building initiatives, rural public libraries may function "not only as the ... information center but [also] as the hub around which community discussion and planning happens" (Kretzmann & McKnight, 1993, p. 173).

What follows is a statistical analysis of rural public library assets, including a discussion of how librarians may be able to better leverage these resources for the benefit of their communities. Each section of the analysis ends with a "Practical Implications" section to summarize the analysis and provide information that may be useful for librarians who wish to argue for greater fiscal and collaborative support for their libraries.

A. Methodology

Rather than focusing on outputs such as circulation and program attendance as indicators of rural library asset usage, the variables selected for this study represent the library assets described in the ABCD literature. Specifically, those variables encompass the economic (annual expenditures), cultural (collections, equipment, and staff expertise), and social (public spaces and open hours, staff, and programs) capital assets held by rural libraries. The variables are mapped to their 2013 IMLS Public Library Data File field names (IMLS, 2015b) in Table 2. To answer research question 2, the nominal IMLS variables used in this study include the geographic region (OBEREG) and governance structure or legal basis (C_LEGBAS) fields. Demographic variables used to answer research question 2 include the poverty rate, percent of adults with a BA degree or higher education, unemployment rate, household median income, and net population change. These variables were obtained from the 2013 USDA Economic Research Service data sets retrieved in 2015, which are no longer available on the USDA site (USDA Economic Research Service, 2015a, 2015b, 2015c, 2015d).

To control for differences due solely to library size, per capita asset variables were calculated by dividing each variable by the unduplicated service

Table 2. Rural Public Library Asset Variables.

Asset	IMLS field name(s)	Description
Outlets	CENTLIB + BRANLIB	Total number of library outlets serving the public (central library and branches)
Bookmobiles	BKMOB	Number of bookmobiles
Hours	HRS_OPEN	Total annual service hours (all outlets)
MLIS	MASTER	FTE staff holding accredited MLIS degree (all outlets)
Staff	TOTSTAFF	FTE paid employees (all outlets)
Inventory	BKVOL + EBOOK + AUDIO_PH + AUDIO_DL + VIDEO_PH + VIDEO_DL + DATABASE + SUBSCRIP	Total number of circulating materials (books, e-books, and physical or downloadable audio and video material), databases, and subscriptions (all outlets)
Programs	TOTPRO	Annual number of library programs (all outlets)
Terminals	GPTERMS	Annual number of public access computers (all outlets)
Expenditures	TOTOPEXP + CAPITAL	Annual operating and capital expenditures (all outlets)

area population size. The per capita approach is compatible with the library ranking methodology developed by Lance and Lyons (2008). Selection of the IMLS public library unduplicated service area population variable (POPU_ UND) rather than the service area field (POPU_LSA) as the divisor in the per capita calculation follows the approach taken by Swan, Grimes, and Owens (2013, p. 6, n. 6; IMLS, 2015a, p. 7). During data verification, the author found that some records in the IMLS file were either missing or contained an invalid unduplicated population service area or other fields that prohibited calculation of per capita variables. Therefore, three fringe, five distant, and six remote libraries were deleted from the data file. The final data set contained 509 fringe, 2,064 distant, and 1,629 remote libraries, for a total of 4,202 rural libraries. Outlying areas, including Puerto Rico, Guam, American Samoa, Northern Mariana Islands, and the Virgin Islands were not considered in this study due to limited data availability.

To control for differences in variable scales during data mining, Z-scores, which transformed the variables to a mean of zero and a standard deviation of one, were calculated for each variable by subtracting variable means from reported values and then dividing by the variable's standard deviation. A review of boxplots and Z-score distributions identified a large number of outliers in the asset variables. Outliers are those observations with a Z-score higher than two standard deviations from the mean of zero (Stevens, 2009, p. 225). Per capita variable histograms revealed positively skewed, leptokurtic distributions, which were confirmed by the descriptive statistics shown in Table 3. Although mitigated by the large number of libraries in the data set, the Shapiro–Wilk normality test p-value for each of the per capita asset variables indicated that the variables were not normally distributed ($p < .001$ for each variable). Given the large number of outlier observations, the positively skewed and leptokurtic distribution of the variables, and the Shapiro–Wilk test results, nonparametric statistical techniques, such as the Kruskal–Wallis rank sum test comparing differences in medians rather than means, were selected to analyze the data set.

Table 3. Descriptive Statistics, Asset Variables.

N = 4202	Inven.	Outlets	BkMob.	Hours	MLIS	Staff	Prog.	Terms.	Expend.
Mean	18.39	0.00	0.00	1.17	0.00	0.00	0.05	0.00	53.75
Median	11.06	0.00	0.00	0.77	0.00	0.00	0.02	0.00	33.52
Std. dev.	26.71	0.00	0.00	2.22	0.00	0.00	0.11	0.01	154.73
Kurtosis	117.55	439.21	512.17	541.32	115.00	156.30	268.35	888.35	797.07
Skew	7.81	15.23	20.23	19.58	7.92	8.81	12.26	23.06	23.66

The random forest decision tree algorithm was selected for use as the non-parametric, supervised data mining classifier during data set exploration. The algorithm is "supervised" because the correct classification (the Locale field) appears in the data set and is available during model training using 10-fold cross-validation. The random forest algorithm was chosen in part because the decision trees in the forest are decorrelated. Decorrelation is accomplished by selecting a random subset of predictors, approximately equal to the square root of the total number of predictors, at each tree split (James, Witten, Hastie, & Tibshirani, 2013, pp. 587–588). As illustrated by the Pearson product–moment correlation coefficient matrix in Table 4, all asset variables except the bookmobile and Master of Library and Information Science (MLIS) variables are either moderately or strongly correlated. The strongest correlations are between outlets and hours (r = .8) and outlets and computer terminals (r = .8). Within the demographic variables, the strongest correlation is between the percentage of the adult population holding a BA degree or higher and median household income (r = .63). Both of those variables are correlated with the MLIS variable (r = .16, respectively). Correlations in the data set are controlled during the construction of random forest classifiers by averaging 100 decorrelated trees. In fact, one criticism of random forest is that particularly "strong features can end up with low scores" due to random selection of split candidates (Saabas, 2014, n.p.). Another criticism is that random forests "can be biased towards variables with many categories" (Saabas, 2014). Despite those criticisms, they "do remarkably well, with very little tuning required" (James, Witten, Hastie, & Tibshirani, 2013, p. 590). Random forest classifiers in this study were built using the Weka data mining software package from the Machine Learning Group at the University of Waikato, New Zealand (http://www.cs.waikato.ac.nz/ml/index.html). All other analyses were performed using Microsoft Excel and the R Project for Statistical Computing (http://www.r-project.org/).

B. Study Limitations

Four limitations arise from the nature of the data collected by third parties. First, the IMLS Public Library Survey aggregates asset variables on a library-wide basis. Of the nine asset variables selected for study, only one (public service hours) is available in the corresponding Outlet Data File that contains branch-level data. Therefore, this study is limited to library system-wide data, although it should be noted that a considerably higher percentage of rural library systems consist of only a single outlet than is typical

Table 4. Variable Correlation Matrix.

	Inv.	Out-lets	Bk Mb	Hrs	MLIS	Staff	Prog	PCs	Exp.	% Pov	% BA or >	% Un-emp.	Med HHI
Inv.	1.00												
Outlets	0.55	1.00											
BkMob	-0.01	-0.03	1.00										
Hours	0.44	0.81	-0.02	1.00									
MLIS	0.18	0.02	0.00	0.03	1.00								
Staff	0.56	0.47	-0.02	0.46	0.30	1.00							
Prog.	0.49	0.44	-0.02	0.37	0.16	0.54	1.00						
PCs	0.52	0.79	-0.02	0.72	0.07	0.56	0.43	1.00					
Expend	0.40	0.56	0.00	0.47	0.15	0.49	-0.03	0.66	1				
% Pov	-0.05	-0.02	0.08	-0.02	-0.03	-0.04	-0.03	0.00	-0.02	1			
% BA or >	0.01	-0.04	-0.01	-0.04	0.16	0.04	0.06	-0.06	0.04	-0.16	1		
% Unemp	-0.07	-0.09	0.02	-0.05	0.03	-0.03	0.00	-0.01	0.07	0.18	-0.27	1	
Med. HHI	0.05	-0.02	-0.04	-0.02	0.16	0.09	0.08	-0.03	0.08	-0.30	0.63	-0.36	1
NetPop	-0.02	-0.02	-0.01	0.00	0.05	0.07	-0.01	0.01	0.01	-0.02	0.24	-0.05	0.20

among town, suburban, or city systems. Rural branch libraries operated by central libraries located outside rural areas are also excluded from this study. Second, 4 fringe libraries, 49 distant libraries, and 53 remote libraries reported 0 employees, although all other data fields appeared to be reported correctly. While a number of those libraries may be staffed solely with volunteers, it is likely that some chose to protect salary information by reporting zero staff. Conservatively, as with other outliers in the Z-scores, libraries reporting zero staff were not removed from the data set. Third, while the IMLS Public Library Data File is dated 2013, the reporting period for several states and individual libraries deviated from a strict January through December reporting period (see IMLS, 2015a, p. 6). However, all libraries reported data for a 12-month period. Finally, the USDA demographic data were reported on county or county-equivalent levels based on the five-digit Federal Information Processing Standard (FIPS) code, which is a higher than optimal level of aggregation given the small population service area of some rural libraries. Therefore, demographic analysis reflects broader trends than may affect the immediate library service area.

Raw library data are reviewed at the state level prior to final submission, and the IMLS conducts extensive editing of the public library survey data, including imputation of nonresponse variables to decrease "the effect of non-response" (IMLS, 2015a, p. 16). Despite those efforts, "some non-sampling error likely remains in the data" (p. 16). Recognizing that limitations and anomalies in the underlying data, as well as choice and applications of analytical methodology, affect "the possibility of biased estimation results" (Hertz, Kusmin, Marré, & Parker, 2014, p. 6), the author accepts all responsibility for errors.

C. Fringe, Distant, and Remote Rural Library Asset Differences

Research question 1 asks: "What are the differences in the asset holdings of fringe, distant, and remote rural libraries?" To begin answering that question, the per capita medians of the nine asset variables appear in Table 5. Median per capita expenditures and MLIS staff are higher in fringe than distant and remote libraries, and median per capita programs are lowest in distant libraries. Unexpectedly, median per capita inventories, outlets, service hours, and terminals increase as distances from urban areas and urban clusters increase. For example, fringe median per capita inventories are 3 units lower than distant and 7.5 units lower than remote rural libraries, and fringe median per capita service hours are .27 hours lower than distant and .61 hours lower

Table 5. Median per Capita Rural Public Library Assets by Locale.

Locale	Inv.	Outlets	BkMob	Hours	MLIS	Staff	Prog.	Term.	Expend.
Fringe	7.2083	0.0002	0.0000	0.4274	0.00003	0.0006	0.0263	0.0015	36.1927
Distant	10.1792	0.0005	0.0000	0.6977	0.00000	0.0006	0.0233	0.0024	31.1153
Remote	14.7574	0.0008	0.0000	1.0330	0.00000	0.0008	0.0244	0.0039	35.5833

than remote libraries. While differences are negligible, median per capita staff is highest in remote libraries. Only 155 bookmobiles operated in rural areas in 2013, and there were no differences in median per capita bookmobiles between fringe, distant, and rural areas.

Omnibus Kruskal–Wallis tests of differences between medians were statistically significant (alpha $= .05$, p-values $< .001$) except for the bookmobile and programs variables. Dunn post-hoc tests conducted with a Bonferroni adjustment to control Type I errors affirmed that differences between fringe, distant, and remote median per capita inventory, outlets, service hours, staff, and terminals were statistically significant. The difference between remote and distant per capita MLIS staff medians is not statistically significant (p-value $= .86$), although differences between fringe and distant as well as fringe and remote libraries are significant. Also, the difference between the fringe and remote expenditures median is not significant (p-value $= 1.00$), although the differences between fringe and distant as well as remote and distant libraries are statistically significant.

While the answer to research question 1 is that there are statistically significant differences between rural fringe, distant, and remote library assets, those differences have small effect sizes. As such, further exploration of asset differences using the research question 2 variable set may provide an additional explanation of asset variances as distances from urban areas and clusters increase.

Practical Implications: Distance from Urban Areas and Urban Clusters

- Median per capita inventories, outlets, service hours, terminals, and staff (in remote libraries) increase as distance from urban areas and urban clusters increase.
- This effect is likely due to lower service area populations in distant and remote areas and the effects of declining populations over the long term (USDA, 2013, p. 5).

D. Data Mining Fringe, Distant, and Remote Rural Public Library Assets

The supervised data mining random forest classification algorithm was selected to help answer research question 2: "What are the relationships between fringe, distant, and remote rural public library asset holdings and library service area population size, geographic regions, political (governance) structures, and community demographics?" The first random forest decision tree was constructed using the Z-scores of the nine per capita asset variables (inventory, outlets, bookmobiles, hours, MLIS, staff, programs, terminals, and expenditures) to classify each rural library into one of the three Locale codes (fringe, distant, or remote). Ten randomly selected training and the corresponding test data sets were simulated through tenfold cross-validation (see James, Witten, Hastie, & Tibshirani, 2013, pp. 241–249). Supervised training used feedback from the Locale field. The final model was constructed from a 100 tree forest. To control collinearity between the trees, each tree split variable was selected from a randomly drawn subset of four variables.

The random forest model correctly classified 2,064, or 55.8%, of the 4,202 rural libraries as fringe, distant, or remote. The confusion matrix shown as Table 6 illustrates that the random forest classifier correctly classified 23% of the fringe, 70% of the distant, and 48% of the remote libraries. These results affirm the earlier finding of asset differences between fringe, remote, and distant libraries, although the differences are not large enough to completely delineate the three Locale categories.

Two metrics, the Kappa statistic and the receiver operating characteristic (ROC) area, help interpret classifier results and facilitate classifier comparisons. The Kappa statistic measures the agreement between the predicted and observed accuracy of the classification "while correcting for an agreement that occurs by chance" (Witten, Frank, & Hall, 2011, p. 166). The random forest classifier based on the nine asset variables has a Kappa statistic of .21, which indicates only fair agreement between the predicted and observed

Table 6. Confusion Matrix, Random Forest Using Nine Asset Variables.

Locale	Classified as		
	Fringe	Distant	Remote
Fringe	121	327	61
Distant	84	1,440	540
Remote	28	819	782
Kappa = .215		ROC area = .655	

accuracy (Landis & Koch, 1977, p. 165). ROC curves plot the true positive rate on the vertical axis against the false positive rate on the horizontal axis. Therefore, the weighted-average ROC area is a measure of the accuracy of the classifier in identifying true positives (pp. 172–173). The ROC area of .66 for the nine-variable random forest classifier indicates that the classifier performed poorly (Tape, n.d.).

Expanding the variable subset to include the unduplicated population service area Z-score slightly improved the accuracy of the classifier from 55.8% to 56.5%. The Kappa statistic and weighted-average ROC areas are also slightly higher (.228 and .664, respectively). The confusion matrix in Table 7a illustrates a slight improvement in classification accuracy with the addition of the unduplicated population variable—accuracy increased from 23% to 25% in the fringe libraries and from 48% to 49% in the remote category. Two additional distant libraries were also correctly classified. While slight, these improvements indicate that population service area size has some relationship to rural library assets beyond the population service area effect controlled by the per capita calculations.

Adding the nominal geographic regions variable increased the accuracy of the random forest classification algorithm by 6.8% (from 56.5% to 63.3%), and the Kappa statistic increased by .13. The weighted-average ROC area of .74 indicated fair rather than poor accuracy in identifying true positives (Tape, n.d.). Most notably, as shown in the Table 7b confusion matrix, 29% of the fringe, 72% of the distant, and 62% of the remote libraries were correctly classified (improvements of 4%, 2%, and 13%, respectively). These results indicate that the differences between fringe, distant, and remote rural libraries are to some extent related to geographic region.

Although negligible, the accuracy of the random forest classifier continued to improve with the addition of the legal basis, or governance nominal, variable—the correct classification of fringe libraries increased by 1%. The confusion matrix appears in Table 7c.

The random forest classifier increased in accuracy by 8.9% (from 63.3% to 72.2%) when the Z-scores for the five demographic variables were added and one additional random feature was considered at each split. As shown in the confusion matrix (Table 7d), the Kappa statistic of .516 indicates moderate rather than fair agreement between the predicted and observed accuracy (Landis & Koch, 1977, p. 165), and the weighted-average ROC area of .83 indicates that the accuracy of the full classifier model is good rather than fair in identifying true positives (Tape, n.d.). Accurate classification of fringe libraries increased from 30% to 42%, distant libraries classification accuracy increased from 72% to 78%, and remote library classification accuracy

Table 7. Confusion Matrices, Random Forest Classifiers.

(a) Asset variables and service area population size				(b) Asset variables, service area population size, and region		

	Classified as				Classified as		
Locale	Fringe	Distant	Remote	Locale	Fringe	Distant	Remote
Fringe	126	328	55	Fringe	150	301	58
Distant	88	1,442	534	Distant	83	1,492	489
Remote	22	802	805	Remote	22	591	1,016
Kappa = .228		ROC area = .664		Kappa = .355		ROC area = .736	

(c) Asset variables, service area population size, region, and legal basis				(d) Asset variables, service area population size, region, legal basis, and demographics		

	Classified as				Classified as		
Locale	Fringe	Distant	Remote	Locale	Fringe	Distant	Remote
Fringe	156	303	50	Fringe	212	272	25
Distant	88	1,494	482	Distant	71	1,614	379
Remote	17	596	1,016	Remote	5	416	1,208
Kappa = .359		ROC area = .747		Kappa = .516		ROC area = .833	

increased from 62% to 74%. These results indicate that the demographic variables are related to differences in rural library assets, with the highest effects related to fringe and remote rural libraries.

To determine whether a random forest model built on fewer attributes (variables) could approach the accuracy of the 17-attribute model just described, the data was preprocessed through the Weka subset evaluator that considers the individual predictive ability of each attribute and the redundancy between attributes in tandem with the Weka "BestFirst" hill-climbing algorithm. Only three of the nine library asset variables were recommended for the reduced set classifier: outlets, MLIS, and terminals. The nominal library region variable and four of the five demographic variables were also recommended: percentage of adults holding a BA degree or higher, unemployment rate, median household income, and net population change. Reviewing the correlation matrix in Table 3, the strongest correlations within this subset of variables are between outlets and terminals (r = .79) and the percentage of adults with a BA or higher degree and median household income (r = .63). The MLIS variable and percentage of adults with a BA or higher degree are the highest correlation between the demographic and library variables (r = .16). Overall, compared to the full variable set, moderate to strong inter-correlations are reduced in this subset of variables.

The random forest classifier built on the eight attributes correctly classified 70.6% of the 4,202 libraries as fringe, distant, or remote—a decrease of only 1.6% in correctly classified libraries from the 17-attribute model. Although it decreased by .0245, the Kappa statistic for the eight-attribute model indicates fair agreement between the predicted and observed accuracy. The weighted-average ROC area decreased by only .006 and can, like the 17-attribute model, be interpreted as a "good" classifier. The confusion matrix in Table 8 illustrates that the reduced attribute model correctly classified 45% of the fringe, 75.5% of the distant, and 72% of the remote libraries, an increase of 3% in correctly classified fringe libraries but decreases of 2.5% and 2% in correctly classified distant and remote libraries, respectively. The results of this model suggest that differences in fringe, distant, and remote library assets are strongly related to the small set of three library variables, the region, and the four demographic variables.

The full variable and the reduced variable random forest classifiers described above successfully classified 72% and 70%, respectively, of the 4,202 rural public libraries within the IMLS fringe, distant, and remote Locale categories. Future studies may identify other variables that increase the accuracy of rural library classification by distance from urban areas and urban clusters. However, "every community, and every library, is unique" (Garcia & Nelson, 2007, p. 7), so outliers and even small differences and combinations of differences in asset variables may explain much of the variation, or "noise," in the data set that results in misclassification. Nevertheless, in terms of answering research question 2, classifier results indicate that there are differences in rural library assets related to region and a small set of demographic variables, which will be further explored in the next section.

Table 8. Confusion Matrix, Eight-Attribute Model.

Locale	Classified as		
	Fringe	Distant	Remote
Fringe	231	252	26
Distant	112	1,558	394
Remote	7	446	1,176
Kappa = .4915		ROC area = .827	

Practical Implications: Data Mining Results

- Assets held by individual rural libraries differ not only by their distance from urban clusters and urban centers but also to some extent by geographic region and local demographic factors, including the percentages of college-educated adults, the unemployment rate, median household income, and net population change.

E. Drilling Down Asset Differences

Of the nine library asset variables explored in answering research question 1, the outlets, MLIS, and terminal variables were of particular importance in the eight-attribute random forest classifier. In answer to research question 2, the random forest classifiers indicate that there are differences between the assets of fringe, distant, and remote rural libraries available for investment in ABCD initiatives that are related to geographic region and demographic variables. Contrastingly, there was little effect of population service area size on classifier accuracy beyond the effect controlled by per capita calculations, and the library governance structure (legal basis) attribute had a negligible effect on classifier accuracy. By "drilling down" into the outlets, MLIS, terminals, region, and demographic variables, specific asset differences that may affect rural library investment in ABCD initiatives will be highlighted.

1. Outlets

The outlets variable was one of the four library variables in the reduced set classifier. Ninety percent of rural libraries do not have branches, and there is little variation by distance from urbanized areas and clusters—91.6% of fringe libraries, 89% of distant libraries, and 90% of remote rural libraries do not have branches, compared to 83% of town, 80% of suburban, and 38% of city libraries that do not have branches. Unsurprisingly, the number of rural libraries with branches increases as population service area size increases (a positive Pearson correlation coefficient of .81). For example, none of the 444 rural libraries serving fewer than 500 people have branches, but only 3 of the 42 rural libraries serving populations of 100,000 or more persons do not have branches. However, as discussed above, median per capita outlets increase as distance from urban areas and urban clusters increase—the median per capita number of outlets increases from .2 per 1,000 residents in fringe, to .5 per

1,000 in distant, to .8 per 1,000 residents in remote rural libraries (Table 5). Mathematically, per capita outlets increase as service area population size decreases (service area population decreases from a median of 4,612 persons in fringe areas, to 2,162 persons in distant areas, to 1,361 persons in remote areas). This effect is compounded by the general decline in rural populations over time (USDA, 2013, p. 5), and 1,086, or 25%, of all rural libraries serve fewer than 1,000 persons. Although there are 10 rural libraries operating book-mobiles without a central location, even the smallest, most remote rural libraries provide at least one public space that could be utilized in ABCD initiatives.

The service hours and outlet variables have a strong positive correlation ($r = .81$; Table 2), so we can expect that as the number of branches increases, access to the public spaces provided by rural libraries would also increase. However, on a per capita basis, rural libraries *without* branches have higher median per capita service hours than rural libraries with branches, and median per capita service hours decrease as the number of branches increases (Table 9). The decline is most dramatic in remote libraries, where the median per capita service hours decrease from a high of 1.1 for libraries without branches to a low of .36 for remote libraries with two or more branches (a decrease in median service hours of .74 hours). Remote rural libraries without branches provide .32 higher median per capita service hours than distant libraries and .65 median per capita higher service hours than fringe libraries without branches. Generally, median per capita service hours increase as distances from urbanized areas and clusters increase and numbers of branches decrease. ABCD initiatives would benefit from full utilization of rural branch service hour capacity through volunteers or additional staff.

The total staff variable is moderately (.5) correlated with both the outlets and service hour variables. As such, we would expect the total number of

Table 9. Median per Capita Service Hours and Staff by Number of Branches.

Number of Branches	Fringe			Distant			Remote		
	Count	Median per capita service hours	Median per capita staff	Count	Median per capita service hours	Median per capita staff	Count	Median per capita service hours	Median per capita staff
0	466	0.45	0.0006	1,837	0.78	0.0006	1,472	1.1	0.0008
1	18	0.33	0.0007	32	0.43	0.0005	44	0.52	0.0005
2	5	0.18	0.0003	49	0.27	0.0005	39	0.48	0.0005
>2	20	0.15	0.0004	146	0.21	0.0004	74	0.36	0.0005

staff to increase as outlets and service hours increase. However, as with distant and remote library service hours, there is a general decrease in median per capita staff as the number of outlets increases (Table 9). While fringe libraries with one branch have a slightly higher median per capita staff than fringe libraries with no branches, lower median per capita staffing levels are found in fringe libraries with two or more branches. Unlocking the full potential of rural branch tangible and social capital assets by increasing staff or volunteers would benefit ABCD initiatives.

Of note, with the exception of the five distant libraries serving populations of 250,000 or more, median per capita staff also decreases as service area populations increase (Fig. 1). The low ratios of per capita staff levels aligns with the findings of other studies, including Fischer's (2015, p. 363) observation that 61% of rural and small library survey respondents "felt that the library did not have an adequate amount of staff working for the library" and Flatley and Wyman's (2009, p. 34) survey of 761 rural libraries (defined as libraries serving populations of 2,500 or fewer) concluding that 80% of respondent libraries had one full-time equivalent (FTE) employee and relied to a large extent on part-time staff and volunteers. Real, Bertot, and Jaeger (2014) expressed concern that inequities between rural and nonrural library staffing levels negatively affected rural Americans' equitable access to online career assistance (p. 13). However, with careful balancing, even rural libraries with low staff-to-population ratios can prioritize community engagement in their mission statements and take advantage of local staff members' pre-existing social network connections to plan programs and services aligned with community goals. For example, the Digital Inclusion Survey, which was

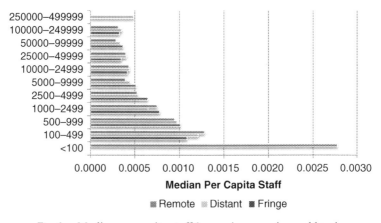

Fig. 1. Median per capita staff by service area size and locale.

conducted by Bertot, Real, Lee, McDermott, and Jaeger (2015) and built off IMLS survey data, identified a wide variety of library programs that are directly relevant to the needs of rural communities. These include formal computer skill classes and assistive technology training (p. 25, Figure 31), website development (p. 30, Figure 36), summer reading programs for children and adults (p. 40, Figure 47), interviewing skills (p. 50, Figure 59), and health or wellness topics (p. 67, Figure 78), among others.

Practical Implications: Rural Library Outlets
(Central Libraries and Branches)

- 91.6% of fringe libraries, 89% of distant libraries, and 90% of remote rural libraries do not have branches, compared with 83% of town, 80% of suburban, and 38% of city libraries that do not have branches.
- 1,086, or 25%, of all rural libraries serve fewer than 1,000 persons.
- While the number of rural libraries with branches increases as population service area size increases, the median per capita number of outlets increases slightly as distance from urban areas and urban clusters increase.
  - This finding is explained by generally decreasing service area sizes as distances from urban areas increase and the general decline in rural populations over time (USDA, 2013, p. 5).
- Rural libraries without branches have higher median per capita service hours than rural libraries with branches, and median per capita service hours decrease as the number of branches increases.
  - This finding is explained by the general decrease in median per capita staff as the number of outlets increases.
- While understaffing is an issue for all rural libraries, rural libraries with branches are understaffed to fully utilize their built assets— physical, public spaces held for the benefit of their communities.
- Advocating for increased staff or volunteers in all rural libraries could unlock the full potential of central outlet and branch assets and increase social capital assets.
- As evidenced by the Digital Inclusion Survey (Bertot et al., 2015), with careful balancing, even rural libraries with low staff-to-population ratios can prioritize community engagement in their mission statements and take advantage of local staff members' preexisting social network connections to plan programs and services aligned with community goals.

---

2. MLIS Degrees
The MLIS variable was the second library variable in the reduced set classifier. Twenty-four percent of rural libraries, or 1,005 total libraries or systems,
reported having at least one MLIS FTE on staff. The high percentage (51%)
of fringe libraries with at least one MLIS FTE most likely explains why the
per capita MLIS variable was one of the few library variables recommended
for use in the streamlined random forest classifier. While the largest numbers
of MLIS-degreed staff serve in distant libraries, only 25% of those libraries have at least one MLIS FTE on staff; 49% of fringe and 86% of remote
libraries did not have a staff member with a MLIS degree. Of note, 374, or
37%, of the reported MLIS staff members were part-time employees.

There is a slight positive correlation between the per capita MLIS variable and the percentage of adults in the library's service area with a bachelor's or higher degree ($r = .16$). On a regional basis, the Southeast has the
lowest percentage of adults holding a bachelor's or higher degree (18% in
fringe, 13% in distant, and 12% in remote rural areas), which is not unexpected given the generally higher poverty rates and lower median household
income in the Southeast region (discussed below). Fringe rural areas in the
Rocky Mountain region have the highest median percentage of adults holding a bachelor's or higher degree (35%), followed by the New England region
(34%). New England distant and remote areas have the highest per capita percentage of adults holding a BA or higher degree (31% and 27%, respectively).

Given the regional distribution of the median percentages of adults holding a BA or higher degree, the regional distribution of MLIS staff (Table 10)
was unexpected. For example, the Southeast has the lowest percentage of
adults holding a BA or higher degree but, compared to the seven other U.S.
geographic regions, the Southeast ranks highest in distant and remote areas
and fourth highest in fringe areas in terms of libraries with some level of
MLIS staff. Further research is needed to determine if the unexpected levels
of Southeast MLIS staff are attributable to IMLS grants encouraging rural
librarians to pursue MLIS degrees (see, e.g., University of Tennessee IMLS

Table 10.   Percentage of Libraries with at Least One MLIS Staff by
Region and Locale.

	All RURAL LIBRARIES	Far West	Great Lakes	Mid-East	New England	Plains	Rocky Mtn.	South East	South West
Fringe	51%	78%	55%	41%	54%	36%	38%	46%	32%
Distant	25%	41%	31%	19%	24%	11%	27%	45%	14%
Remote	14%	25%	26%	14%	11%	7%	21%	33%	8%

grants RE-01-09-0031-09 at https://www.imls.gov/grants/awarded/re-01-09-0031-09 and RE-71-12-0014-12 at https://www.imls.gov/grants/awarded/re-71-12-0014-12). Possibly due to the effect of Alaska libraries' high state and federal income levels (discussed further below), the Far West fringe area ranked first in libraries with some level of MLIS staff, although it ties with the Southeast as the lowest-ranking region in the percentage of adults holding a BA or higher degree.

Practical Implications: MLIS-Degreed Full Time Equivalents (FTEs)

- 24% of rural libraries have at least one MLIS-degreed FTE on staff.
- 37% of reported MLIS-degreed staff are part-time employees.
  - These findings may be explained by Fischer (2015, pp. 362–363; citing earlier studies), who suggests that low salaries in small and rural libraries make it difficult to hire staff holding MLIS degrees.
- The Southeast has the lowest percentage of adults holding a BA or higher degree, but, compared to the seven other U.S. geographic regions, the Southeast ranks highest in distant and remote areas and fourth highest in fringe areas in terms of libraries with some level of MLIS staff.
  - This finding may be explained by IMLS grants that supported MLIS students in the rural Southeast region.
- Library schools and library organizations should work to secure scholarships and grants supporting higher education for rural librarians to promote effective use of rural library assets.
- From the ABCD perspective, whether or not MLIS-trained personnel are present, library staff should draw on outside resources, such as online training programs, to expand their skills for the benefit of the community.

---

3. Public Access Terminals

The public access terminal variable was the third library asset variable in the reduced set classifier. As shown previously in Table 5, the median per capita number of public access terminals increases slightly as distance from urbanized areas or urban clusters increases—from 1.5 terminals per 1,000 persons in fringe libraries, to 2.4 per 1,000 in distant libraries, to 3.9 terminals per 1,000 persons in remote libraries. The trend toward generally higher numbers

of median per capita terminals in remote libraries is also evident when analyzed by population service area size, region, or legal basis, which may explain
why the terminal variable was recommended for use in the streamlined random forest classifier.

As expected, due to the strong correlation between unduplicated population service area and terminals (r = .81), the median number of public access
terminals generally increases as service area size increases. For example,
the smallest rural libraries (those serving fewer than 1,000 residents) have a
median of 4 terminals, whereas rural libraries serving populations of more
than 10,000 but fewer than 25,000 residents have a median of 18 terminals.

Practical Implications: Public Access Terminals

- The number of rural public library computer terminals increases as
  service area size increases.
- The per capita number of computer terminals increases slightly
  as distances from urban areas and urban clusters increase due to
  decreases in service area sizes.
- As a group, libraries serving fewer than 1,000 persons had a median
  of 4 terminals per library.
- These results complement Real, Bertot, and Jaeger's (2014, p. 11)
  conclusion that "rural libraries lead their nonrural counterparts" in
  providing sufficient terminal access and Fischer's (2015, p. 365) finding that 71% of the small and rural libraries in her sample were satisfied with the number of terminals.
- As discussed below, funds from state and federal agencies helped
  provide public access terminals and broadband access in the smallest
  rural libraries in 2013. Advocacy campaigns documenting the positive community outcomes generated by those investments will help
  ensure the sustainability of public access terminal assets.

F. Regions and Demographics

The regions variable increased the random forest classifier accuracy by 8.9%
and was one of the four library variables in the reduced set classifier. The
overall large number of Plains rural libraries (28% of the total, including
IA, KS, MN, MO, NE, ND, and SD rural libraries) and the high percentage

of remote Plains libraries (44% of all remote libraries) may explain why the region variable was a strong predictor of locale. The Great Lakes region (IL, IN, MI, OH, and WI) contains 19% of the remote libraries, 16% are located in New England (CT, ME, MA, NH, RI, and VT), 11% in the Southeast (AL, AR, FL, GA, KY, LA, MS, NC, SC, TN, VA, and WV), 10% in the Mideast (DE, DC, MD, NJ, NY, and PA), 7% in the Southwest (AZ, NM, OK, and TX), 5% in the Rocky Mountain region (CO, ID, MT, UT, and WY), and 4% of all rural libraries are located in the Far West region (AK, CA, HI, NV, OR, and WA). The New England region contains the largest percentage of fringe libraries (37% of all fringe libraries), the Great Lakes region contains the largest percentage of distant libraries (26% of all distant libraries), and, as mentioned previously, 44% of all remote libraries are located in the Great Plains region.

The five 2013 demographic variables improved the full model's accuracy by 8.9%, and all but one of the demographic variables, the overall poverty percentage, was recommended for inclusion in the reduced variable set classifier. As seen in Table 11, there is little variation in the median poverty rate between rural fringe, distant, and remote libraries, which may explain why that variable was not recommended for the reduced variable set classifier. In general, the 2013 unemployment rate increased while the median household income decreased as distance from urban areas and urban clusters increased—median rural remote unemployment was 1.6% higher than the rural fringe unemployment rate and 1.4% higher than the distant unemployment rate, and remote median household income was $10,649 lower than the fringe median household income and $3,534 lower than the distant median household income. Consistent with the moderate correlation ($r = .63$) between median household income and the percentage of adults holding a BA or higher college degree, the percentage of adults with a BA or higher degree also decreases as distances from urban areas and urban clusters increase—11% more fringe and 2% more distant residents hold a BA or higher degree than remote residents, contributing to the lower numbers of MLIS staff in remote rural libraries, discussed previously.

Table 11.   2013 Demographic Variables.

	Median % poverty	Median % adults BA or higher	Median % unemployment	Median household income	Median net 2013 pop. change
Fringe	13%	29%	7.1%	$55,020	187
Distant	14%	20%	6.9%	$47,895	−56
Remote	14%	18%	5.5%	$44,361	−21

Practical Implications: Regions and Demographics

- The New England region contains the largest percentage (37%) of all fringe rural libraries (those closest to urban areas and urban clusters and the most likely to lose their rural designation after the 2020 census).
- The Great Lakes region contains the largest percentage (26%) of rural distant libraries.
- 44% of all remote libraries (those farthest from urban populations) are located in the Great Plains region.
- The 2013 unemployment rate increased while the median household income decreased as distance from urban areas and urban clusters increased.
- The percentage of adults with a BA or higher degree decreases as distances from urban areas and urban clusters increase—11% more fringe and 2% more distant residents hold a BA or higher degree than remote residents.
  o This factor contributes to the lower numbers of MLIS-degreed staff in remote rural libraries.

1. Regional and Demographic Interactions: Library Expenditures

The interaction effects of region and locale by the expenditure variable appear in Fig. 2. Although the remote Far West region has the highest unemployment rate (9.9%) and the third-highest poverty rate (16.8%), libraries in the Far West region have the highest median per capita library spending ($96.14). This is largely due to state and federal income contributions to the 67 remote Alaska rural libraries—each library received a minimum of $6,500 in income from the state of Alaska, and 61 of those libraries received a median of $9,574 in federal income. The state and federal contributions to remote Alaska libraries resulted in high levels of per capita staff, inventory, and programs, leading to the remote Far West's number one ranking in those variables. From the ABCD perspective, the Alaska libraries' state and federal incomes are examples of economic capital produced by a local institution drawing on outside resources for the

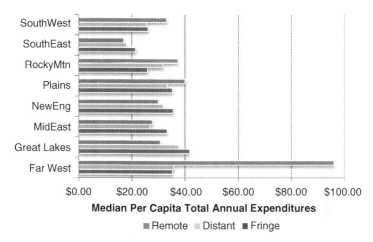

Fig. 2.   Median per capita expenditures by region and locale.

benefit of the community. At least some portion of the income remains in the community in the form of local expenditures and local salaries, and the economic multiplier effect creates new economic assets within the community (see Arns, 2013, pp. 20–22, reviewing public library expenditures and economic multipliers).

Fringe, distant, and remote libraries in the Southeast region have the lowest median per capita spending levels at $21.50, $17.98, and $17.02, respectively. Consistent with low median per capita expenditures, Southeast rural libraries also have the lowest median per capita inventory units, staff, service hours, and programs. When analyzing the demographic variables by region, the Southeast had the highest poverty rates, ranging from 18% for fringe, 19.9% for distant, and 23.8% for remote areas. Southeast unemployment rates were also high—7.1% for fringe, 8.1% for distant, and 9.3% for remote areas. Finally, the Southeast region ranked lowest in fringe, distant, and remote median household incomes. Clearly, the Southeast region's high rank in unemployment and poverty coupled with its low rank in median household income help explain the finding of low median per capita library expenditures coupled with low median per capita staff, hours, inventory, and programs.

Practical Implications: Regional and Demographic
Interactions—**Library Expenditures**

- Remote rural libraries in the Far West region had the highest unemploy-ment rate (9.9%) and the third-highest poverty rate (16.8%) in 2013.
- Contrastingly, rural libraries in the Far West region had the highest 2013 median per capita library expenditures ($96.14).
  - This is explained by state and federal revenue contributions to 67 remote Alaska rural libraries—each library received a minimum of $6,500 in income from the state of Alaska, and 61 of those libraries received a median of $9,574 in federal income.
- State and federal contributions to remote Alaska libraries resulted in high levels of per capita staff, inventory, and programs, leading to the remote Far West's number one ranking in those assets.
- From the ABCD perspective, the Alaska libraries' state and federal incomes are examples of economic capital produced by a local insti-tution drawing on outside resources for the benefit of the community.
- The Southeast region ranked low in median per capita library expenditures coupled with low median per capita staff, hours, inventory, and programs.
  - This is explained by the Southeast region's high rank in unemployment and poverty coupled with its low rank in median household income.
  - The Southeast's region's high rank in numbers of MLIS-degreed staff, discussed previously, may mitigate these demographic effects over the long term as MLIS staff effectively deploy library assets to benefit their communities.

2. Regional and Demographic Interactions: Rural Populations
Consistent with the .09% overall decline in rural populations (USDA, 2013, p. 5), median remote and distant net populations declined slightly during 2013. The median fringe net population change was positive by 187 persons. However, 212 (42%) of the fringe, 1,249 (61%) of the distant, and 995 (61%) of the remote rural libraries operated in areas with declining populations dur-ing 2013. While median net population changes in fringe, distant, and remote areas were small overall, there were larger regional differences in net popula-tion changes, as shown in Fig. 3. Net population growth in 2013 was highest in the fringe Southwest, Rocky Mountain, and Plains regions. If growth levels continue, it is likely that at least some of those rural libraries will be reclas-sified as nonrural in the 2020 census. In the meantime, rural librarians in those areas should find demand increasing for their services. Net population declines were largest in the remote and distant Southeast region—those areas

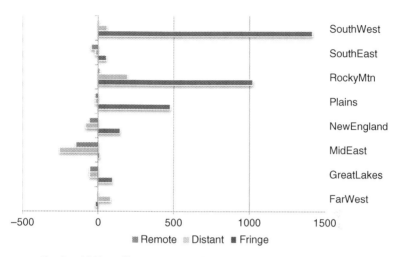

Fig. 3. 2013 median net population change by region and locale.

with the lowest median per capita expenditures, staff, service hours, programs, and inventory—demonstrating the efficacy of IMLS investment in Southeast rural MLIS librarians to promote the effective use of library assets in areas further stressed by population declines. The importance of each community asset increases in areas of low population density further stressed by declining populations (Snow, 2001, p. 6), and, regardless of their rank, all rural libraries possess valuable assets that can be contributed to ABCD initiatives.

Practical Implications: Regional and Demographic Interactions—Rural Populations

- Net population growth in 2013 was highest in the fringe Southwest, Rocky Mountain, and Plains regions.
  - Rural librarians in those areas should find demand increasing for their services.
- Net population declines in 2013 were largest in the remote and distant Southeast region.
  - Southeast rural population declines further stressed those libraries with the lowest median per capita expenditures, staff, service hours, programs, and inventory.
  - These factors support the efficacy of IMLS investment in MLIS librarians in the rural Southeast to promote the effective use of library assets in impoverished areas further stressed by population declines.

VI. CONCLUSIONS

In answer to research question 1, the comparison of per capita library asset medians revealed that there are statistically significant, yet small, differences between fringe, distant, and remote library inventories, outlets, service hours, staff, terminals, MLIS staff (fringe/distant and fringe/remote only), and expenditures (fringe/distant and remote/distant only). Of the three library asset variables used in the reduced set random forest classifier (outlets, MLIS staff, and public access terminals), only the terminal variable yielded an expected result—the actual median number of public access terminals generally increases as service area size increases. Unexpectedly, median per capita outlets (along with service hours and staff) increase as distances from urban areas and urban clusters increase. This effect is most likely attributable to lower service area populations and generally declining populations in distant and remote areas. Larger rural libraries face additional challenges, as per capita service hours tend to decrease as the number of branches increases. Also contrary to expectations, the Southeast and Far West regions ranked high in levels of MLIS staff, although they rank low in the percentage of adults holding a BA or higher degree. Whether due to IMLS grants to MLIS programs in the Southeast—such as those discussed by Mehra, Singh, Hollenbach, and Partee in the chapter "Rural Librarians as Change Agents in the 21st Century" in this volume—or higher state and federal income contributions in the Far West, the potential contributions of MLIS staff to ABCD initiatives in those high-poverty areas cannot be overestimated.

In answer to research question 2, the random forest classifiers indicated that region and demographic variables were related to asset differences between fringe, distant, and remote rural libraries, whereas population service area size and governance structure had little effect. Two important findings emerged from the interaction between distance from urban areas, geographic region, and demographic variables. First, the Southeast region's high rank in unemployment and poverty coupled with its low rank in median household income helped explain the Southeast's low median per capita library expenditures coupled with low median per capita staff, hours, inventory, and programs. Over time, the Southeast's high ranking in MLIS staff may lead to library asset increases. Second, state and federal contributions to Alaska libraries explained the remote Far West's high rank in per capita library expenditures despite high poverty and unemployment rates. The state and federal contributions to remote Alaska libraries can also be seen in the remote Far West's number one ranking in median per capita staff, inventory, and programs. Aligned with the ABCD framework, the state and federal economic capital invested in the remote Alaska libraries created cultural and social capital for the benefit of the local communities, and the economic multiplier effect created new economic assets from the portion of state and federal funds remaining in the local community through local purchases and salaries. Although 13 of the remote Alaska libraries serve fewer than 100 persons, their ability to connect their communities to outside resources and create new economic, cultural, and social assets from those resources demonstrates that even the smallest rural library can make important contributions to ABCD initiatives.

Future research is planned to extend analysis of the interactions between locale and regions to multiple years using additional demographic variables. Comparing median per capita assets to minimum standards for library operation (such as the New York standards available at http://www.nysl.nysed.gov/libdev/ministan.htm) may provide further explanation of the unexpected increases in several of the median per capita asset variables as distances from urban areas and clusters increased. Continuing the quantitative analysis of rural libraries through the asset-based community development framework may also lay the groundwork for the development of new benchmarking techniques for identifying undercapitalized and highly capitalized rural public libraries, in terms of both individual libraries and clusters of libraries, while providing likely candidates for further study and enriching the advocacy tool set available to practitioners.

REFERENCES

Alemanne, N. D., Mandel, L. H., & McClure, C. R. (2011). Chapter 3: The rural public library as leader in community broadband services. *Library Technology Reports*, *47*(6), 19–28.

Arns, J. W. (2013). *Assessing the value of public library services: A review of the literature and meta-analysis (META)*. Retrieved from http://www.libsci.sc.edu/metaweb/ValuingPublicLibraries_FinalReport.pdf.

Becker, S., Crandall, M, D., Fisher, K. E., Kinney, B. Landry, C., & Rocha, A. (2010). *Opportunity for all: How the American public benefits from Internet access at U.S. libraries*. Washington, DC: Institute of Museum and Library Services. Retrieved from https://www.imls.gov/assets/1/AssetManager/OpportunityForAll.pdf.

Bertot, J. C., Real, B., Lee, J., McDermott, A. J., & Jaeger, P. T. (2015, October 1). *2014 digital inclusion survey: Survey findings and Results*. College Park, MD: Information Policy & Access Center. Retrieved from http://digitalinclusion.umd.edu/sites/default/files/uploads/2014DigitalInclusionSurveyFinalRelease.pdf.

Blejwas, E. (2010). Asset-based community development in Alabama's black belt: Seven strategies for building a diverse community movement. In G. P. Green & A. Goetting (Eds.), *Mobilizing communities: Asset building as a community development strategy* (pp. 48–67). Philadelphia, PA: Temple University Press.

Bourdieu, P. (1985). The forms of capital. In J. Richardson (Ed.), *Handbook of theory and research for the sociology of education* (pp. 241–258). New York, NY: Greenwood Press.

Burt, R. S. (1992). *Structural holes: The social structure of competition.* Cambridge, MA: Harvard University Press.

Dewar, T. (1997, July). *A guide to evaluating asset-based community development: Lessons, challenges, and opportunities.* Chicago, IL: ACTA Publications.

Duncan, C. M. (2001). Social capital in America's poor rural communities. In S. Saegert, J. P. Thompson, & M. R. Warren (Eds.), *Social capital and poor communities* (pp. 60–86). New York, NY: Russell Sage Foundation.

Fischer, R. K. (2015). Rural and small town library management challenges *Public Library Quarterly*, *34*, 354–371.

Flaherty, M. G., & Miller, D. (2016, April). Rural public libraries as community change agents: Opportunities for health promotion. *Journal of Education for Library and Information Science*, *57*, 143–150.

Flatley, R., & Wyman, A. (2009). Changes in rural libraries and librarianship: A comparative survey. *Public Library Quarterly*, *28*, 24–39.

Garcia, J., & Nelson, S. (2007). *2007: Public library service responses.* Chicago, IL: Public Library Association.

Ginger, J. A. (2015). *Capturing the context of digital literacy: A case study of Illinois public libraries in underserved communities* (Doctoral dissertation). Retrieved from http://hdl.handle.net/2142/88063.

Goulding, A. (2004). Editorial: Libraries and social capital. *Journal of Librarianship and Information Science*, *36*, 3–6.

Green, G. P. (2010). Community assets: Building the capacity for development. In G. P. Green & A. Goetting (Eds.), *Mobilizing communities: Asset building as a community development strategy* (pp. 1–13). Philadelphia, PA: Temple University Press.

Granovetter, M. S. (1973). The strength of weak ties. *American Journal of Sociology*, *78*, 1360–1380.

Hancks, J. W. (2011). *Keepin' it rural: The role of rural public library educational programming and outreach in community economic sustainability efforts.* Retrieved from ProQuest Dissertations and Theses. (874246054).

Hertz, T., Kusmin, R., Marré, A., & Parker, T. (2014, August). *Rural employment trends in recession and recovery.* Economic Research Report No. 172. Washington, DC: Economic Research Service, United States Department of Agriculture.

Heuertz, L. (2009). *Rural libraries building communities.* Retrieved from ProQuest Dissertations and Theses (AAT 305016178).

Hildreth, S. (2007). Rural libraries: The heart of our communities. *Public Libraries*, *46*(2), 7–11.

Institute of Museum and Library Services. (2015a, July). *Data file documentation public libraries survey fiscal year 2013.* Retrieved from https://www.imls.gov/sites/default/files/fy2013_pls_data_file_documentation.pdf.

Institute of Museum and Library Services. (2015b, July). *Public libraries in the United States survey: Fiscal year 2013* [Data file]. Retrieved from https://www.imls.gov/publications/public-libraries-united-states-survey-fiscal-year-2013.

James, G., Witten, D., Hastie, T., & Tibshirani, R. (2013). *An introduction to statistical learning: With applications in R.* New York, NY: Springer.

Johnson, C. A. (2012). How do public libraries create social capital? An analysis of interactions between library staff and patrons. *Library & Information Science Research*, *34*, 52–62.

Khan, S. R., Rifaqat, Z., & Kazmi, S. (2007). *Harnessing and guiding social capital for rural development.* New York, NY: Palgrave MacMillen.

Kretzmann, J. P., & McKnight, J. L. (1993). *Building communities from the inside out: A path toward finding and mobilizing a community's assets.* Skokie, IL: ACTA Publications.

Kretzmann, J. P., & Rans, S. A. (2005). *The engaged library: Chicago stories of community building.* Evanston, IL: Urban Libraries Council.

Lance, K. C., & Lyons, R. (2008, June 15). The new LJ index. *Library Journal, 133*(11), 38–41. Retrieved from http://lj.libraryjournal.com/2008/06/ljarchives/the-new-lj-index/.

Landis, J. R., & Koch, G. G. (1977). The measurement of observer agreement for categorical data. *Biometrics, 33,* 159–174.

Lin, N. (2001). *Social capital: A theory of social structure and action.* New York, NY: Cambridge University Press.

Majekodunmi, A. (2011). *Examining the role of rural community libraries: Social connectedness and adult learning.* Retrieved from ProQuest Dissertations and Theses (AAT 921360301).

Mathie, A., & Cunningham, G. (Eds.). (2008). *From clients to citizens: Communities changing the course of their own development.* Warwickshire, UK: Practical Action Publishing.

McKnight, J. L. (1996). *A twenty-first century map for healthy communities and families.* Evanston, IL: Asset Based Community Development Institute.

McKnight, J. L. (2003). *Regenerating community: The recovery of a space for citizens.* Evanston, IL: Institute for Policy Research, Northwestern University.

Phillips, R., & Shockley, G. (2010). Linking cultural capital conceptions to asset-based community development. In G. P. Green & A. Goetting (Eds.), *Mobilizing communities: Asset building as a community development strategy* (pp. 92–111). Philadelphia, PA: Temple University Press.

Rans, S. A., & Altman, H. (2002). *Asset-based strategies for faith communities.* Evanston, IL: Asset Based Community Development Institute.

Real, B., Bertot, J. C., & Jaeger, P. T. (2014, March). Rural public libraries and digital inclusion: Issues and challenges. *Information Technologies and Libraries, 3*(1), 6–24.

Russell, C., & Nurture Development (2009, June). *Communities in control—Developing assets.* Liverpool, UK: Carnegie UK Trust.

Saabas, A. (2014, December 1). Selecting good features—Part III: Random forests [Web log comment]. Retrieved from http://blog.datadive.net/selecting-good-features-part-iii-random-forests/.

Scales, T. L., Streeter, C. L., & Cooper, H. S. (Eds.). (2014). *Rural social work: Building and sustaining community capacity* (2nd edn.). Hoboken, NJ: Wiley.

Smith, S. A. (2014). The future of small rural public libraries in America: A report prepared for the Board of the Langlois Public Library. *Public Library Quarterly, 33*(1), 83–85. doi:10.1080/01616846.2013.848138

Snow, L. K. (2001). *The organization of hope: A workbook for rural asset-based community development.* Chicago, IL: ACTA Publications.

Swan, D. W., Grimes, J., & Owens, T. (2013, September). *The state of small and rural libraries in the United States.* Research Brief No. 5. Washington, DC: Institute of Museum and Library Services. Retrieved from http://www.imls.gov/assets/1/AssetManager/Brief2013_05.pdf

Stevens, J. P. (2009). *Applied multivariate statistics for the social sciences* (5th edn.). New York, NY: Routledge.

Tape, T. G. (n.d.). *The area under the ROC curve.* Retrieved from http://gim.unmc.edu/dxtests/roc3.htm.

United States Department of Agriculture. (2013, November). *Rural America at a glance: 2013 edition.* Economic Brief No. EB-24.

United States Department of Agriculture Economic Research Service. (2015a). *Poverty estimates for the U.S., states, and counties, 2013* [Data file]. Retrieved March 23, 2015.

United States Department of Agriculture Economic Research Service. (2015b). *Population estimates for the U.S., states, and counties, 2010–13* [Data file]. Retrieved March 23, 2015.

United States Department of Agriculture Economic Research Service. (2015c). *Unemployment and median household income for the U.S., states, and counties, 2000–2013* [Data file]. Retrieved March 23, 2015.

United States Department of Agriculture Economic Research Service. (2015d). *Educational attainment for the U.S., states, and counties, 1970–2013* [Data file]. Retrieved March 23, 2015.

Vårheim, A. (2007). Social capital and public libraries: The need for research. *Library & Information Science Research, 29,* 416–428.

Witten, I. H., Frank, E., & Hall, M. A. (2011). *Data mining: Practical machine learning tools and techniques* (3rd edn.). Burlington, MA: Morgan Kaufmann Publishers.

A GAP ANALYSIS OF THE PERSPECTIVES OF SMALL BUSINESSES AND RURAL LIBRARIANS IN TENNESSEE: DEVELOPMENTS TOWARD A BLUEPRINT FOR A PUBLIC LIBRARY SMALL BUSINESS TOOLKIT

Bharat Mehra, Bradley Wade Bishop, and Robert P. Partee II

ABSTRACT

This chapter presents a gap analysis of the perspectives of small businesses and rural librarians in Tennessee in order to develop an implementation blueprint of a public library small business toolkit, a resource that the state's rural public libraries can create for small businesses in the future.

Rural and Small Public Libraries: Challenges and Opportunities
Advances in Librarianship, Volume 43, 97–121
ISSN: 0065-2830/doi:10.1108/S0065-283020170000043005

The chapter reports on select comparison data sets collected via two exploratory online surveys with small businesses and rural public librarians, respectively, in an externally funded planning grant awarded by the Institute of Museum and Library Services' National Leadership Grants for Libraries (Research category) to the School of Information Sciences at the University of Tennessee.

Findings from the gap analysis of the perspectives of small businesses and rural librarians provide similarities and differences between the two stakeholder groups in terms of

- *existing assistance needs of small businesses,*
- *information-related challenges small businesses experience,*
- *desired public library use, and*
- *information-related components of a public library small business toolkit.*

The study is a unique example of action research based on varied levels of participation in rural research and action, learning through collaboration, community inquiry into everyday experiences and potential impact, use of mixed methods, and the situated nature of applications and concrete outcomes. It serves as a pilot case experience and prototype assessment test bed to expand strategies for the entire Appalachian region and other rural environments in the future.

Keywords: Small businesses; rural libraries; Tennessee; gap analysis

I. INTRODUCTION

This chapter presents a gap analysis of the perspectives of small businesses and rural librarians in Tennessee in order to develop an implementation blueprint of a small business public library toolkit, a resource that the state's rural public libraries can create for small businesses in the future.[1] It is based on select research findings in an externally funded planning grant entitled "The Role of Rural Public Libraries in Small Business Economic Development in the Appalachian Region: A Case Study of Tennessee (PLSB-TN)"[2] recently (October 2014 to September 2016) awarded by the Institute of Museum and Library Services' National Leadership Grants for

Libraries (Research category) to the School of Information Sciences at the University of Tennessee. PLSB-TN has involved collecting quantitative and qualitative feedback about the needs, expectations, and experiences of small businesses and rural public libraries in the state. It serves as a pilot case experience and prototype assessment test bed to expand approaches in the future for the whole Appalachian region and similar rural settings (Mehra, Bishop, and Partee II, 2016a).

The planning grant is a unique example of action research as defined in terms of collaborations between a "professional action researcher and members of an organization or community seeking to improve a situation" (Greenwood & Levin 1998; Mehra & Braquet, 2007). In the PLSB-TN, the research team has collected data that will be used to develop a product to improve the experiences of small businesses in rural Tennessee via partnering with public libraries in the state (Mehra, Bishop, & Partee II, 2016b). The PLSB-TN gap analysis has involved organizing preliminary planning activities; analyzing existing needs and feasibility; solidifying community partnerships; and developing initial work plans, blueprints, and a strategic action plan of a public library small business toolkit that will engage, energize, and strengthen ties between various rural stakeholders (Mehra, Bishop, & Partee II, 2016c). Kemmis and McTaggart (1988) identified the objects of action research as social practice and its transformations, the changes that occur in social institutions, and relationships that support this (Mehra & Braquet, 2014). Action research characteristics fitting the PLSB-TN activities include varied levels of participation in rural research and action, learning through collaboration, community inquiry into everyday experiences and potential impact, use of mixed methods, and the situated nature of applications and concrete outcomes (Mehra, 2006; Rahman, 2008; Stringer, 1999).

II. RURAL CONTEXT IN TENNESSEE

There are several points to recognize regarding the research context of rural Tennessee. It forms part of the Appalachian region (namely, the Southern and Central Appalachian [SCA] belt)[3] that has traditionally faced challenging economic, social, and cultural conditions adversely affecting the population living in these areas (Appalachian Regional Commission, 2010; Eller, 2008; Mehra, 2014; Scruggs, 2010). These hardships have included historical and ongoing issues of crippling poverty, high unemployment, low information literacy levels and educational attainment, a lack of access to information technology resources, and other debilitating socioeconomic conditions that are unique to the region (American Library Association Office for Literacy and Outreach Services, 2011; Mehra et al., 2014; Lichter & Campbell, 2005). Entrenched in larger typecasting and ostracizing of the "South" (Cooper & Terrill, 2009; Escott, Goldfield, McMillen, & Turner, 1999), American popular culture and the news media have cultivated a provincial image of the SCA region and its rural library milieus (Cash, 1991; Cobb, 2007; Wyatt-Brown, 2008) with their deprived circumstances and inadequate resources (Fritsch & Gallimore, 2007; Mehra et al., 2012; Mehra, Black, Singh, & Nolt, 2011) in a religiously and politically conservative climate with habitually unfriendly cultural responses toward people on the peripheries of society (Fisher & Smith, 2012; Ludke & Obermiller, 2012; Mehra & Gray, 2014).

Embedded in these harsh, pervasive conditions of struggle and survival, rural libraries can potentially play a leadership role in economic development and the sustainable economic viability of the region (Mehra & Singh, 2015; Real, Bertot, & Jaeger, 2014). As part of the state's educational centers of learning and information providers, Tennessee's rural public libraries in particular represent untapped possibilities to develop collaborations with the workforce industry and promote economic development and cultural growth in the region's smaller communities (Economic Development Research Group, 2007). They have recognized the need to venture out of their traditional bastions of middle-class power and privilege (Mehra, Rioux, & Albright, 2009) to build bridges with external constituencies and play a greater role in community building and community revitalization (Mehra, Black, & Lee, 2010). This chapter reports on one such initiative that explores perspectives of the small business community and rural public libraries about gaps and possible areas for future strategic direction to proactively partner with and contribute to community development efforts in the state (Mehra & Singh, 2014).

III. TENNESSEE'S REGIONAL LIBRARIES

The Tennessee State Library and Archives consists of nine multicounty regions serving 211 small and medium-sized public libraries throughout Tennessee.[4] These regions are geographically defined and are applicable to small businesses and public libraries alike.[5] These areas are the Buffalo River Region, Clinch River Region, Falling Water River Region, Hatchie River Region, Holston River Region, Obion River Region, Ocoee River Region, Red River Region, and Stones River Region.

Tennessee's Regional Library System has been in existence since 1939, and its mission is to (1) provide supplementary library materials to member public libraries, (2) assist local governments in public library development and expansion, (3) provide continuing education to local library staff and trustees, (4) assist in the selection and maintenance of library technology, and (5) provide library services to disadvantaged community members who have difficulty using local public libraries.[6] During the beginning of the 21st century, 69 of the 95 (National Association of Counties Rural Action Caucus, 2002), indicating a role for regional and county public library systems to shape the lives of their community members. A rural public library in Tennessee is defined as one that does not belong to any of the four metropolitan public library systems in the state (i.e., Memphis Public Library, Knox County Library, Nashville Public Library, and the Chattanooga–Hamilton County Bicentennial Public Library).

Rural libraries in Tennessee face hurdles as they attempt to provide small businesses with access to updated and authoritative information; help them judiciously use the information, based on their requirements, in light of ever-increasing information rates (Lang, 1999); deliver the advantages of technology, computers, and the Internet to small business in geographically dispersed areas; and collaborate with other community-based agencies and organizations to provide better systems, programs, and services for all small business community members (Rosser-Hogben, 2004). Fig. 1 shows the rural public library outlets within and beyond the Appalachian region, with a focus on the state of Tennessee. Out of Tennessee's 95 counties, 41 are in Appalachia (http://www.arc.gov/counties), and a population of 2,785,342 out of Tennessee's total population of 6,346,105 live in Appalachian counties (http://www.arc.gov/data). During the past decade, sixty-six counties (U.S. Census Bureau, 2010). All rural libraries were included in this study, as they shared similar experiences and conditions with the Appalachian rural libraries. The research team will use the implications from this research to benefit libraries and communities in the Appalachian region and other rural communities around the country.

Fig. 1. Rural public library outlets with a focus on Tennessee.

IV. RESEARCH METHODS

This chapter reports on select comparison data sets collected via two exploratory online surveys with small businesses and rural public librarians, respectively.[7] The small business survey inquired about their information needs and
perspectives about the role of public libraries in economic development, providing baseline data to develop further work with the small business community (Mehra, Bishop, & Partee II, 2017). The public library survey was
piloted to research the current practices of rural public librarians in assisting
small businesses (Bishop, Mehra, & Partee II, 2016). We administered the
survey and informed consent forms through an Internet-based software system hosted on a secure server.

   We formed an advisory committee of 10 small business and rural library
representatives to consult and guide us in the dissemination of the surveys.
Using snowballing techniques, we recruited a convenience sample of small
business representatives connected to Tennessee's chambers of commerce
and economic development councils to participate in the small business
survey (Babbie, 2001). They received a recruitment email with a description
of the study to forward to small businesses in their professional circles. The
authors also contacted various Tennessee librarians to assist in distributing
the surveys to small businesses in their regions. For the public library survey,
we sent a recruitment email and survey link via state library listservs, along
with emails to rural public libraries, PLSB-TN partners, and advisory board
members.

   This research adopted an original strategy in collecting data using web-
based surveys, a method that has conventionally been employed to collect
quantitative data sets (Barrios et al., 2011), to garner qualitative feedback
in comment boxes for almost all nondemographic questions. Although
open-ended questions for amassing qualitative data are common in surveys,
they are used selectively and in a limited manner, whereas this survey-based
research was designed with a majority of open-ended questions. The resulting
advantage was that the research involved a larger number of respondents who
provided detailed qualitative feedback in the survey comment boxes (Creswell
& Clark, 2007).

   We also employed a "mixed methods" approach in the data analysis of
survey feedback using content analysis that has traditionally been applied in
qualitative research (Glaser, 1965; Neuendorf, 2002) to generate quantitative
response counts for the categories and themes identified for each question.
The resulting advantage in the analysis and generation of results was an integration of both quantitative and qualitative characteristics (Mertens, 2010).

Open, axial, and selective coding facilitated the application of grounded theory generated categories and the wide-ranging themes that were quantitatively recoded as response counts to each question, which we have selectively presented in tables in this chapter. Many respondents provided a rich variety of more than one response to each survey question. An understanding of similar meanings in the respondents' varied choice of words and the grouping of respondents' specific responses under broader, narrower, and related concepts provided the basis for our generation of categories and themes. For each question, the coding steps included (1) compiling the response text, (2) sequentially ordering each respondent's content separated in response counts (C1, C2, etc.), (3) classifying each response count under specific categories related to the themes (if applicable), (4) developing and refining a key of categories and themes, and (5) totaling counts for each with specific examples. The following illustrates how select coding was applied to generate categories and themes from respondent (P1 and P2) feedback on the kinds of information-related assistance that they would find useful (Q1 on data collection instrument):

> [P1: "I mainly need tax information (C1)...information when I opened my business (C2) including laws/regulations (C3), tax forms (C4)." P2: "Government rules (C5)...business registration (C6), licenses (C7), sales tax application/filing (C8), federal wage/tax filing (C9)"].

In the above example, C1, C4, C8, and C9 are connected to the theme "Tax information." Likewise, C2 is connected to the theme "Start-up information," C3 and C5 are connected to the theme "Legal information," and C6 and C7 to "Business registration and licenses." Documenting particular details while compiling the feedback (e.g., examples of a specific theme), often reflecting the respondent's choice of words, ensured reliability, validity, and relevance of the categories and themes for each question across the two researchers.

The following are overlapping topics that both stakeholder groups volunteered, allowing us to generate the comparable data sets:

1. Existing assistance needs of small businesses
2. Information-related challenges small businesses experience
3. Desired public library use
4. Information-related components of a public library small business toolkit

Appendix 1 compares the specific questions that were asked in the two surveys to collect the comparable data sets. These questions allowed each respondent to describe the small business and economic development efforts in their terms and gave the researchers data on the resources and services each library provided (or lacked). The research team developed a codebook after reviewing all responses. Each utterance (i.e., expression) in the open-ended responses was counted. Although several categories emerged through thematic coding of similarly phrased expressions, a few mentions remained uncategorized and were coded as "other."

V. FINDINGS

A. Participant Demographics

Of the 120 small business representatives who responded to the survey, many did not select a gender or a race/ethnicity. Forty-four (59%) selected male and 30 selected female (41%). Respondents were allowed to enter their race/ethnicity using their own words to determine the categories with which they self-identified. Of the 74 that indicated a race/ethnicity, only one each self-identified as African American Black, White/Native American, Hispanic/Mexican, and "human." One each self-identified (in their own words) as White/Anglo Saxon, White/Anglo, Caucasian/American, American, and European/American. In addition, 25 identified as "Caucasian" and 40 identified as "White," with a total of 69 self-identifying a term associated with White/Caucasian. Of the 65 public librarians who responded to the survey, most gave feedback regarding their demographic characteristics, with seven (11%) selecting male and 58 (89%) selecting female for gender, and 65 of the 66 who responded indicating their race/ethnicity as Caucasian/White while one self-identified as American Indian. The age ranges for the two groups are listed in Table 1.

Table 1. Age Range of Respondents.

Age range	Small business representatives	Public library representatives
18–29 years	2 (3%)	7 (11%)
30–39 years	8 (11%)	10 (15%)
40–49 years	22 (30%)	9 (14%)
50–59 years	18 (24%)	26 (40%)
60 years and above	24 (32%)	13 (20%)
Total	74	65

The average number of years owning (or working at) a small business was 17.72 from the 71 usable responses. Forty-five of the respondents (63.4%) had worked at or owned small businesses for more than 10 years. For the librarians, the average number of years working in public libraries was 11.13 years from the 67 usable responses. Twenty-eight (43.08%) of the respondents indicated more than 10 years and 39 (60%) less than 10 years, representing a good mix of experienced and newer librarians. Fifty-four (73%) of the 74 respondents indicated their small business was in a U.S. Bureau of the Census "rural" area, with all of these small businesses being in the Tennessee Appalachian region. Forty-six (71%) of the respondents indicated their public library was in the Tennessee Appalachian region, and 43 (66%) indicated their public library was in a U.S. Bureau of the Census "rural" area. The 74 responses from small business representatives were from 22 of the 52 Appalachian Region Counties in Tennessee. Nineteen (25.7%) public libraries of the total 74 that responded were not from the Appalachian counties, but these librarians can still provide valuable insight because they operate in similar areas. They lack the federal designation of "Appalachian" because they are not part of the contiguous Appalachian mountainous areas, but they are still part of the same local culture. The 33 responses (44.60%) from public library representatives were from 18 of the 52 Appalachian Region Counties in Tennessee.

B. Existing Information-Related Assistance Needs of Small Businesses

Table 2 summarizes respondent feedback regarding existing information-related assistance needs to manage small businesses. We framed the question differently for the business and librarian groups to match their respective professional expectations and knowledge. We asked small businesses about their existing use and need of information-related assistance, while we asked public libraries about the existing ways they support small businesses. An important finding is that small business operators did not identify public libraries as an existing information-related agency that was relevant to their needs and could provide information resources related to starting or managing their small business.

Both the small business and public library respondents ranked Internet use as the highest count category of information-related assistance needs (22.04%), contributing to a significantly larger total count gap compared to the other categories. Overall, the next three highest count categories included legal (6.86 %), tax (6.24%), and business registration and licenses (6.24%),

Table 2.   Existing Information-Related Assistance Needs
of Small Businesses.

Category	Small business count	Public library count	Total
Internet	22.43%	21.56%	22.04%
Legal	7.22%	6.42%	6.86%
Tax	8.37%	3.67%	6.24%
Business registration and licenses	10.27%	0.00%	5.61%
Education	1.14%	10.09%	5.20%
Printing	1.14%	10.09%	5.20%
Functionalities to maintain business	9.13%	0.00%	4.99%
Local information	7.98%	0.92%	4.78%
Marketing	1.52%	8.26%	4.57%
Business-related community resources	6.46%	1.83%	4.37%
Other	3.04%	5.96%	4.37%
Space	0.00%	9.63%	4.37%
Reference	1.14%	6.88%	3.74%
Book	1.14%	6.42%	3.53%
Developing business plans	5.70%	0.00%	3.12%
Finance information	5.32%	0.00%	2.91%
Employment	1.90%	2.75%	2.29%
None	1.90%	2.29%	2.08%
Programming	0.00%	3.21%	1.46%
News and trends	2.28%	0.00%	1.25%
Trade information	1.14%	0.00%	0.62%
Start-up information	0.76%	0.00%	0.42%
Total	100.00%	100.00%	100.00%

providing a total count of less than that for Internet use. However, small business representatives ranked business registration and licenses (10.27%), functionalities to maintain business (9.13%), and tax (8.37%) in their next three highest count usage categories, while public library representatives ranked education (10.09%), printing (10.09%), space (9.63%), and marketing (8.26%) in their next three highest ranked count categories of how they assisted small businesses.

C. Respondent Feedback Regarding Information-Related Challenges

Table 3 summarizes respondent feedback regarding recent information-related challenges. We asked small business operators what information-related

Table 3. Challenges Faced by Small Businesses.

Themes	Small business count	Public library count	Total
Legal information	14.46%	7.50%	12.20%
Finance information	16.87%	0.00%	11.38%
External environment	13.25%	0.00%	8.94%
Functionalities to maintain business	13.25%	0.00%	8.94%
None	12.05%	0.00%	8.13%
Internet	0.00%	22.50%	7.32%
Business information	0.00%	17.50%	5.69%
Personnel management	8.43%	0.00%	5.69%
Tax/insurance	4.82%	5.00%	4.88%
Health information	6.02%	0.00%	4.07%
Employment	0.00%	10.00%	3.25%
Information infrastructure	4.82%	0.00%	3.25%
Marketing	0.00%	10.00%	3.25%
Reference	0.00%	10.00%	3.25%
Access networks	3.61%	0.00%	2.44%
Unknown	0.00%	7.50%	2.44%
Local events	2.41%	0.00%	1.63%
Printing	0.00%	5.00%	1.63%
Space	0.00%	5.00%	1.63%
Total	100.00%	100.00%	100.00%

challenges they faced in managing their operations, while we asked public librarians what information-related challenges they faced in serving the needs of local small businesses in their communities.

We found significant differences in the overall number of responses from each group, with those from small business representatives (66.94%) more than doubling those collected from public library representatives (32.52%). Small business operators ranked finance information as the highest count category of information-related challenges they experienced (16.87%), while public libraries ranked Internet use as the highest count category of information-related challenges small businesses experienced (22.5%). Overall, the three highest count categories included legal information (12.20%), finance information (11.38%), external environment (8.94%), and functionalities to maintain business (8.94%), although public library representatives provided a minimal count for these three categories (5.88%). Public library representatives ranked Internet (22.50%), business information (17.50%), employment (10.00%), marketing (10.00%), and reference (10.00%) in their three highest ranked count categories of challenges small businesses experienced.

D. Desired Public Library Use

Table 4 compiles respondent feedback about the methods of library assistance (Q4, 21 respondents), the provision of specific services/resources (Q5, 23 respondents), and the desired improvements (Q6, 16 respondents). We asked small businesses how they would like public libraries to assist them, while we asked public libraries about the ways they could improve their efforts to assist small businesses. Again, nearly twice as many small business representatives (69.81%) responded to this question versus public library representatives (30.19%). Small businesses ranked functionalities to maintain business (22.97%), none (16.22%), and technology (10.81%) as their three highest count categories in the ways that public libraries could assist them, while public libraries regarded education (34.38%), functionalities to maintain business (14.06%), business-related community resources (14.06%), needs (9.38%) and other (9.38%) as their three highest ranked count categories of ways to improve assistance to small businesses.

Table 4. Desired Ways for Public Libraries to Improve
Their Efforts in Assisting Small Business.

Themes	Small business perspective	Public library perspective	Total
Functionalities to maintain business	22.97%	14.06%	20.28%
None	16.22%	3.13%	12.26%
Education	0.00%	34.38%	10.38%
Technology	10.81%	0.00%	7.55%
Legal/physical	8.78%	1.56%	6.60%
Rules/requirements	9.46%	0.00%	6.60%
Finance information	6.76%	1.56%	5.19%
Access networks	6.76%	0.00%	4.72%
Outreach	6.76%	0.00%	4.72%
Business-related community resources	0.00%	14.06%	4.25%
Tax information	5.41%	1.56%	4.25%
Needs	0.00%	9.38%	2.83%
Other	0.00%	9.38%	2.83%
Personnel management	2.03%	3.13%	2.36%
Start-up services	2.03%	0.00%	1.42%
Health information	1.35%	0.00%	0.94%
Space	0.00%	3.13%	0.94%
Who	0.00%	3.13%	0.94%
Internet	0.00%	1.56%	0.47%
Local information	0.68%	0.00%	0.47%
Total	100.00%	100.00%	100.00%

E. Information-Related Components of a
Public Library Small Business Toolkit

Table 5 summarizes respondent feedback about essential components of a public library small business toolkit (Q8). Overall, functionalities to maintain business (17.39%), local information (15.65%), finance information (9.57%), and tax information (9.57%) were the categories with the highest overall response counts. In addition to the categories of functionalities to maintain business (19.05%), local information (11.11%), and tax information (11.11%), small business representatives ranked the category of "none" (12.70%) in their top three ranked components of a toolkit. Public librarians, on the other hand, ranked the categories of local information (21.15%), functionalities to maintain business (15.39%), finance information (9.62%), business events (9.62%) and advanced marketing (9.62%) as their top three ranked toolkit components.

VI. DISCUSSION

This section draws on the previously mentioned implications for the implementation of a blueprint to develop a public library small business toolkit. The gap analysis from the findings is clear when reviewing the differing survey

Table 5. Components of a Public Library Small Business Toolkit.

Theme	Small business perspective	Public library perspective	Total
Functionalities to maintain business	19.05%	15.38%	17.39%
Local information	11.11%	21.15%	15.65%
Finance information	9.52%	9.62%	9.57%
Tax information	11.11%	7.69%	9.57%
Business events	7.94%	9.62%	8.70%
None	12.70%	1.92%	7.83%
Advanced marketing	4.76%	9.62%	6.96%
Internet resources	4.76%	7.69%	6.09%
Rules/requirements	6.35%	3.85%	5.22%
Technology skills	4.76%	3.85%	4.35%
Miscellaneous	3.17%	1.92%	2.61%
Legal	0.00%	3.85%	1.74%
Personnel management	3.17%	0.00%	1.74%
Physical	0.00%	3.85%	1.74%
Health information	1.59%	0.00%	0.87%
Total	100.00%	100.00%	100.00%

responses between the two stakeholder groups. The following are discussion points organized by themes from the findings, namely: (1) existing information assistance needs, (2) information-related challenges, (3) desired public library use, and (4) information-related components of a toolkit.

A. Existing Information Assistance Needed by Small Businesses

The researchers expected gaps to emerge between the two stakeholder surveys, as responses to information assistance needs reflect the differing understandings of starting and operating a small business. Business representatives know their information needs because they operate their businesses, but public librarians may not be informed of all the resources they need. Despite two different professional groups responding to questions in the domain of business, there were many similarities in the needs discussed by both types of stakeholders.

The responses converged the most on Internet use. As it is the dominant communication infrastructure for everyday life tasks, including much of consumer behavior, the small business representatives and public librarians both listed Internet use as the most crucial need. This was mentioned nearly three times as often as the second most common response. No wonder programs such as BroadbandUSA in the U.S. Commerce Department's National Telecommunications and Information Administration (NTIA; "About," n.d.) go beyond connectivity to provide "assistance to communities that want to expand their broadband capacity and promote broadband adoption" and help with "planning new infrastructure and engaging a wide range of partners in broadband projects" based on a need to address the question, "how can people in rural communities effectively USE technologies to make a real difference in their everyday lives?" (Mehra, 2017). Multnomah County Library, the oldest public library west of the Mississippi, located in Oregon, was selected by the Benton Foundation and the National Digital Inclusion Alliance in its efforts to explore the "origins, strategies, challenges and funding mechanisms for successful digital inclusion organizations" (Siefer, 2017) to meet identified goals that include access to affordable high-speed Internet and devices for those in need; training and support to ensure that everyone has the skills to use digital technology to enhance their quality of life; empowerment of community partners to bridge the digital divide through funding, coordination, training, and staff resources; opportunities for jobs in the digital economy for underserved populations; and policy framework that supports digital equity and meaningful Internet adoption/use, leading to better community outcomes. Further, in a report entitled "Digital Inclusion and Meaningful Broadband Adoption Initiatives" published by the Benton Foundation, Rhinesmith (2016) highlights the following four digital inclusion activities for helping low-income individuals and families "adopt broadband in ways that were most appropriate to their personal needs and contexts": (1) providing low-cost broadband; (2) connecting digital literacy training with relevant content and services; (3) making low-cost computers available, and (4) operating public access computing centers. The Federal Communications Commission's *2016 Broadband Progress Report* retains the existing speed benchmark of 25 Mbps download/3 Mbps upload for fixed services for which the following two findings are relevant: (1) 39% of rural Americans (23 million people) are denied this access, compared to only 4% of urban Americans, and (2) the availability of fixed terrestrial services in rural America continues to lag behind urban America at all speeds: 20% lack access even to service at 4 Mbps/1 Mbps, down only 1% since 2011, and 31% lack access to 10 Mbps/1 Mbps, down only 4% since 2011.

The next three categories most mentioned in total were legal, tax, and business registration and licenses. These information assistance needs were indicated by many small business representatives; only registration and licenses was not included by any public librarians. An important point to note here is that a difference in these numbers across the two stakeholders might be related to different perceptions and uses of vocabularies associated with these categories; research limitation in separating legal, tax, and business information from Internet availability based on existing methods used in data collection; and/or barriers to finding these types of information related to issues of the digital divide and digital literacy.

That category and many that follow for starting and operating a small business begin to reveal a knowledge gap for librarians to overcome to assist in local economic development. Certainly, public librarians can locate and compile resources that would address the common legal, tax, and other registration and licensing information needs of small businesses. The contrast is most striking in small business responses to the category of functionalities to maintain business—with 24 mentions from small business (9.13%) and zero from public libraries. Public librarians listed education, printing, marketing, and space much more than small businesses. Since emerging from the Great Recession in 2009, new business formation in the United States has been "highly concentrated, clustered mostly in high-density urban or suburban areas" (e.g., half of the net increase of business establishments in 2010 to 2014 occurred in only 20 counties, of which 17 were in just four states—California, Florida, New York, and Texas), and "small counties have experienced net negative growth" with acute circumstances in rural areas not even participating in this "scant amount of new business formation" (Dearie, 2016). Rural libraries can be possible partners in helping small businesses emerge and stay afloat in such a dismal scenario, as affirmed in other findings like those published by the Appalachian Regional Commission (ARC). Based on 2017 estimates, of the 420 designated Appalachian counties, 84 counties with a total population of 1,668,358 are economically distressed, and another 114 counties with a total of 3,621,825 residents are economically at risk (Appalachian Regional Commission, n.d.), while the region's labor force participation stays low, at 59.5% compared with 64.2% nationally (ARC, 2015).

It is important to note that the three highest count categories (after the top ranked) for one stakeholder group was scored with quite a low count by the other group. This indicates a lack of differential awareness, perceptions, and reality of experience across the two groups about the existing information-related assistance needed to maintain small businesses and that provided by public library representatives. It calls for research to explore perspectives and conduct need analysis and marketing of existing resources provided by public libraries to bridge the gaps between the two stakeholder groups.

Moreover, a toolkit may address these gaps in small business owners' understanding of the services beyond Internet use that public libraries offer for free. If small business operators were to recognize public libraries as valuable resources, then these libraries would be able to facilitate community economic development, especially for new businesses that may not have resources to print, market, or even hold space for meetings when first starting. The categories of listed information across the two stakeholder groups will form the structure of a toolkit blueprint in providing an identification of key fields underlying the database design. This toolkit will facilitate better conversations between small business operators and public libraries, allowing them to meaningfully discuss how they can work together.

B. Respondent Feedback Regarding Information-Related Challenges

The researchers again could safely assume small business representatives would be more forthcoming with information-related challenges than public librarians. Public librarians in total listed less than half the number of challenges that small business representatives did. The public librarians most often mentioned the challenge of Internet access. In part, this is because public libraries serve as an anchor institution and in many rural communities are the only free Internet access point. However, no small business person listed the Internet as a challenge. Without this challenge being overcome, it would have been difficult to complete or receive an online survey. Perhaps, the method limits the actual number of businesses that do face challenges related to Internet connectivity and costs.

It is worth repeating that the three highest count categories for each stakeholder group were scored with a low count by the other group. Again, there are significant gaps in awareness across the two groups and there is a need for research and education to bridge the differential knowledge and realities of experience. The small business challenges most listed were legal information, finance information, external environment, and functionalities to maintain business. Public librarians indicated only legal information from this set. This gap was expected, but can inform other parts of the toolkit given that public librarians appear seemingly unaware of the information-related challenges of small business representatives. Only small business representatives listed personnel management and health information. Again, these challenges related to human resources and their health insurance are gaps to be addressed in a toolkit if public librarians will play a role in assisting the economic development in their communities. Some requirements of the Affordable Care Act, the comprehensive healthcare reform law enacted in March 2010 (sometimes known as ACA, PPACA, or "Obamacare"), were in place when the data were collected in this research (i.e., October 2014 to September 2016), though the future implications of the political aftermath of the 2016 presidential election are uncertain. But no matter what healthcare policy exists, small businesses will still have some questions about it AND librarians will be able to help answer their questions. Public librarians also list several potential challenges that small businesses did not mention, and they reflect areas where a public library's services and resources could help economic development (e.g., marketing, reference, printing, and space). There is a good chance that small business representatives do not know that a reference librarian at a public library may be able to answer their questions more quickly than using their own personnel. The gap in understanding the challenges is clear, but the small business representatives' challenges must be addressed first in a toolkit to lead those stakeholders to understand the other challenges public librarians may help with (even if they do not perceive these challengers at the moment).

C. Desired Public Library Use

Small business representatives and public librarians diverge the most in the responses to desired public library usage. The second most common response count from small business representatives for desired public library use was "none." The response reflects a lack of awareness, again, about what public libraries offer to all community users. Fortunately, many other responses from both stakeholders matched. The most common was functionalities to maintain business, and this category captures many of the information needs and challenges outlined in the prior question set and analysis. The small business representatives list many of the other needs again as desired public library use, such as legal/physical, rules/requirements, finance information, and tax information. The order of questions may have given respondents time to refine their needs to overcome challenges into well-formulated desired use at this point in the survey. A few new categories emerged as well, with technology, access networks, and start-up services appearing for the first time.

Once again, the public librarians may not have a handle on the exact desired public library use by the community of users from small businesses, as indicated by their responses. The gap is large, with public librarians listing education by far the most times as a desired public library use, and small business representatives never mentioned it. Public libraries serve a primary purpose of providing access to information in many communities, but the secondary objectives related to education that stem from literacy through all potential lifelong learning activities may not be widely known in all sectors of the community. The public librarians also listed functionalities to maintain business and business-related community resources several times to encompass many of the potential uses that small business representatives may desire.

D. Information-Related Components of a Public Library Small Business Toolkit

Perhaps through the survey questions and responses, the needs, challenges, and desires began to merge in the responses to this final set of questions related to the toolkit components. Certainly, the small business representatives and public librarians began to have synergistic responses and counts of those essential components for inclusion in a public library small business toolkit. Both stakeholder groups list functionalities to maintain business, local information, finance information, tax information, advanced marketing, and rules/requirements. A toolkit must include the links or data to address these common information needs listed by the stakeholders. The knowledge gap in some ways is filled through the methodology of the two surveys, but a toolkit being built would better assist the public librarians to provide help to small businesses in their communities. It must be noted that there are fewer responses from small business representatives to this question than others in the survey. This may indicate that responses are only from those most willing to use public libraries and likely do not include those that do not desire help from them.

VII. CONCLUSION

The findings from the gap analysis of the exploratory survey feedback collected from small business and public library representatives were insightful and practically oriented. Our research affirmed that it is necessary to identify gaps between the two stakeholder groups and better develop communication and information bridges for any potential collaborations and future directions for partnerships to be able to emerge. Identifying these gaps is only the first step in bridging the free and valuable resources and services of public libraries to best match the information needs and desires of small business representatives. It is worth strongly driving home the point that librarians do not fully understand small business operators' needs and are thus having a different conversation. Similarly, policymakers, local/state/ federal economic programs, chamber of commerce agencies, etc. are developing initiatives to support small businesses in which rural libraries (or any other library type) are often conspicuous in their absence. The implications for toolkit blueprint design in this research were an action-focused effort that can lead to the development of an information resource that might form a step in the right direction toward building future alliances and partnerships between small businesses and rural libraries. Of course, questions of operationalization and implementation, including intellectual property ownership, responsibility, technical infrastructure, use policies, and rights management, among other areas, will need to be examined more closely to move forward. A focus on Tennessee as a test bed allowed the research team to explore an action research approach and methods, strategies, and partnering initiatives that have strong potential to be translated and applied at a national level based on reflections and lessons learned during this process.

ACKNOWLEDGMENTS

The authors appreciate the recently awarded PLSB-TN grant from the Institute of Museum and Library Services' National Leadership Grants for Libraries (Research category) reported in this chapter. We also gratefully acknowledge the generous contributions of various library stakeholders, PLSB-TN partners, and collaborators as well as respondents from the small business community who participated in this research. Thanks to Abbey Elder for loaning her calculation skills.

NOTES

1. The U.S. Bureau of the Census defines "rural" as areas with fewer than 2,500 people and open territory (Economic Research Service, 2007). *The Encyclopedia of Rural America* defines the related concept of "nonmetropolitan" counties to describe the spread of housing developments outside the boundaries of metro areas that have no cities with 50,000 or more residents (Rathge, 1997, p. 627) in addition to being non-urbanized (Office of Management and Budget, 1998). The word "rural" in this chapter is used with regard to both meanings.

2. For more details about PLSB-TN, see http://scholar.cci.utk.edu/plsb-tn.

3. The Appalachian Regional Commission (ARC, 1974), created as a Unites States federal–state partnership, defines Central Appalachia to include West Virginia's nine southernmost counties, eastern Kentucky, Virginia's southwestern tip, and the northwestern portion of Tennessee's Appalachian area (Bush, 2003), while Southern Appalachia includes most of Appalachian Virginia and Tennessee as well as the western Carolinas and the northern parts of Georgia, Alabama, and Mississippi.

4. http://sos.tn.gov/tsla.

5. http://sos.tn.gov/products/tsla/public-library-services-resources.

6. http://sos.tn.gov/products/tsla/tennessee-regional-library-system.

7. Researchers received approval from their university's institutional review board before implementing the surveys. All participating individuals provided informed consent.

REFERENCES

Appalachian Regional Commission. (n.d.). County economic status and distressed areas in Appalachia. Retrieved April 20, 2017, from http://www.arc.gov/appalachian_region/countyeconomicstatusanddistressedareasinappalachia.asp.

Appalachian Regional Commission. (2015). *Investing in Appalachia's future: The Appalachian Regional Commission's five-year strategic plan for capitalizing on Appalachia's opportunities*

2016–2020. Washington, DC: Appalachian Regional Commission. Retrieved March 10, 2012, from https://www.arc.gov/images/newsroom/publications/sp/Investingin AppalachiasFutureARCs2016-2020StrategicPlan.pdf.

Appalachian Regional Commission. (2010). *Moving Appalachia forward: Appalachian Regional Commission Strategic Plan 2011–2016*. Washington, DC: Appalachian Regional Commission. Retrieved March 10, 2012, from http://www.arc.gov/images/newsroom/publications/sp/ARCStrategicPlan2011-2016.pdf.

American Library Association Office for Literacy and Outreach Services. (2011). The small but powerful guide to winning big support for your rural library. Chicago, IL: American Library Association. Retrieved March 10, 2012, from http://www.ala.org/offices/sites/ala.org.offices/files/content/olos/toolkits/rural/2011RuralWeb_FINAL.pdf.

Appalachian Regional Commission. (1974). The new Appalachian subregions and their development strategies. *Appalachia, a Journal of the Appalachian Regional Commission, 8*, 11–27.

Babbie, E. (2001). *The practice of social research* (9th edn.). Belmont, CA: Wadsworth Thomson.

Barrios, M., Villarroya, A., Borrego, A., & Castellà, C. O. (2011). Response rates and data quality in web and mail surveys administered to PhD holders. *Social Science Computer Review, 29*, 208–220.

Bishop, B. W., Mehra, B., & Partee II, R. (2016). The role of rural public libraries in small business development. *Public Library Quarterly, 35*(1), 1–14.

Bush, W. S. (2003). *Bridging the gap between culture and mathematics: The Appalachian perspective*. Athens, GA: Appalachian Collaborative Center for Learning, Assessment, and Instruction in Mathematics, Ohio State University.

Cash, W. J. (1991). *The mind of the South*. New York, NY: Vintage Books.

Cobb, J. C. (2007). *Away down south: A history of Southern identity*. Oxford, UK: Oxford University Press.

Cooper, W. J. Jr., & Terrill, T. E. (2009). *The American South: A history* (Vol. 2, 4th edn.). Lanham, MD: Rowman and Littlefield Publishers.

Creswell, J. W., & Clark, V. L. P. (2007). *Designing and conducting mixed methods research*. Thousand Oaks, CA: Sage.

Dearie, J. R. (Policy Council Member, Economic Innovation Group). (September 8, 2016). *Struggling to grow: Assessing the challenges for small businesses in rural America*. Testimony before The Subcommittee on Small Business, United States House of Representatives. Retrieved April 29, 2017, from http://smallbusiness.house.gov/uploadedfiles/dearie_-_house_small_business_committee_sept_8_2016.pdf.

Economic Development Research Group, Regional Technology Strategies, Massachusetts Institute of Technology Department of Urban Studies Planning. (2007). *Sources of regional growth in non-metro Appalachia*. Retrieved March 12, 2014, from http://www.arc.gov/research/researchreportdetails.asp?REPORT_ID=84.

Economic Research Service. (2007). *Measuring rurality: What is rural?* Washington, DC: Economic Research Service, The Economics of Food, Farming, Natural Resources, and Rural America, U.S. Department of Agriculture. Retrieved March 10, 2012, from http://www.ers.usda.gov/Briefing/Rurality/WhatIsRural/.

Eller, R. D. (2008). *Uneven ground: Appalachia since 1945*. Lexington, KY: The University Press of Kentucky.

Escott, P. D., Goldfield, D. R., McMillen, S. G., & Turner, E. H. (1999). *Major problems in the history of the American South: Documents and essays, Volume II: The New South* (2nd edn.). Boston, MA: Houghton Mifflin Harcourt.

Federal Communications Commission. (2016). *2016 Broadband Progress Report.* Retrieved April 29, 2017, from https://www.fcc.gov/reports-research/reports/broadband-progress-reports/2016-broadband-progress-report.

Fisher, S. L., & Smith, B. E. (Eds.). (2012). *Transforming places: Lessons from Appalachia* (1st edn.). Champaign, IL: University of Illinois Press.

Fritsch, A., & Gallimore, P. (2007). *Healing Appalachia: Sustainable living through appropriate technology.* Lexington, KY: The University Press of Kentucky.

Greenwood, D., & Levin, M. (1998). *Introduction to action research: Social research for social change.* Thousand Oaks, CA: Sage.

Glaser, B. G. (1965). The constant comparative method of qualitative analysis. *Social Problems, 12*(4), 436–445.

Lang, B. (1999). Bricks and bytes: Libraries in flux. In S. Graubard & P. LeClerc (Eds.), *Books, bricks & bytes: Libraries in the twenty-first century* (pp. 221–235). New Brunswick, NJ: Transaction.

Kemmis, S., & McTaggart, R. (1998). *The action research planner.* Victoria: Deakin University Press.

Lichter, D. T., & Campbell, L. A. (2005). *Changing patterns of poverty and spatial inequality in Appalachia.* Washington, DC: Appalachian Regional Commission. Retrieved November 2, 2008, from http://www.arc.gov/index.do?nodeID=2914

Ludke, R. L., & Obermiller, P. J. (Eds.). (2012). *Appalachian health and well-being* (1st edn.), Lexington, KY: The University Press of Kentucky.

Mehra, B. (2017). Digital inclusion of rural libraries to promote effective broadband use and further economic growth & community development in the southern and central Appalachian region. Presentation in the *BroadbandUSA webinar: Broadband adoption and digital inclusion in rural communities.* U.S. Commerce Department's National Telecommunications and Information Administration (NTIA), April 19, 2017. Retrieved April 20, 2017, from https://www2.ntia.doc.gov/node/1006.

Mehra, B. (2014). Perspectives of rural librarians about the information behaviors of children with special needs in the southern and central Appalachian region: An exploratory study to develop user-centered services. In D. Bilal & J. Beheshti (Eds.), *New directions in children and adolescents' information behavior research.* Cambridge, MA: Emerald Publishing.

Mehra, B. (2006). An action research (AR) manifesto for cyberculture power to "marginalized" cultures of difference. In D. Silver & A. Massanari (Eds.), *Critical cyber-culture studies* (pp. 205–215). New York: New York University Press.

Mehra, B., Bishop, B. W., & Partee II, R. (2017). Small business perspectives about the role of rural libraries in economic development. *Library Quarterly, 87*(1), 17–35.

Mehra, B., Bishop, B. W., & Partee II, R. (2016a). Community partnerships to further the role of rural public libraries in small business economic development: A case study of Tennessee (poster paper). In X. Lin & M. Khoo (Eds.), *Proceedings of the iconference 2016: Partnership with society.* Philadelphia, PA, March 20–23, 2016. Retrieved April 20, 2017, from https://www.ideals.illinois.edu/bitstream/handle/2142/89386/Mehra465.pdf?sequence=1.

Mehra, B., Bishop, B. W., & Partee II, R. P. (2016b). Information science professionals as community action researchers to further the role of rural public libraries in small business economic development: A case study of Tennessee. [Best overall conference paper.] In Proceedings of the Annual Conference of the 2016 Canadian Association for Information Science/L'Association canadienne des sciences de l'information (CAIS/ACSI): Information Science in our Communities: Reflections on our Work and the People, Places and Institutions Around Us, Calgary, Alberta, Canada, June 1–3, 2016.

Mehra, B., Bishop, B. W., & Partee II, R. P. (2016c). Information science professionals as community action researchers to further the role of rural public libraries in small business economic development: A case study of Tennessee. *Canadian Journal of Information and Library Science*, *40*(4) [Accession Number: E16045].

Mehra, B., Black, K., & Lee, S. 2010. Perspectives of east Tennessee's rural public librarians about the need for professional library education: An exploratory study. *Journal of Education for Library and Information Science*, *51*(3), 142–157.

Mehra, B., Black, K., Singh, V., & Nolt, J. (2011). What is the value of LIS education? A qualitative analysis of the perspectives of rural librarians in southern and central Appalachia. [Best paper for the 2011 Association for Library and Information Science Education (ALISE) Annual Conference.] *Journal of Education for Library and Information Science*, *52*(4), 265–278.

Mehra, B., Black, K., Singh, V., Nolt, J., Williams, K. C., Simmons, S., & Renfro, N. (2014). The social justice framework in the information technology rural librarian master's scholarship program: Bridging the rural digital divides. *Qualitative and Quantitative Methods in Libraries Journal*, Special Issue 2014: Social Justice, Social Inclusion (pp. 5–11). Retrieved February 25, 2014, from http://www.qqml.net/papers/Special_Issue_2014_Social_Justice_Social_Inclusion/QQML_Journal_2014_SpecialIssue_5-11_Mehraetal.pdf.

Mehra, B., & Braquet, D. (2014). Marriage between participatory leadership and action research to advocate benefits equality for lesbian, gay, bisexual, and transgender people: An extended human rights role in library and information science. In: B. Eden & J. Fagan (Eds.), *Leadership in academic libraries today: Connecting theory to practice* (pp. 185–212). Toronto, Canada: Scarecrow Press.

Mehra, B., & Braquet, D. (2007). Library and information science professionals as community action researchers in an academic setting: Top ten directions to further institutional change for people of diverse sexual orientations and gender identities. *Library Trends*, *56*(2), 542–565.

Mehra, B., & Gray, L. (2014). "Don't say gay" in the State of Tennessee: Libraries as virtual spaces of resistance and protectors of human rights of lesbian, gay, bisexual, transgender, and queer (LGBTQ) people, LGBTQ Users Special Interest Group [Theme: Addressing the silence: How Libraries can serve their LGBTQ users]. In *Proceedings of the World Library and Information Congress: 80th International Federation of Library Associations and Institutions (IFLA) General Conference and Council* [Conference Theme: Libraries, Citizens, Societies: Confluence for Knowledge], August 16–22, 2014, Lyon, France. Retrieved April 20, 2017, from http://library.ifla.org/1011/1/151-mehra-en.pdf.

Mehra, B., Rioux, K., & Albright, K. S. (2009). Social justice in library and information science. In M. J. Bates & M. N. Maack (Eds.), *Encyclopedia of library and information sciences* (pp. 4820–4836). New York: Taylor & Francis Group.

Mehra, B., & Singh, V. (2015). A social justice framework to further community engagement in Pakistan's information management and library professions. In *Proceedings of the International Conference on Information Management and Libraries*, Department of Information Management, University of Punjab, Quaid-i-Azam Campus, Lahore-Pakistan, from November 10–13, 2015.

Mehra, B., & Singh, V. (2014). Recruitment and retention in the information technology rural librarian master's scholarship program (Part I and Part II): Implications of social justice in the southern and central Appalachian region. *Qualitative and Quantitative Methods in Libraries Journal*, 13–22. Retrieved February 25, 2014, from http://www.qqml.net/

papers/Special_Issue_2014_Social_Justice_Social_Inclusion/QQML_Journal_2014_
SpecialIssue_13-22_MehraandSingh.pdf.

Mehra, B., Singh, V., Mitchell, C., Williams, K. C., Simmons, S., & Renfro, N. (2012). Empowering
rural librarians as change agents in the 21st century: Development of community-based
technology literacy and management outcomes in the southern and central Appalachia
(poster abstract). In World Library and Information Congress: 78th International
Federation of Library Associations and Institutions (IFLA) General Conference and
Assembly, Helsinki, Finland, August 11–17, 2012.

Mertens, D. M. (2010). *Research and evaluation in education and psychology: Integrating diversity
with quantitative, qualitative, and mixed methods.* Thousand Oaks, CA: Sage.

National Association of Counties Rural Action Caucus. (2002). *County data.* Washington, DC:
NACRAC.

National Telecommunications and Information Administration, U.S. Department of Commerce.
(n.d.). BroadbandUSA: Connecting America's communities, "about." Retrieved April 24,
2017, https://www2.ntia.doc.gov/about.

Neuendorf, K. A. (2002). *The content analysis guidebook.* Thousand Oaks, CA: Sage.

Office of Management and Budget. (1998, December 21). Part III alternative approaches to
defining metropolitan and nonmetropolitan areas. Federal Register. 63 (6370526-70561).
Retrieved March 10, 2012, from http://www.whitehouse.gov/omb/inforeg/msa.pdf.

Rahman, M. A. (2008). Some trends in the praxis of participatory action research. In P. Reason
& H. Bradbury (Eds.), *The SAGE handbook of action research* (pp. 49–62). London: Sage.

Rathge, R. W. (1997). Rural demography. In *Encyclopedia of rural America: The land and the
people* (pp. 626–629). Santa Barbara, CA: ABCCLIO.

Real, B., Bertot, J. C., & Jaeger, P. T. (2014). Rural public libraries and digital inclusion: Issues
and challenges. *Information Technology and Libraries, 33*(1), 1–19.

Rhinesmith, C. (2016, January). Digital inclusion and meaningful broadband adoption initiatives. Evanston, IL: Benton Foundation. Retrieved April 24, 2017, from benton.org/
broadband-inclusion-adoption-report.

Rosser-Hogben, D. M. (2004). Meeting the challenge: An overview of the information needs of
rural America. *Rural Libraries, 24*(1), 25–49.

Scruggs, C. E. (2010). *The view from Brindley Mountain: A memoir of the rural south.* North
Charleston, SC: BookSurge Publishing.

Siefer, A. (April 20, 2017). *Innovators in digital inclusion: Multnomah county library.* Benton
Foundation. Retrieved from https://www.benton.org/blog/innovators-digital-inclusion-
multnomah-county-library.

Stringer, E. (1999). *Action research.* Thousand Oaks, CA: Sage.

U. S. Census Bureau. (2010). 2010 census urban area facts. United States Department of
Commerce.

Wyatt-Brown, B. (2008). *Southern honor: Ethics and behavior in the Old South. History e-book
project reprint series.* New York, NY: ACLS Humanities E-Book.

APPENDIX 1: COMPARISON OF SPECIFIC QUESTIONS IN THE TWO SURVEYS TO DEVELOP THE COMPARABLE DATA SETS

1. Existing assistance needs of small businesses

Small business survey: Existing assistance needed	What kinds of information-related assistance do you need to manage your small business? [Q1SB]
	Within the last month, identify at least FIVE examples of specific services, resources, and places where you found information to manage your small business. [Q2SB]
Public library survey: Existing assistance provided by agency	Identify FIVE existing ways you assist small businesses in your community (e.g., developing a business plan, identifying the laws governing your small business, filing tax forms related to your small business, etc.). [Q1PL]
	What services and programs do you have to assist small businesses in your community? [Q2PL]
	What resources do you have to assist small businesses in your community? [Q3PL]
	What activities, access, training, support, or other ways do you provide to small businesses in your community? [Q4PL]
	List at least FIVE small businesses you have assisted in your community. What kinds of assistance did you provide them? [Q5PL]
	How has your public library collaborated and partnered with small businesses in your community? Provide examples. [QPL9]

2. Information-related challenges small businesses experience

Small business survey	Identify FIVE information-related challenges/barriers you have faced in managing your small business. [Q3SB]
Public library survey	Identify the FIVE most critical information-related challenges experienced by small businesses in your community. [Q6PL]

3. Desired public library use

Small business survey	Identify FIVE ways you would like the public library to assist you in managing your small business. [Q4SB]
	How can the public library provide you specific information-related services, programs, and resources to assist you to manage your small business? Prompt: Provide examples of specific services, programs, resources, and other ways the public library can assist you to manage your small business. [Q5SB]
	Identify FIVE ways the public library can improve its efforts to assist small businesses in your community. [Q6SB]
Public library survey	Identify FIVE ways your public library can improve its efforts to assist small businesses in your community. [Q8PL]
	What plans (if any) does your public library have to assist small businesses in your community? [Q10PL]

4. Information-related components of a public library small business toolkit

Small business survey	What are FIVE essential information-related components of a small business toolkit that will help you in managing your small business? [Q8SB]
Public library survey	What are FIVE essential components of a public library small business toolkit to assist small businesses in your community? [Q11PL]

RURAL LIBRARIANS AS CHANGE AGENTS IN THE TWENTY-FIRST CENTURY: APPLYING COMMUNITY INFORMATICS IN THE SOUTHERN AND CENTRAL APPALACHIAN REGION TO FURTHER ICT LITERACY TRAINING

Bharat Mehra, Vandana Singh, Natasha Hollenbach, and Robert P. Partee II

ABSTRACT

Purpose – *This chapter discusses the application of community informatics (CI) principles in the rural Southern and Central Appalachian (SCA) region to further the teaching of information and communication*

Rural and Small Public Libraries: Challenges and Opportunities
Advances in Librarianship, Volume 43, 123–153
Copyright © 2018 by Emerald Publishing Limited
All rights of reproduction in any form reserved
ISSN: 0065-2830/doi:10.1108/S0065-283020170000043006

technologies (ICT) literacy concepts in courses that formed part of two externally funded grants, "Information Technology Rural Librarian Master's Scholarship Program Part I" (ITRL) and "Part II" (ITRL2), awarded by the Institute of Museum and Library Services' (IMLS) Laura Bush 21st Century Librarian Program to the School of Information Sciences (SIS) at the University of Tennessee (UT).

Design/Methodology/Approach *– The chapter documents ICT use in ITRL and ITRL2 to extend librarian technology literacy training, allowing these public information providers to become change agents in the twenty-first century. It discusses aspects of CI that influenced these two projects and shaped the training of future rural library leaders embedded in traditionally underrepresented areas to further social justice and progressive changes in the region's rural communities.*

Findings *– The chapter demonstrates the role that CI principles played in the context of ITRL and ITRL2 from project inception to the graduation of the rural librarians with examples of tangible IT services/products that the students developed in their courses that were directly applicable and tailored to their SCA contexts.*

Originality/Value *– ITRL and ITRL2 provided a unique opportunity to apply a CI approach to train information librarians as agents of change in the SCA regions to further economic and cultural development via technology and management competencies. These change agents will continue to play a significant role in community building and community development efforts in the future.*

Keywords: Rural libraries; change agents; information and communication technology; literacy training; Southern and Central Appalachian region; community informatics

I. INTRODUCTION

Recent community informatics (CI) discourse reintroduces the notion that this concept should "be used for the benefit of global communities as well as 'local' ones" (Horelli & Schuler, 2012). The term "glocal" negotiates these intersections between the local and regional or the national and global dimensions of people's information and communication technology (ICT) use and its embedment within contemporary cultural processes as experienced in the complex ecologies of meaning-making within the context of globalization and transnationalism (Baumann, 2000; Mehra & Papajohn, 2007; Sassen, 2014; Wellman, 2002). Further, in its "glocal" nature, CI provides "even in the most 'rural' and remote settings continuous and powerful connections to the global and the opportunity to be present in the global at will," using modern technological platforms "to empower and self-manage the transformation of even the most isolated and closed off of social contexts" (Gurstein, 2012).

This chapter discusses the application of CI principles in the rural Southern and Central Appalachian (SCA) region to further teaching of ICT literacy concepts in courses that formed part of two externally funded grant projects, "Information Technology Rural Librarian Master's Scholarship Program Part I" (ITRL, http://www.sis.utk.edu/rural-librarianship) and "Part II" (ITRL2, http://www.sis.utk.edu/13-scholarships-available-itrl2), awarded by the Institute of Museum and Library Services' (IMLS) Laura Bush 21st Century Librarian Program to the School of Information Sciences (SIS) at the University of Tennessee (UT). The purpose of ITRL and ITRL2 was to recruit and train rural library paraprofessionals working in the SCA region to complete their Master of Science in Information Sciences degree part time in the UT SIS's synchronous online distance education program. Sixteen ITRL students completed their graduate education from June 2010 to August 2012, combining work experience in regional libraries with a curriculum that focused on information technology (IT) and rural library management, while 13 ITRL2 students were enrolled in a similarly structured program from June 2013 to August 2015.

This chapter documents ICT use in ITRL and ITRL2 to extend librarian technology literacy training, allowing these public information providers to become change agents in the twenty-first century. It discusses aspects of CI that influenced these two projects and shaped the training of "future library leadership as embedded change agents to work in traditionally underserved and/or underrepresented areas (i.e., rural SCA regions)" and further social justice to "bring a life-anchoring perspective to their regional work environments and surrounding communities" (Mehra & Singh, 2017). The chapter demonstrates the role that CI principles played in the context of ITRL and ITRL2 from program inception to the graduation of the rural librarians with examples of tangible IT services or products that the students developed in their courses that were directly applicable and tailored to their SCA contexts. Appendix 1 includes a list of acronyms commonly used in this chapter and their definitions or explanations for readers' reference.

II. A COMMUNITY INFORMATICS PERSPECTIVE

This section briefly highlights salient aspects of CI that were directly relevant in the context of ITRL and ITRL2. Drawing on these characteristics and traits of CI, we will also identify, describe, and analyze how they were a driving force shaping conceptualization, application, and implementation of the two grant projects.

CI is a field of study, analysis, and practice for developing ICT applications to enable these community processes and the achievement of community objectives for the empowerment of communities (compiling Gurstein, 2000, 2007, and others). It was developed from the broader concept of social informatics, defined as the "body of research that examines the design, uses, and consequences of ICT in ways that take into account their interaction with institutional and cultural contexts" (Kling, 2000). While social informatics is concerned with the social aspects of computerization (Kling, 2007), CI has a stronger connection to democracy (e.g., Jansson, 2013), grassroots mobilization (e.g., Wickramasinghe & Ahmad, 2014), and local sustainable communities (e.g., Grunfeld, 2014). There are, however, many variations in its definitions, core questions, theories, methodological techniques, and practices (Bradley, 2006). For example, the Gyandoot rural technology project in the Indian state of Madhya Pradesh is a CI effort that builds on local community support and involvement to focus attention on local health and economic concerns (Warschauer, 2003).

In ITRL and ITRL2, CI was applied in more significant and meaningful ways (beyond organizational and institutional settings) in response to the SCA situational context and cultural dynamics within which community and technology interactions took place (e.g., power and empowerment; see Arnold & Stillman, 2013); how these came together as interpreted by the librarian-in-training students; and the ways that they evolved in different kinds of local and regional settings, both place-based (e.g., Mirani & Mirani, 2013) and online (e.g., Ghobadi, 2013), reflected in (and shaping) the uniqueness of the IT and management products rural librarians-in-training developed.

Social capital is a common topic of discussion within the CI literature. During modern times, sociologists Bourdieu (1986) and Coleman

(1998) popularized the concept in the 1980s in their work on social ties and networks that help generate trust and social reciprocity. Since then, much debate has occurred among various scholars across disciplinary backgrounds regarding conceptualization of social capital. The following broad working definition covers its most common elaborations: "Social capital refers to the extent, nature and quality of social ties that individuals or communities can mobilize in conducting their affairs" (Zinnbauer, 2007, p. 16). According to the Information Economy Division within the Australian Government's Department of Communications, Information Technology, and the Arts (2005), the common assumption seems to be that one of the benefits of ICT deployment is to increase community social capital. However, there has been some difficulty in determining whether this assumption is accurate.

Pigg (2001) concluded that information exchanged through electronic networks was not sufficient to build or maintain a community. Kavanaugh and Patterson (2001) presented two hypotheses: (1) as the number of community network users increases, the greater the community involvement and attachment within the community; (2) as the number of community network users increases, so will the use of the network to build social capital by communicating with other community members. Interestingly, while the network was used more to build social capital, there was not an increase in community involvement or attachment. In a later article, Pigg and Crank (2004) determined through meta-analysis of the literature that more research needed to be done to determine whether ICTs can create social capital: "... our analysis suggests ICT has the capability to contribute to enhancing and extending social networks, providing access to resources that can be mobilized for action, enhancing solidarity in social groups, and supporting mechanisms of enforceable trust and reciprocity in transactions" (p. 69). In other words, while ICTs can enhance networks that already exist, they cannot build communities in and of themselves. In ITRL and ITRL2, the measurement and analysis of social capital to study the impact of ICTs was determined through evidence provided by librarian-in-training students (e.g., number of actual and potential primary, secondary, and tertiary users at the library; collection of quantitative and qualitative feedback collected from various patron communities; etc.), justifying the development of the individual IT and management products they created in their information science courses.

The value and place of technology in developing and maintaining communities has been one of the core areas of investigation confronting the CI field. Stoeker (2005) pointed out that there was an incorrect assumption among researchers that technology would build community. Instead, researchers and practitioners should ensure that community goals drive technology rather than the other way around: "Information is often confused with technology, in the sense that once you have the technology it is assumed you will get the information." It is not enough to have access to technology—instead, people must be trained in its use and develop the skills to get the most out of it. Day (2005) stated that technology should be viewed as "a tool to be designed, used, and shaped by humans for human purposes." This was a driving force in ITRL and ITRL2, where a strong expectation of the rural librarian-in-training students was to integrate the involvement and feedback collected from various user communities in the processes of assessment, evaluation, and development of their IT products.

More recently published CI research takes the idea of community involvement further in recognizing that for ICTs to create social capital and be truly effective in terms of real impacts, they have to be sustainable. This can be achieved by focusing on "building the capacity of local people for community interaction to collaborate and work together to find solutions to local problems, and to work toward shared objectives that contribute to the well-being of the local community as a whole" (Simpson, 2005). This is tied to the concept of empowerment of the community defined as the "processes by which those who have been denied the ability to make choices acquire such an ability" (Kabeer, 1999, p. 437). In building social capital at a community level, the concept of empowerment, therefore, relates specifically to the critical and reflective expansion of strategic choices, not just any set of choices (Batliwala, 1994). Sustainability and community empowerment in ITRL and ITRL2 was ensured via ongoing inclusion of the SCA library partners and their embedded communities in all decision making and the requirement that the librarian-in-training students actually be employed in the SCA libraries in order to be eligible to participate in the two programs. The application of the "train the trainer" philosophy ensured that the rural librarian-in-training students continuously took what they learned and developed in the classroom into their work environments and communities. The ongoing involvement of the practitioner mentors from the SCA regions in ITRL and ITRL2 activities related to the training of the students also echoed the idea of integrating the community as the center of technology-based change via development of relevant products and processes.

III. ICTS AND RURAL COMMUNITIES

The importance of sustainability and community empowerment has also been addressed from another perspective, through the research and policy development work done since the 1990s surrounding the concept of the "digital divide," especially when discussing ICTs in the context of rural communities. Digital divides—intentionally plural—are based on geography and other variables such as race, ethnicity, gender, sexual orientation, income, education, age, and disability. These divides are identified as the gaps between the "haves" and "have-nots" in their knowledge; adoption; access; and use of computers, the Internet, and ICTs (Hilbert, 2011; Mehra, Bishop, Bazzell, & Smith, 2002; U.S. Department of Commerce, 1995), be it at the local, regional, national, or global levels of comparison (Chinn & Fairlie, 2004; Norris, 2001). Traditionally, digital divides have revolved around the idea of access. The central idea behind these earlier studies is that if everyone had access to technology, then that alone would lead to technology use. Gurstein (2003) took issue with this and stated that there are several related issues that need more attention. For example, resource allocators provide support for the creation of ICT infrastructure and access points without considering the need to expand local capacity for developing, managing, and maintaining ICT capabilities in a manner that could lead to a shift in focus from access to "effective use" in terms of "the capacity and opportunity to successfully integrate ICTs into the accomplishment of self or collaboratively identified goals."

More current CI work takes this idea further in identifying that for ICTs to be truly effective in terms of community impacts specifically in rural development efforts, they must be sustainable at the social, cultural, institutional, economic, political, and technological levels in order to overcome challenges that include access to infrastructure, limited formal education, insufficient training and capacity building, financial and political constraints, and other social and cultural challenges (Pade, Mallinson, & Sewry, 2006). CI prioritizes community-led solutions in ICT development that seek to create local economic and social opportunities to minimize the digital divides between rural and urban users (McMahon, O'Donnell, Smith, Walmark, Beaton, & Simmons, 2011). Rural broadband has recently become an "important means by which rural communities around the world can gain access to global networks of knowledge and communication" (Adria & Brown, 2012). A concrete recommendation in a grassroots community movement for successfully developing rural broadband is the identification of community intermediaries who "not only provide communities with expert knowledge and advice but also create one of the means by which communities can envision the relationship between the global effects of broadband technology and their potential application for local benefits" (*ibid*). Community intermediaries can also play a role in strengthening community relationships and nurturing needed connections that would lead to the creation of essential networks considered to build social capital (Flora & Flora, 2004). The rural librarians-in-training in ITRL and ITRL2 served in some ways as information professional intermediaries who were living and working in local communities that desired specific technology-related changes.

IV. THE ROLE OF RURAL LIBRARIES

Discussions of the digital divide and the development of ICTs in general have greatly impacted the role of libraries, especially in rural settings (Mehra et al., 2012). One of the primary methods of providing access has been the establishment of public computing facilities in rural libraries. Chigona (2006) discusses how such computer facilities are often created in existing public facilities in order to lower setup and operating costs and to provide easy access for intended users. According to IMLS (2016), (1) the 278,733 public-access Internet computers available at public libraries reflected a one-year increase of 2.8 percent and a 10-year increase of 98.5 percent; (2) the 333.9 million user sessions on public-access computer terminals in public libraries represented a decrease of 9.2 percent from FY 2010, which may be related to increases in the use of personal devices; (3) future data will identify how public libraries continue to offer Wi-Fi connectivity and broadband accessible by library computers and through patrons' personal devices. An earlier study by Stevenson (2007) focused on Phase II of a technology grant program for public libraries funded by the Bill and Melinda Gates Foundation and called for rural public libraries to embrace CI and the Free Software Foundation to change the digitally divided have-nots from passive recipients and consumers of information to active learners and creators of information. Bishop, Bruce, and Jones (2006) created a suite of free open-source web-based software for community inquiry. This suite came out of research focusing on how people and communities (including those embedded in rural environments) learn, what tools facilitate learning within communities, and which communities can share knowledge, skills, and tools.

This need for, and the importance of, community involvement has carried through over the years and is integrated in the findings reported in the recent 2015 Library Resource Guide, "Libraries' New Balancing Act: Investing in Technology with Restrained Resources" (Community Public Libraries Edition), based on a new study of 574 public libraries by Joseph McKendrick (2015) that includes the following: (1) with stable budgets over the past year, public libraries are arriving at an optimal mix of print and digital offerings; (2) demand for digital services, materials, and features continues to rise;

(3) cloud computing continues to be a viable option for more libraries; (4) libraries also continue to invest in PCs and devices for patrons; (5) the recent accelerated pace of change brought about by IT now poses the greatest challenge to public libraries. Mchra, Black, and Lee (2010) conducted a study examining the existing conditions experienced in rural libraries and perspectives of librarians in East Tennessee. The authors discussed technology from several angles in library and information science (LIS) education and practice, namely, the information needs of rural librarians, key library activities that were enacted using ICTs, and the training and skills acquisition needed by information professionals in the region.

McClure et al. (2011a, 2011b) conducted two parallel studies of broadband connectivity and use at rural Florida anchor institutions and reported that participating rural libraries struggled with adequate broadband to meet service needs. They found that multiple situational factors affected broadband adoption, including administrative support, funding, broadband availability, and the general public's understanding of the importance of broadband. McClure et al. (2012) conducted a follow-up study of Indiana public library e-government services, costs, and benefits and documented the following regarding rural libraries: (1) the situational nature of e-government service provisions varied from library to library across the state—urban library staff members spent about 40% of their time and rural library staff members spent about 15% of their time on e-government transactions; (2) on a per-staff-member basis, the average costs for urban and rural professional and paraprofessional staff are $15,556.06 for urban professionals, $11,704.52 for urban paraprofessionals, $4,358.10 for rural professionals, and $4,419.85 for rural paraprofessionals. Meanwhile, Chigona (2006) determined that the four factors for success of communal computing facilities interpreted in the context of rural libraries are community buy-in, local champions, location of the agency, and marketing and public awareness. As the following discussions demonstrate, the frameworks outlined above were integral to the development of ITRL and ITRL2 activities.

V. DISTANCE EDUCATION TO TRAIN LIBRARIANS

Elliott (2010) discusses how digital technologies and other ICTs make distance education a practical option for students in rural and urban settings. While the focus is on students from low socioeconomic backgrounds, most of the discussion is relevant to other types of distance education students as well. Community-embedded learning via online distance education in real time using interactive ICTs and voice over Internet protocol (VoIP) in LIS has proven to provide the community clienteles served by the students taking these courses a network and access to educators, student's colleagues, curriculum materials, and knowledge "that is indirectly available to friends, coworkers, and community members who live and work" near the students (Kazmer, 2005). For example, graduate online education in the Graduate School of Library and Information Science at the University of Illinois at Urbana-Champaign has offered the highly successful Library Education Experimental Program (LEEP) since 1996, leading to a master's degree in LIS, and by the 2010–2011 school year had enrollment exceeding 300 students (Estabrook, 2003). LEEP continues to train highly motivated students who are independent learners; are often employed full time; have strong technological capabilities; and become information champions in their local and regional communities via effective communication, collaboration, and community building (Haythornthwaite & Kazmer, 2004, 2002).

Distance education applications in LIS are especially important to generate community impact, owing to the process of enculturation where students are provided with, or are already working in, real-world settings. This allows them to make connections between information constructs and work practices on an everyday basis while developing tangible products in their courses that are usable, used, and useful to the community (Fischer, Rohde, & Wulf, 2006). Tomkinson (2009) describes a program (Youth ICT Training initiative, YICT) that features both elements. YICT is centered in a rural area of Canada where there is a significant lack of technology and technological infrastructure. The purpose of the program is to provide IT training through a distance-education format and short-term employment in the community utilizing the learned skills. This program has the double outcome of teaching students IT skills that they would not have been able to obtain otherwise while also aiding the development of the IT infrastructure. The students in the ITRL and ITRL2 programs found the use of synchronous and asynchronous distance education tools critical in the completion of their online learning experience. They discussed how they developed IT products during the courses that were tailored to their specific rural communities as a result of learning through the UT SIS course delivery experience.

Sometimes community organizations provide the training instead of the universities. Heaton et al. (2013) examined the Animacoop training program aimed at group facilitators. This program provided several tools and allowed students to select those that were most relevant to them. Such levels of flexibility are a major element in Merkel et al. (2005), where a web design course was offered for people of different organizations, and the focus was on the skills, as everyone had a different vision for their own organization website. However, the problem with having a champion is, what happens when they leave? This study discovered that often community organizations end up relying on one person for technology skills, and when that person leaves the organization has no idea what they have or how to support it.

VI. THE RURAL DIGITAL DIVIDES IN THE SCA REGION

The U.S. Bureau of the Census defines "rural" areas as those with fewer than 2,500 people and open territory (Economic Research Service, 2007). *The Encyclopedia of Rural America* defines the related concept of "nonmetropolitan" counties to accurately describe the spread of housing developments outside the boundaries of metro areas that have no cities with 50,000 or more residents (Rathge, 1997), in addition to being nonurbanized (Office of Management and Budget, 1998). The word "rural" in this article is used with regard to both meanings.

The Appalachian Rural Commission, a United States federal–state partnership, identifies Central Appalachia to include (1974) West Virginia's nine southernmost counties, eastern Kentucky, Virginia's southwestern tip, and the northwestern portion of Tennessee's Appalachian area (Bush, 2003), while southern Appalachia includes most of Appalachian Virginia and Tennessee; the western Carolinas; and the northern parts of Georgia, Alabama, and Mississippi.

The SCA region has historically experienced debilitating information poverty and unemployment, economic challenges, low levels of information literacy and educational attainment (Spatig et al., 2009), a lack of access and use of IT (Mehra, Black, Singh, & Nolt, 2011a; Mehra, Singh, & Parris, 2010), and other unique environmental circumstances (Appalachian Regional Commission, 2002, 2004; Bardwell et al., 2009; Black, Mather, & Sanders, 2007; Herzenberg, Price, & Wial, 2005; Kusmin, 2008; Lichter & Campbell, 2005; Schwartz, 2004). As a result of their location in the impoverished SCA belt, a region that has also been ignored and traditionally marginalized owing to stigma and lack of national attention, support, and distribution of resources (Eller, 2008; Scruggs, 2010), SCA rural librarians have been on the disadvantaged side of the digital divides, experiencing critical information needs and concerns that have been inadequately represented in the LIS professions (Mehra et al., 2014). These problems are only recently beginning to get some attention in LIS education and practice (Mellon & Kester,

2004). For example, recent research indicates that the SCA librarians have a strong desire to access professional library education that integrates IT and rural library management competencies to help their communities effectively address some of their challenges and circumstances (Mehra, Black, Singh, & Nolt, 2011b). This article focuses broadly on the use of ICTs in the development and implementation of ITRL and ITRL2 in serving this need.

VII. THE ITRL AND ITRL2 CONTEXT

ITRL and ITRL2 are training SCA rural library paraprofessionals in IT literacy and management competencies, allowing them to become change agents and bring a life-anchoring perspective to their regional work environments and surrounding communities. According to Page and Scott (2001), a change agent "facilitates a 'bedding down' of new practices within organizations" (p. 530), develops skills they learn and pass on to others based on "changed work practices … and changes in their relationship to colleagues" (p. 548), and an "ability to take understandings arising in one 'world'" (p. 548) and use them to initiate change in another. ITRL and ITRL2 participants are also developing tangible IT and management services and products in their courses that are directly applicable and tailored to their SCA contexts. IT deliverables for rural libraries include (1) technology infrastructure planning and analysis; (2) web design, development, and usability; (3) database design and implementation; (4) building digital library and web portals; (5) establishing hardware and software networking; and (6) creating Library 2.0 tools. Management outcomes include service evaluation in rural libraries; management of a rural library program for adults, children, and young adults; reader's advisory; and grant writing and collection development. The teaching of management-related topics in ITRL and ITRL2 is reported elsewhere (Mehra & Singh, 2017). This chapter discusses the teaching of IT-related courses to further ICT training as relevant to a CI perspective. Through the entire ITRL and ITRL2 experience, however, student training was geared toward transforming participating paraprofessional librarians into change agents who learned to introduce new approaches, strategies, practices, and specific deliverables in response to how the particular challenges of the twenty-first century impact their SCA libraries and communities.

ITRL and ITRL2 have structured course requirements where the students are expected to take three required courses (providing knowledge of the core functionalities in the profession, namely, Information Environments, Information Representation and Organization, and Information Access and

Retrieval), six courses focusing on IT, and five courses on rural library management and services (Mehra & Singh, 2014). The curricula, however, also integrated an element of flexibility and was individually tailored based on the (1) sequence and choice of courses, which could be changed on a limited basis after considering an individual student's interests, skills, specific career path, and prior experiences, as well as the schedule of course offerings during various semesters; (2) analysis of students experiences in their unique SCA environments, as the course deliverables and tangible products that students individually developed in their assignments were expected to be useful and applied to the local contexts of their rural libraries and communities; (3) requirement for students in the school media track that stipulated a partially altered list of courses based on the state certification requirements. The 29 student librarians, chosen from the 51 applicants, came from 7 states and 24 cities, representing 5 academic libraries (college and university libraries), 18 public libraries (including individual libraries, county libraries, and regional library systems), 4 school libraries or county schools, 1 special library, and 1 community agency. Table 1 presents this information as well as some demographic and other characteristics of the librarians-in-training, including their sex, race or ethnicity, and work title.

The partners in the two projects were the Blount County Public Library in Maryville, Tennessee; Clinch-Powell Regional Library (now the Clinch River Regional Library) in Clinton, Tennessee; Fort Loudoun Regional Library (now the Ocoee River Regional Library) in Athens, Tennessee; Nolichucky Regional Library in Morristown, Tennessee; Sevier County Public Library System in Sevierville, Tennessee; the Watauga Regional Library (now the Holston River Regional Library) in Johnson City, Tennessee; and their leadership personnel. Project partners were selected to participate based on their leadership, role, knowledge, networks, experience, and interests to participate in promoting IT-based development and change in the SCA libraries and their communities. Though all the project partners were located in the East Tennessee region, representatives from other regional or county library systems in the SCA region also participated in the various grant activities. This included practitioner mentors who were assigned to each student librarian and worked with the educators to advise, mentor, train, and tailor individual student's academic program, integrating IT competencies to meet the needs of their rural library and community. This ensured that the IT outcomes generated by each student in the courses were relevant, usable, and meaningful to the context of each SCA rural library and community setting. Table 2 presents demographic and other characteristics of the practitioner mentors including their sex, geography, type of library, and work title.

Table 1.   Demographic Characteristics of ITRL and
ITRL2 Student Librarians.

Sr. no.	Demographic category	Comments
1.	Sex	Female (26), male (3)
2.	Race/ethnicity	African American (1), White/Caucasian (28)
3.	Work geography [state (city/town)]	GA (Dahlonega) = 1, KY (Barbourville-1, Harlan-1) = 2, MD (Hancock-1) = 1, NC (Marshall-1) = 1, TN (Athens-1, Bristol-1, Cleveland-1, East Ridge-1, Harrogate-1, Kingsport-2, Knoxville-3, Lebanon-1, Maryville-1, Mountain City-1, New Market-1, Sevierville-2, Watertown-1) = 17, VA (Big Stone Gap-1, Glade Spring-1, Goshen-2, Lexington-1, Wise-1) = 6, WV (Harmon-1) = 1
4.	Type of library	Community agency (1), community college library (3), county public library (7), county school system (2), elementary school library (2), public library (10), regional library (1), research and education center (1), university library (2)
5.	Work title	Acquisitions assistant (1), branch manager/program specialist (6), business and program administrator (1), circulation assistant (1), children's library assistant (1), children's room assistant (1), director (3), elementary school teacher/media team member (1), emerging technologies specialist (1), information specialist (1), instructional supervisor for materials and supplies (1), library assistant (2), library media specialist (1), library technical assistant (1), library technologist (1), public services coordinator (1), resource center/education coordinator (1), reference librarian (1), systems business coordinator (1), technology software support specialist (1), youth program specialist (1)

VIII. MEASURING THE IMPACT OF ITRL AND ITRL2

The experiences documented in this chapter are based on research data
sets collected during ITRL and ITRL2 to measure the impact of the grant
activities on the rural SCA libraries and communities via the IT and management skills and course products developed by the student librarians working in those settings. Methods involved ongoing evaluation and assessment
of the impact on the rural library and community conducted continuously
throughout the grant duration. The research team collected data sets from
student librarians, practitioner mentors, course instructors and program

Table 2. The Demographic Characteristics of ITRL and ITRL2 Practitioner Mentors.

Sr. no.	Demographic category	Comments*
1.	Sex	Female (19), male (7)
2.	Work geography [state (city/town)]	KY (Combs-1, London-1) = 2, NC (Boone-1) = 1, TN (Athens-2, Chattanooga-1 Clinton-1, Johnston City-1, Harrogate-1, Kingsport-1, Knoxville-3, Morristown-1, Sevierville-2, Watertown-1) = 14, VA (Abingdon-1, Big Stone Gap-1, Clifton Forge-1, Cumberland-1, Lexington-2, Norton-1, Richmond-1) = 8
3.	Type of library	Regional library (6), county public library (5), community college library (2), elementary school library (2), public library (5), state library (1), university library (3)
4.	Work title	Branch manager (1), cataloging specialist (1), continuing education consultant (1), director (10), district director (1), electronic services librarian (1), librarian (1), library systems and tech unit head (1), media specialist (2), music librarian (1), professor and librarian (1), reference librarian (2), system director (2)

* There were three individuals who were practitioner mentors in both ITRL and ITRL2, hence the totals do not add to 29.

administrators, and community members via formative and summative evaluations (Mehra, Black, Singh, & Nolt, 2011c). Mixed methods provided complementary quantitative and qualitative feedback from various stakeholders throughout the five phases in each project and include student recruitment, information needs analysis, implementation of education and training, mentoring, program outcomes evaluation, and results dissemination. This data collection and analysis proved effective, especially owing to the computer-enabled strategies and approaches that provided a holistic picture of the grant evaluation based on integration of multiple viewpoints. The various efforts in data collection and data analysis identified and evaluated expectations and accomplishments of all participants involved in the program throughout the process and timeframe of the grant.

Initially, the student librarians (i.e., the librarians-in-training) provided feedback via an in-depth narrative essay that was submitted as part of their application packet. Additional student assessment was collected via strategic academic plans, advising sessions and ongoing communication, course participation and interactions, formal course evaluations, and course grades. The research team conducted qualitative narrative interviews during odd-numbered semesters, and they delivered pre- and post-course quantitative surveys in even-numbered semesters. The researchers also collected student feedback during annual summits.

Practitioner mentors provided feedback during structured information flow and communication at least once a semester with educator advisors and students individually or collectively, through email surveys, and in ongoing interactions as matters arose. Educators and administrators provided feedback during weekly meetings, email surveys, and in an ongoing manner as matters arose. Other SCA rural librarians and community members provided feedback via a listserv and during meetings (face-to-face, phone, email, Skype) to promote information and communication exchanges; during various presentations and publications at professional conferences and venues to facilitate networking and data collection; and in response to press releases, feature stories, and information shared on the website development to facilitate networking and data collection. Such feedback helped inform the course design in terms of its objectives, content coverage, assignments, topic scheduling, readings, grading policies, and other areas. It has also helped inform our understanding of how to keep improving the student librarians' overall experiences as well as ensure the deliverables they were generating were having positive effects in their rural library and community. In addition, it allowed the team to better understand the technology and management needs of rural librarians in the SCA region.

IX. ICT INNOVATIONS IN ITRL AND ITRL2 COURSE DELIVERY MECHANISM

The use of the UT SIS's cutting-edge synchronous distance education communication technology allowed for real-time online interactions between the instructor and the student librarians in the virtual classroom via VoIP, which made the interactive experience a truly unique offering in this part of the country (Kumbhar, 2009; Marek, 2009). Interacting via distance education technologies contributed to the educational and training process of the rural library paraprofessionals who became proficient in IT-related best practices in the information sciences as a result, and it also contributed in their confidence level and skills in improving information access and ICT use in the SCA rural communities. The online courses were initially delivered synchronously using Saba Centra 7.6 software (online delivery system for the SIS distance education program), "an online learning environment that combines a highly interactive virtual classroom learning, e-meeting, and web seminar platform with a learning content management system to deliver optimal blended learning" (Saba Centra, n.d.). Recently, the university shifted to Blackboard Collaborate, a similar platform with additional functionalities that was used to deliver live, interactive classes via the Internet. It offered "a more collaborative, interactive, and mobile learning experience with a collaborative learning platform that constantly evolves, and you'll keep everyone engaged like never before" (Blackboard, 2015). Such a learning environment provided a combination of real-time voice, video, and text ability, where an interface screen gave opportunities for everyone to participate, collaborate, and engage with each other in a classroom-like experience in addition to viewing PowerPoint slides. Blackboard 7.0 (Blackboard, n.d.) and email also served as asynchronous communication and information-sharing tools.

The SCA student librarians appreciated the mixed use of these synchronous and asynchronous distance education tools in making their learning experiences possible online, and, in addition, the student librarians believed their IT products developed during the courses were more relevant to their rural communities as a result of learning through the UT SIS course delivery experience. As Becky Grindstaff, a software support specialist in the Knox County Schools, Tennessee, and participating student librarian noted, "The organization and management of UT's Distance Education classes in the SIS Department will impact my thinking as I assist with Knox County Schools' Distance Learning Program. The addition of a Distance Learning Program within Knox County Schools should have a significant impact, especially on class offerings at high schools on the rural outskirts of Knox County. Rural school districts outside Knox County Schools might connect to our distance learning courses in the future, and therefore the impact will be even larger on rural communities. I am very thankful to be part of the ITRL program" (private communication). In addition, face-to-face and phone interactions have helped extend the nature and significance of the learning experience outside the virtual classroom for the student librarians.

X. COMMUNITY-DRIVEN ICT DELIVERABLES FOR RURAL SCA LIBRARIES

As ITRL and ITRL2 student librarians worked as paraprofessionals in rural SCA libraries prior to and while completing the programs, they had direct knowledge of the needs, wants, expectations, and circumstances experienced in their local and regional communities. This embedment in the SCA communities provided strong validity to their role as intermediaries and ensured that the tangible course products they developed were relevant and useful to the rural library and community. For example, during the audio-recorded asynchronous sessions for the 2011 ITRL Annual Summit,[1] student librarians described various ICT-related benefits, impacts, outcomes, and deliverables they created in their courses that were significant for the rural SCA libraries and communities.[2] The following is a brief thematic description related to the select community-driven ICT deliverables the student librarians created in their ITRL and ITRL2 courses.

A. Improved Technological Skills to Provide More Effective ICT Services

This included improving and expanding existing computer systems, networks, and computing applications as well as developing new innovative ICTs in the SCA rural libraries. For example, Julie Forkner, Director of the E.G. Fisher Public Library in Athens, Tennessee, applied her ITRL knowledge to develop a mobile laptop lab with 12 computers, including one for the visually impaired, at her library. The new lab, in turn, helped develop a professional relationship with TechSoup, a nonprofit that helps public libraries get the technology resources they need to operate at their full potential. As a result of developing a better understanding of ICT policies and procedures, she was able to update, maintain, and troubleshoot new public access computers; develop network configurations (e.g., updating public library desktops to Windows 2010); and improve the mobile lab to reach out to other community libraries. During fall 2010 in IS 585 (Information Technologies), Forkner developed the "Laptop Checkout Program/Computer Learning Grant" to make laptops available for checkout and increase computer access in her community. Likewise, ITRL2 student librarian Rebecca Tedesco improved skills in web design to better serve the Cleveland State Community College Library in Cleveland, Tennessee. Catherine Tyler gained skills in computer hardware and software troubleshooting in ITRL2 to help patrons resolve issues at Rockbridge Regional Library in Goshen, Virginia.

B. Provided Strategic Assessment of ICT Services

This included developing a critical understanding of the ICT context (social and technical infrastructure) in a rural library setting in order to help close the rural digital divide. For example, ITRL student librarian Angela Glowcheski, Information Specialist at the Lumpkin County Public Library in Dahlonega, Georgia, conducted a user-centered assessment of the computer classes offered to the community as part of adult programming in IS 554 (Public Library Management and Services) during spring 2011. Based on her analysis of the findings, Glowcheski implemented a reorganization plan of the computer classes to better serve the library's rural clients.

C. Developed Online Communication and ICT Evaluation Instruments to Collect Feedback from Various Constituencies

Lauren Long, a library technologist at the Madison County Public Library in Marshall, North Carolina, developed the first online user and staff surveys at her library. During spring 2011 in IS 554 (Public Library Management and Services), as part of the ITRL curriculum, Long focused on identifying the current configuration of the library's desktop public access computers and how the user community utilized these computers based on qualitative and quantitative methods of data collection. During fall 2010 in IS 585 (Information Technologies), ITRL student librarian Fran Owen, an instructional supervisor for materials and supplies at the Sevier County Schools in Sevierville, Tennessee, created a wiki for school librarians to share curriculum development and designed and implemented an evaluation instrument to improve communication between the school system and a software vendor. In ITRL2, Anjanae Brueland created a system-wide technology inventory for the Sevier County Public Library System in Tennessee. In the same program, Rebecca Tedesco created a crowdsourcing web mapping application to include user-generated content for the Cleveland State Community College Library in Cleveland, Tennessee.

D. Participated in "Hands-on Learning" ICT Projects

For ITRL, during spring 2012, in IS 590 (Social Informatics), Brittany Fletcher, an elementary school teacher and media team member at the Mountain City Elementary School in Mountain City, Tennessee, developed an iPad use and implementation plan in the K-12 school classroom environment. During fall 2010, in IS 567 (Information Networking Applications), Becky Grindstaff, a software support specialist in the Knox County Schools, Tennessee, created a podcasting tutorial for open-source Audacity software as part of the ITRL curriculum. Using Camtasia Studio 7 for Windows, she also created three screencast videos showing the installation process for Drupal 6, a content management system for websites. In ITRL2, Anjanae Brueland facilitated the circulation and implementation of Kindle Fire e-readers at the Sevier County Public Library in Sevierville, Tennessee.

E. Adopted Alternative and Cheaper ICT Resources

This included promoting awareness and developing use of open-source software (OSS) applications. For example, during fall 2010 in IS 585 (Information Technologies), ITRL student librarian Susan Macrellis, the director of East Ridge City Library in East Ridge, Tennessee, evaluated the suitability of OSS Evergreen as the integrated system for her library.

F. Designed and Developed Rural Library Websites

During fall 2013, Anjanae Brueland, ITRL2 student and systems business coordinator in human resources for the Sevier County Public Library System in Sevierville, Tennessee, revamped her library website and created four themed webpages that included participating in the Geek the Library Campaign, a page on the American Affordable Care Act, a programming supplies wish list page, and a page to spotlight system partners. Additionally, she created a SpiceWorks account for conducting a system-wide technology inventory. Rebecca Tedesco improved skills in web design in ITRL2 to better serve the Cleveland State Community College Library in Cleveland, Tennessee. ITRL2 student librarian Rebecca Baker gained skills to perform a technology assessment to redesign the library website at Blount County Public Library in Maryville, Tennessee. ITRL2 student librarian Casey Fox gained skills to evaluate and redesign system websites for Lawson McGhee Library, a Knox County Public Library in Knoxville, Tennessee. Fellow ITRL2 student librarian Ryan Congdon developed a website that instructs on the use of e-readers for Rockbridge Regional Library in Lexington, Virginia.

G. Developed Information Retrieval Skills Online

Examples of such work included using professional methods when aiding users in research and answering questions and providing faster search results. ITRL2 student Pamela Wiggins developed skills to successfully negotiate user search queries for the patrons of the Watertown Public Library in Watertown, Tennessee.

H. Improved Skills to Allow Better User Electronic Access

Students learned about various selection–reference–evaluation tools important to all libraries and the ethics involved in providing virtual reference services, developed online forms to provide laptops for checkout to increase computer access for users, and learned how to properly assign subject headings and vocabulary control to improve online public access catalog entries. Anjanae Brueland assisted in developing the policy for lending e-readers, iPads, and notebooks for the Sevier County Public Library System in Tennessee.

I. Integrated IT into Student Perspectives and Shaped Community Expectations of an LIS Professional

Significant topics in this area included conceptualization of a paraprofessional versus a future information professional; the ability to think about tasks in new ways; broadened horizons; real-world effects on the rural library; ways for the student and rural community to examine the nature of the community, rural library, and the individual staff member's role; and how to make the work environment more enjoyable and productive. Tonia Kestner created an instructional PowerPoint on IT and User Instruction for Library Patrons to help the patrons of Washington County Public Library, Glade Spring Branch, in Glade Spring, Virginia. Mary Rayme was recognized for her presentation in February 2014 at the Big Talk From Small Libraries conference, sponsored by the Nebraska Library Commission and the Association for Rural and Small Libraries.

XI. PLACING ITRL AND ITRL2 IN A COMMUNITY INFORMATICS CONTEXT

Fig. 1 is an exploratory representation of ITRL and ITRL2 in a CI context. Based on our findings from ITRL and ITRL2, we believe we have a deeper understanding of the role of students in empowering their communities using ICTs. Looking back, we can clearly demonstrate how CI-related concepts helped us design and implement the IT components that formed important parts of these programs. The conceptualization of the ITRL and ITRL2 project, starting from the technology and management focus of the program, was a result of consultation and collaboration with community stakeholders, including practitioner mentors, community members, instructors, library staff, and

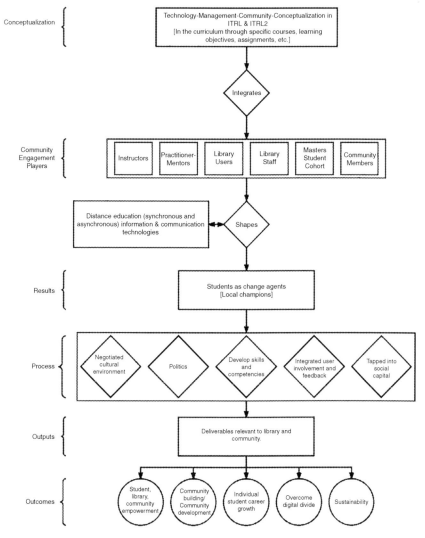

Fig. 1. Representation of community informatics in the ITRL and ITRL2.

library users. The research team engaged stakeholders in discussions to shape the focus of the ITRL and ITRL2 program. Next, we trained the students in the ITRL and ITRL2 programs with a focus on technology and management through the custom, tailored curriculum; specific courses; learning objectives;

and learning outcomes. When ITRL and ITRL2 students took these courses, they used their own experiences and contexts to shape their assignments. The assignments encouraged them to develop products customized to their work places, their communities, and their library patrons. The student librarians took these concepts and implemented them using their own experience and in consultation with other various stakeholders from their communities (other staff members at their libraries, patron user communities, etc.).

The aspect of students developing skills and competencies that are needed by their communities is reflective of the community embedment of ITRL and ITRL2. The deliverables that the student librarians created during their courses in ITRL and ITRL2 were developed as a result of applying skills related to negotiating with their environment, working with the local political structure, and responding to the challenges and opportunities in a management framework. During their time in the ITRL and ITRL2 program, students experienced a range of opportunities and challenges at their workplaces, with their efforts to resolve these issues and document their decisions contributing to their successful completion of the program. This provided for a very rich embedded learning experience.

As the student librarians were developing content for their workplace, in many instances they interviewed their colleagues or patrons and used the feedback to develop the assignment deliverables. This was a clear demonstration of community members' empowerment; their feedback led to customized services or other library-related products. The student librarians tapped into their local social capital and became change agents for community empowerment.

The student librarians' technical skills and competencies are demonstrated in the results presented as course deliverables and products. During ITRL and ITRL2, the resulting opportunities for the student librarians and their work with various stakeholders also served as an individual career-growth incentive. Multiple ITRL and ITRL2 students were given increased responsibilities, including promotions and new roles, because of their experience in this program. The experience of the ITRL and ITRL2 students was also enhanced by the course delivery mechanism. The ITRL and ITRL2 programs were taught in an online environment using distance education technologies, which served a dual purpose. The students did not have to leave their workplace, and they became adept at using online collaborative tools and technologies to learn and collaborate with their distant cohort members. The experience of cultivating a community at a distance will be beneficial to them in their future work environments.

Thus, on one hand the students served as change agents for their community, and, on the other hand, they developed skills and competencies that led to personal growth and improved career opportunities. This example of community engagement and empowerment through student librarians serves as a positive model for overcoming the digital divide and for sustained community involvement in the life of the library. This approach of enabling students to become agents of change using technology and embedding the experience in community was based on applying CI principles.

XII. CONCLUSION

ITRL and ITRL2 provided a unique opportunity to apply a CIs approach to train information librarian agents of change in the SCA regions to further economic and cultural development via technology and management competencies. These change agents will continue to play a significant role in community building and community development efforts. The experiences in ITRL and ITRL2 will allow them to consolidate their activities and extend the roles of the libraries as community anchors in future directions of growth. Insights gained during the two programs will allow the team to apply similar efforts in other rural parts of the country.

NOTES

1. URL: http://asp8.centra.com/GP/main/0000008aeed00000013325341d9e95f8.
2. For detailed description of ICT deliverables, see URL: http://www.sis.utk.edu/itrl-program-deliverables.

ACKNOWLEDGMENTS

We are thankful to IMLS for awarding us the two grants that funded the projects discussed in this chapter.

REFERENCES

Adria, M., & Brown, D. (2012). Ambiguity and uncertainty in the "last mile": Using sense-making to explore how rural broadband networks are created. *The Journal of Community Informatics, 8*(3). Retrieved from http://ci-journal.net/index.php/ciej/article/view/587/940.

Appalachian Regional Commission. (1974). The new Appalachian subregions and their development strategies. *Appalachia, a Journal of the ARC, 8*, 11–27.

Appalachian Regional Commission. (2002). *Evaluation of the Appalachian Regional Commission's vocational education and workforce training projects.* Washington, DC: Appalachian Regional Commission. Retrieved from http://www.arc.gov/images/reports/education/arcvoced.pdf.

Appalachian Regional Commission. (2004). *Appalachia: Turning assets into opportunities.* Washington, DC: Appalachian Regional Commission. Retrieved 12 September, 2011, from http://www.arc.gov/publications/TurningAssetsintoOpportunitiesPDF.asp.

Arnold, M. V., & Stillman, L. (2013). Power, communities, and community informatics: A meta-study. *Journal of Community Informatics, 9*(1). Retrieved from http://ci-journal.net/index.php/ciej/article/view/577/957.

Australian Government, Information Economy Division within the Department of Communications, Information Technology and the Arts. (2005). *The role of ICT in building communities and social capital: A discussion paper.* Retrieved from http://www.social-capital.net/docs/The_Role_of_ICT_in_Building_Communities_and_Social_Capital.pdf.

Bardwell, G., Morton, C., Chester, A., Pancoska, P., Buch, S., Cecchetti, A., Vecchio, M., Paulsen, S., Groak, S., & Branch, R. A. (2009). Feasibility of adolescents to conduct community-based participatory research on obesity and diabetes in rural Appalachia. *Clinical and Translational Science, 2*(5), 340–349.

Batliwala, S. (1994). The meaning of women's empowerment: New concepts from action. In G. Sen, A. Germain, & L. C. Chen (Eds.), *Population policies reconsidered: Health, empowerment and rights* (pp. 127–138). Cambridge: Harvard University Press.

Baumann, M. P. (2000). The local and the global: Traditional music instruments and modernization. *The World of Music, 42*(3), 121–144.

Bishop, A. P., Bruce, B. C., & Jones, M. C. (2006). Community inquiry and informatics: Collaborative learning through ICT. *Journal of Community Informatics, 2*(2). Retrieved from http://ci-journal.net/index.php/ciej/article/view/349/253.

Black, D. A., Mather, M., & Sanders, S. G. (2007). *Standards of living in Appalachia, 1960 to 2000.* Washington, DC: Appalachian Regional Commission. Retrieved from http://www.arc.gov/ images/reports/2007/standardsliving/Standards_ Living_Appalachia.pdf.

Blackboard. (n.d.). *Blackboard.* Retrieved from http://www.blackboard.com.

Blackboard. (2015). *Blackboard collaborate: Online collaboration tools that engage everyone, every time, everywhere.* Retrieved from http://www.blackboard.com/Platforms/Collaborate/Overview.aspx.

Bourdieu, P. (1986). The forms of capital. In J. Richardson (Ed.), *Handbook of theory and research for the sociology of education* (pp. 241–258). New York, NY: Greenwood Press.

Bradley, G. (2006) *Social and community informatics, Humans on the net.* London: Routledge.

Bush, W. S. (2003). *Bridging the gap between culture and mathematics: The Appalachian perspective.* ACCLAIM.

Chigona, W. (2006). Should communal computing facilities cohabit with public facilities? *Journal of Community Informatics, 2*(3). Retrieved from http://ci-journal.net/index.php/ciej/article/view/276/260.

Chinn, M. D., & Fairlie, R. W. (2004). *The determinants of the global digital divide: A cross-country analysis of computer and Internet penetration.* New Haven, CT: Economic Growth Center, Yale University. Retrieved 12 November, 2011, from http://www.econ.yale.edu/growth_pdf/cdp881.pdf.

Coleman, J. (1998). Social capital in the creation of human capital. *American Journal of Sociology, 94*(1), 95–120.

Day, P. (2005). Sustainable community technology: The symbiosis between community technology and community research. *Journal of Community Informatics, 1*(2). Retrieved from http://ci-journal.net/index.php/ciej/article/view/217/177.

Economic Research Service. (2007). *Measuring rurality: What is rural?* Washington, DC: Economic Research Service, The Economics of Food, Farming, Natural Resources, and Rural America, U. S. Department of Agriculture. Retrieved 12 September, 2011, from http://www.ers.usda.gov/Briefing/Rurality/WhatIsRural/.

Eller, R. D. (2008). *Uneven ground: Appalachia since 1945.* Lexington, KY: The University Press of Kentucky.

Elliott, A. (2010). Equity, pedagogy and inclusion: Harnessing digital technologies to support students from low socio-economic backgrounds in higher education. *Journal of Community Informatics, 6*(3). Retrieved from http://ci-journal.net/index.php/ciej/article/view/751/643.

Estabrook, L. (2003). Distance education at the University of Illinois. In D. B. Barron (Ed.), *Benchmarks in distance education: The LIS experience* (pp. 63–73). Westport, CT: Libraries Unlimited.

Fischer, G., Rohde, M., & Wulf, V. (2006). Spiders in the net: Universities as facilitators of community-based learning. *Journal of Community Informatics, 2*(2).

Flora, C., & Flora, J. (2004). *Rural communities: Legacy and change.* Boulder, CO: Westview Press.

Ghobadi, S. (2013). Application of activity theory in understanding online communities of practice: A case of feminism. *Journal of Community Informatics, 9*(1). Retrieved from http://ci-journal.net/index.php/ciej/article/view/828.

Grunfeld, H. (2014). ICT for sustainable development: An example from Cambodia. *Journal of Community Informatics, 10*(2). Retrieved from http://ci-journal.net/index.php/ciej/article/view/900.

Gurstein, M. (2000) *Community informatics: Enabling communities with information and communications technologies.* Hershey, PA: Idea Group Publishing.

Gurstein, M. (2003). Effective use: A community informatics strategy beyond the digital divide. *First Monday, 8*(12).

Gurstein, M. (2012). Glocality: Thinking about community informatics and the local in the global and the global in the local. *Journal of Community Informatics, 8*(3). Retrieved from http://ci-journal.net/index.php/ciej/article/view/946/942.

Gurstein, M. (2007). *What is community informatics (and why does it matter)?* Milano: Polimetrica.

Haythornthwaite, C., & Kazmer, M. (2002). Bringing the Internet home: Adult distance learners and their Internet, home and work worlds. In B. Wellman & C. Haythornthwaite (Eds.), *The Internet in everyday life* (p. 443). Oxford, UK: Blackwell.

Haythornthwaite, C., & Kazmer, M. (Eds.). (2004). *Learning, culture and community in online education: Research and practice.* New York, NY: Peter Lang.

Heaton, L., Millerand, F., Prouix, S., & Crespel, E. (2013). Facilitating community innovation: The Outils-Réseaux Way. *The Journal of Community Informatics, 9*(3). Retrieved from http://ci-journal.net/index.php/ciej/article/view/711/1019.

Herzenberg, S. Price, M., & Wial, H. (2005). *Displacement in Appalachia and the non-Appalachian United States, 1993–2003: Findings based on five displaced workers surveys.* Washington, DC: Appalachian Regional Commission. Retrieved from http://www.arc.gov/images/reports/2006/ displacement/pdf/displacement_arc.pdf.

Hilbert, M. (2011). The end justifies the definition: The manifold outlooks on the digital divide and their practical usefulness for policy-making. *Telecommunications Policy*, *35*(8), 715–736. Retrieved December 15, 2011, from: http://martinhilbert.net/ManifoldDigitalDivide_Hilbert_AAM.pdf.

Horelli, L., & Schuler, D. (2012.) Editorial: Linking the local with the global within community informatics. *Journal of Community Informatics*, *8*(3). Retrieved from http://ci-journal.net/index.php/ciej/article/view/939/931.

Institute of Museum and Library Services. (2016, March). *Public libraries in the United States survey: Fiscal year 2013*. Washington, DC: Institute of Museum and Library Services. Retrieved 12 May, 2017, from https://www.imls.gov/sites/default/files/publications/documents/plsfy2013.pdf.

Jansson, G. (2013). Local democratic values and e-government: Barrier or promoter? A case study of a multicultural Swedish municipality. *Journal of Community Informatics*, *9*(1). Retrieved from http://ci-journal.net/index.php/ciej/article/view/872.

Kabeer, N. (1999). Resources, agency, achievements: Reflections on the measurement of women's empowerment. *Development and Change*, *30*(1), 435–464.

Kavanaugh, A. L., & Patterson, S. J. (2001). The impact of community computer networks on social capital and community involvement. *American Behavioral Scientist*, *45*(3), 496–509.

Kazmer, M. M. (2005). Community-embedded learning. *Library Quarterly*, *75*(2), 190–212.

Kling, R. (2000). Learning about information technologies and social change: The contribution of social informatics. *The Information Society*, *16*(3), 217–232.

Kling, R. (2007) What is social informatics and why does it matter? *Information Society*, *23*(4), 205–220.

Kumbhar, R. (2009). Use of e-learning in library and information science education. *DESIDOC Journal of Education in Library and Information Science Education*, *29*(1), 37–41.

Kusmin, L. (2011). Rural America at a glance: 2011 edition. *Economic Information Bulletin*, *85*, 1–6.

Lichter, D. T., & Campbell, L. A. (2005). *Changing patterns of poverty and spatial inequality in Appalachia*. Washington, DC: Appalachian Regional Commission. Retrieved from http://www.arc.gov/index.do?nodeID=2914.

Marek, K. (2009). Learning to teach online: Creating a culture of support for faculty. *Journal of Education for Library and Information Science*, *50*(4), 275–292.

McClure, C. R., Mandel, L. H., Saunders, J. D., Alemanne, N. D., Spears, L. I., & Bishop, B. W. (2011a). *Florida Rural Broadband Alliance, LLC FRBA Florida Middle Mile Networks – Northwest and south central regions project: Broadband needs assessment, diagnostics, and benchmarking of selected anchor institutions: Fourth interim report*. Tallahassee, FL: Information Use Management and Policy Institute. Retrieved from http://ii.fsu.edu/content/download/71196/785546/file/FRBA_4thInterim_Report_FINAL_Dec31_11a.pdf.

McClure, C. R., Mandel, L. H., Saunders, J. D., Alemanne, N. D., Spears, L. I., & Bishop, B. W. (2011b). *North Florida Broadband Authority (NFBA) Ubiquitous Middle Mile Project: Broadband needs assessment, diagnostics, and benchmarking of selected anchor institutions: Final report*. Tallahassee, FL: Information Use Management and Policy Institute. Retrieved from http://nfba.ii.fsu.edu/docs/NFBA_Final_Report_Dec31_11b.pdf.

McClure, C. R., Mandel, L. H., Guenther, D., Carmichael, L. R., & Spears, L. I. (2012). *Describing Indiana public library e-government services, costs, and benefits: An exploratory study*. Tallahassee, FL: Information Use Management and Policy Institute. Retrieved from http://ii.fsu.edu/content/download/86555/907606/file/ISL_E-Gov_Final_Report_Sep5_12a.pdf.

McKendrick, J. (2015). *Libraries' new balancing act: Investing in technologies with restrained resources, community public libraries edition.* Medford, NJ: Library Resource Guide.

McMahon, R., O'Donnell, S., Smith, R., Walmark, B., Beaton, B., & Simmonds, J. (2011). Digital divides and the 'first mile': Framing First Nations broadband development in Canada. *The International Indigenous Policy Journal, 2*(2). Retrieved from http://ir.lib.uwo.ca/iipj/vol2/iss2/2/.

Mehra, B., Bishop, A. P., Bazzell, I., & Smith, C. (2002). Scenarios in the Afya project as a participatory action research (PAR) tool for studying information seeking and use across the "digital divide." *Journal of the American Society of Information Science and Technology, 53*(14), 1259–1266.

Mehra, B., Black, K., & Lee, S. (2010). Perspectives of East Tennessee's rural public librarians about the extent of need for professional library education: A pilot study. *Journal of Education for Library and Information Science, 51*(3), 142–157.

Mehra, B., Black, K., Singh, V., & Nolt, J. (2011a). Collaboration between LIS education and rural libraries in the Southern and Central Appalachia: Improving librarian technology literacy and management training [Brief communications and research in progress]. *Journal of Education for Library and Information Science, 52*(3), 238–247.

Mehra, B., Black, K., Singh, V., & Nolt, J. (2011b). What is the value of LIS education? A qualitative analysis of the perspectives of rural librarians in Southern and Central Appalachia. *Journal of Education for Library and Information Science, 52*(4), 265–278.* [Best paper for the 2011 Association for Library and Information Science Education (ALISE) Annual Conference].

Mehra, B., Black, K., Singh, V., & Nolt, J. (2011c). Mapping the education of rural librarians' technology literacy and management training: Use of mixed data collection methods in the ITRL program. In *Proceedings of the World Library and Information Congress: 77th International Federation of Library Associations and Institutions General Conference and Assembly* [Library Theory and Research Section and Statistics and Evaluation Section], August 13–18, 2011, San Juan, Puerto Rico.

Mehra, B., Black, K., Singh, V., Nolt, J., Williams, K.C., Simmons, S., & Renfro, N. (2014). The social justice framework in the information technology rural librarian master's scholarship program: Bridging the rural digital divides. *Qualitative and Quantitative Methods in Libraries Journal,* Special Issue 2014: Social Justice, Social Inclusion (pp. 5–11). Retrieved February 25, 2014, from http://www.qqml.net/papers/Special_Issue_2014_Social_Justice_Social_Inclusion/QQML_Journal_2014_SpecialIssue_5-11_Mehraetal.pdf.

Mehra, B., Black, K., Singh, V., Nolt, J., Williams, K.C., Simmons, S., & Renfro, N. (2012). Computer-enabled innovations in the information technology rural librarian master's scholarship program: Bridging rural digital divides in the Southern and Central Appalachia. In *Proceedings of the 57th Indian Library Association Annual Conference,* February 23–25, 2012, Mangalore, Karnataka.

Mehra, B., & Papajohn, D. (2007). "Glocal" patterns of communication-information convergences in Internet use: Cross-cultural behavior of international teaching assistants in a culturally alien information environment. *The International Information and Library Review, 39*(1), 12–30.

Mehra, B., & Singh, V. (2017). Library leadership-in-training as embedded change agents to further social justice in rural communities: Teaching of library management subjects in the ITRL and ITRL2. In N. A. Cooke & M. E. Sweeney (Eds.), *Teaching for Justice: Implementing Social Justice in the LIS Classroom.* Sacramento, CA: Library Juice Press.

Mehra, B., & Singh, V. (2014). Recruitment and retention in the information technology rural librarian master's scholarship program (part I and part II): Implications of social justice in the Southern and Central Appalachian Region. *Qualitative and Quantitative Methods in Libraries Journal*, Special Issue 2014: Social Justice, Social Inclusion (pp. 13–22). Retrieved February 25, 2014, from http://www.qqml.net/papers/Special_Issue_2014_Social_Justice_Social_Inclusion/QQML_Journal_2014_SpecialIssue_13-22_MehraandSingh.pdf.

Mehra, B., Singh, V., & Parris, H. (2010). Open source software collaborations in Tennessee's regional library system: An exploratory study. *Library Review*, 59(9), 690–701.

Mellon, C. A., & Kester, D. D. (2004). Online library education programs: Implications for rural students. *Journal of Education for Library and Information Science*, 45(3), 210–220.

Merkel, C. B., Clitherow, M., Farooq, U., Xiao, L., Ganoe, C. H., Carroll, J. M., & Rosson, M. B. (2005). Sustaining computer use and learning in community computing contexts: Making technology part of "who they are and what they do." *The Journal of Community Informatics*, 1(2), 158–174.

Mirani, Z. (2013). Perception of farmers and extension and research personnel regarding use and effectiveness of sources of agricultural information in Sindh province of Pakistan. *Journal of Community Informatics*, 9(1). Retrieved from http://ci-journal.net/index.php/ciej/article/view/680/962.

Norris, P. (2001). *Digital divide: Civic engagement, information poverty and the Internet worldwide*. Cambridge, MA: Cambridge University Press.

Office of Management and Budget. (1998, December 21). Part III alternative approaches to defining metropolitan and nonmetropolitan areas. *Federal Register*, 63(6370526-70561). Retrieved September 12, 2011, from http://www.whitehouse.gov/omb/inforeg/msa.pdf.

Pade, C. I., Mallinson, B., & Sewry, D. (2006). An exploration of the categories associated with ICT project sustainability in rural areas of developing countries: A case study of the Dwesa project. In *Proceedings of the 2006 annual Research Conference of the South African Institute of Computer Scientists and Information Technologists on IT Research in Developing Countries* (pp. 100–106). Somerset West, South Africa: South African Institute for Computer Scientists and Information Technologists.

Page, M., & Scott, A. (2001). Change agency and women's learning new practices in community informatics. *Information, Communication & Society*, 4(4), 528–559.

Pigg, K. (2001). Applications for community informatics for building community and enhancing civic society. *Information, Communication, & Society*, 4(4), 507–527.

Pigg, K. E., & Crank, L. D. (2004). Building community social capital: The potential and promise of information and communications technologies. *The Journal of Community Informatics*, 1(1), 58–73.

Rathge. R. (1997). Rural demography. In G. A. Goreham (Ed.), *Encyclopedia of rural America: The land and the people* (pp. 626–629). Santa Barbara, CA: ABC-CLIO.

Saba Centra. (n.d.). *Saba. The people management solution*. Retrieved from http://na1.saba.com/try.aspx.

Sassen, S. (2015, January 29). *The larger ecologies of meaning within which we use technology and experience globalization*. Speech presented at the 2005 Association for Library and Information Science Education annual conference, Boston, MA.

Schwartz, J. H. (2004). *Development and progress of Appalachian higher education network*. Washington, DC: Appalachian Regional Commission. Retrieved from http://www.arc.gov/images/news-andevents/publications/ahen/AHENetwork.pdf.

Scruggs, C. E. (2010). *The view from Brindley Mountain: A memoir of the rural South* (Kindle Edition). New York, NY: BookSurge.

Simpson, L. (2005). Community informatics and sustainability: Why social capital matters. *The Journal of Community Informatics, 1*(2). Retrieved from http://ci-journal.net/index.php/ciej/article/view/210/169.

Spatig, L., Gaines, S., MacDowell. R., Sias. B., Olson, L., & Adkins, C. (2009). Like a mountain: Performing collaborative research with youth in rural Appalachia. *Collaborative Anthropologies, 2*(1), 177–212.

Stevenson, S. (2007). Public libraries, public access computing, FOSS and CI: There are alternatives to private philanthropy. *First Monday, 12*(5). Retrieved from http://firstmonday.org/ojs/index.php/fm/article/view/1833/1717.

Stoeker, R. (2005). Is community informatics good for communities? Questions confronting an emerging field. *The Journal of Community Informatics, 1*(3), 13–26.

Tomkinson, K. (2009). In search of community champions: Researching the outcomes of K-Net's Youth Information and Communications Technology Training Initiative. *The Journal of Community Informatics, 5*(2). Retrieved from http://ci-journal.net/index.php/ciej/article/view/555/449.

U.S. Department of Commerce, National Telecommunications and Information Administration (NTIA). (1995). Falling through the net: A survey of the "have nots" in rural and urban America. Retrieved November 12, 2011, from http://www.ntia.doc.gov/ntiahome/fallingthru.html.

Warschauer, M. (2003). Social capital and access. *Universal Access in the Information Society, 2*(4), 315–330. doi: 10.1007/s10209-002-0040-8

Wellman, B. (2002). Little boxes, glocalization, and the networked individualism. In M. Tanabe, P. Van den Besselaar, & T. Ishida (Eds.), *Digital cities II: Computational and sociological approaches* (pp. 11–25). New York, NY: Springer.

Wickramasinghe, C. N., & Ahmad, N. (2014). How does Internet usage influence on social capital, connectedness, success and well-being of grassroots level inventors in Sri Lanka? *Journal of Community Informatics, 10*(1). Retrieved from http://ci-journal.net/index.php/ciej/article/view/817/1035.

Zinnbauer, D. (2007). *What can social capital and ICT do for inclusion?* Seville: JRC Institute for Prospective Technological Studies. Retrieved from http://ftp.jrc.es/EURdoc/eur22673en.pdf.

APPENDIX 1: LIST OF ACRONYMS COMMONLY USED IN THIS CHAPTER AND THEIR DEFINITIONS OR EXPLANATIONS

Acronym	Definition/explanation
CI	Community informatics
ICT	Information and communication technology
IMLS	Institute of Museum and Library Services
IT	Information technology
ITRL	Information Technology Rural Librarian Master's Scholarship Program, Part I (Official Name: Rural Library Professionals as Change Agents in the 21st Century: Integrating Information Technology Competencies in the Southern and Central Appalachian Region), funded by the Institute of Museum and Library Services' Laura Bush 21st Century Librarian Program to the School of Information Sciences at the University of Tennessee for $567,660 during October 2009 to September 2013 (Principal Investigator B. Mehra; Co-Principal Investigators: K. Black, V. Singh).
ITRL2	Information Technology Rural Librarian Master's Scholarship Program, Part II (Official Name: Rural Library Professionals as Change Agents in the 21st Century: Integrating Information Technology Competencies in the Southern and Central Appalachian Region, Part II), funded by the Institute of Museum and Library Services' Laura Bush 21st Century Librarian Program to the School of Information Sciences at the University of Tennessee for $478,258 during October 2012 to September 2016 (Principal Investigator: B. Mehra; Co-Principal Investigator: V. Singh).
LIS	Library and information science
SCA	Southern and Central Appalachian
UT SIS	University of Tennessee's School of Information Sciences

DEFINING COMMUNITY ARCHIVES WITHIN RURAL SOUTH CAROLINA

Travis L. Wagner and Bobbie Bischoff

ABSTRACT

This chapter deploys qualitative interviews with employees of rural South Carolina cultural institutions to assess the state of their rural community archives in order to understand both the practices and needs of the institutions within their relationship to larger, traditional archives with the aim to better understand national trends around community archives.

The research uses open-ended qualitative interviews based on snowball sampling focused on cultural institutions in populations defined as "rural" by the state of South Carolina. Using snowball sampling allowed for communities to self-identify other cultural institutions previously overlooked in surveys of rural South Carolina archival holdings.

Findings from the interviews provide new community-defined understandings of both practices and needs of rural community archives. Valuable insights include the following:

- *A clear awareness on the part of rural community archives of their relationship to larger practices of archiving*

Rural and Small Public Libraries: Challenges and Opportunities
Advances in Librarianship, Volume 43, 155–180
Copyright © 2018 by Emerald Publishing Limited
All rights of reproduction in any form reserved
ISSN: 0065-2830/doi:10.1108/S0065-283020170000043007

- *Notable moments of creativity by rural community archives concerning long-term self-sustenance*
- *A continued need for low-cost, low-barrier methods of digital outreach for both preservation and communication*
- *A more direct stream of access to grant funding favoring community archival practitioners over user-based research funding*

While many examples of community-based archival practice exist within British, Australian, and New Zealand research, such studies remain sparse and entity specific within the United States. This continued lack of case studies and models for understanding and aiding rural, community archives within the United States is only amplified when divided by regions and states. By focusing directly on the concerns of practitioners working to preserve and make available localized histories, this research illuminates both the incredible agency of rural community cultural institutions while re-conceptualizing the needs of such groups.

Keywords: Cultural heritage; community archives; local history; resource sharing; digitization

I. INTRODUCTION

South Carolina is home to seven rural counties, defined by the Institute of Museum and Library Services (IMLS) as being more than 25 miles from urbanized areas (Swan et al., 2013). In these counties, libraries are often understaffed, underfunded, and lack much of the infrastructure to reach their full potential as cultural institutions. Other chapters within this volume explore such issues, suggesting solutions, advocacy, and resources for those working with community libraries. We build on these discussions to explore how archives and institutions that effectively operate as archives face similar challenges in these communities.

Much like discussions involving rural libraries, it is not that such archives do not exist, but instead that their presence is often different from what one might consider a "traditional" repository. By evoking the notion of community archives within the context of rural counties, we examine how such collections emerge and function within rural South Carolina. By looking at institutions that include, but are not limited to, churches, historical societies, welcome centers, and, of course, rural libraries, we argue that rural communities build archives that do not wholly reflect institutionalized standards.

Yet, even while existing outside of the parameters of "traditional," these archives offer history, tangible artifacts, and research equitable to established repositories.

We posit that factors limiting rural archives' viability and visibility mirror those present within rural libraries. We interrogate how issues of low staffing, nontraditional hours of operation, and the lack of a stable digital presence result in small, rural community archives remaining detached from discussions of archival needs and practices. Through qualitative, interview-based investigations of the institutions in question, we describe not only the many looks and styles of community archives in the rural Southeast but also, more importantly, establish the user needs and the role such archives play in information literacy and collective memory. Because of the qualitative basis of this particular approach, we explore how each archives perceives such gaps and barriers, including challenges such as digital curation, controlled storage, processing, deaccessioning, and copyright. Though exploratory in nature, we advocate broadening discourses with the already large umbrella of community archives to more clearly incorporate rural instantiations.

Furthermore, although this chapter focuses specifically on examples within South Carolina rural communities, we argue that such challenges transcend regionality, becoming replicable nationally. Accordingly, we offer examples and discussions that reflect such sentiments. Ultimately, we hope that this chapter helps facilitate an exploration of alternative methods implemented by communities without the resources or training to properly create a collection or space indicative of a traditional archives. In turn, our goal is to reorient how others engage with communities whose histories remain dangerously close to being lost, and we hope to advocate for the ability of people outside of major urban population centers to enjoy future access to their cultural heritage.

II. SITUATING COMMUNITY AND RURALITY IN DEFINITIONS OF ARCHIVES

Heritage agencies choose numerous ways to define themselves. Among the most common are historical society, cultural center, genealogical society, and historical museum. The majority of heritage agencies are not intimate with pioneering archival practices and do not intentionally apply professional archival methods to collections of materials (Flinn, 2007). In order to aptly use the word "archives" and establish a definition for rural community archives, we begin this chapter by defining "traditional archives" as those operated by professional archivists with persons who are likely to possess at least a graduate degree in some variant of library and information sciences or have worked for some time in an information specialist capacity. Ideally, a professional archivist and their potential coworkers possess both of these prerequisites, though a considerable amount of the latter often makes up for an individual lacking the former.

The professional and more formal definition of "archives" states that an archives is a repository of documents produced "in the course of the conduct of the activities of the body that produces them and according to its needs" (Eastwood, 2010, p. 6). This definition comfortably encompasses archives within state and local governments as well as the archives of organizations, corporations, businesses, and academia. The basic functions of "legitimized" archives are accession, arrangement, description, preservation, and provision of access to collections of materials. More ideally, these materials should represent some governing body, broadly defined. Within this formal definition, much is written about theory, practice, memory, accountability, power, and social justice in the mainstream archives.[1]

However, by focusing less on formal definitions to what an archives should look like and instead examining the relationship between collections of documents and cultural memory, the archival world and what constitutes our heritage considerably expands. No longer is an archives merely an institution functioning singularly as a repository for objective historicity. An archives with a more decentralized definition is one with a fluid relationship between itself and communities it serves. The National Archives of the United Kingdom provides a useful alternative definition, simply describing an archives as a "collection of information known as records" (What Are Archives?, 2015). When deploying the expanded definition of information as provided by Buckland (1991) to include more than merely written historical documents, records come in many iterations and possess both physical manifestations and intangible interactions. Indeed, the National Archives of the United Kingdom's emphasis on a record being known affords a considerable expansion of information to include the communal interactions latent in rural community archives, as obviously implied in the evocation of "community" as opposed to "institutional" archive. Admittedly, archival discourse from the United Kingdom is not synonymous with U.S. contexts, yet the sentiment remains crucial to how one can advocate for and imagine the needs of rural archives.

Fortunately, the Society of American Archivists (SAA) expands this definition to include relationships among the records, families, communities, and memory. SAA adopted a definition of archives to reflect "a place to go where people find information" (What is An Archives?, 2007). SAA makes reference to collective memory with examples like "your family history becom[ing] a part of your community's—and America's—collective memory" (What is An Archives?, 2007). These definitions demonstrate that a relationship exists between the archival record and memory, which is an important concept in creating a working definition of rural community archives. Exploring the relationality of community and known information provides a productive framework for defining entities that warrant inclusion within the expanse that is rural community archives.

III. METHODOLOGY

This study employs qualitative open-ended interviews with employees and curatorial staff at eight rural South Carolina cultural institutions. While the institutional representatives we interviewed all professed to possess archival collections, the term "cultural institution" is used here to account for many iterations of what archival spaces can and do look like. Indeed, of the institutions represented in this study, archival spaces included: historical societies, church archives, library-based history rooms, and basements in welcome centers.

To determine which towns and subsequent cultural spaces counted for inclusion within the project, potential participating communities needed to adhere to Bunch's (2008) definition of "rural" as it pertains to South Carolina. Bunch identifies any county with an adjusted population density (APD) of fewer than 155 people per square mile as being rural, with this method allowing marked differentiation between small, suburban counties that are still "urban because of their proximity to a major metropolitan area" (2008, p. 1).[2] By deploying such a definition, the aforementioned archives, despite their varying physical spaces, become distinguished and unified as relating uniquely to their community in question. This distinction demarcates and often affords them the unique advantage of avoiding tangential inclusion—or co-opting—by larger metropolitan collections. Indeed, regardless of the formal title of the institutions included in this study, each represents a rural community archives.

Participants were approached via searches for historical societies, information centers, archives, and other cultural spaces through both web searches and archival databases within the counties whose APDs reflect the scope of Bunch's definition of rurality for South Carolina. We contacted participants via methods available to researchers who used these institutions, with this information commonly appearing on their websites. We conducted most interviews by phone or email. We used a snowball sampling method following our first several interviews, as many participants suggested other institutions to interview and contact.[3]

The interview structure was entirely open-ended, affording the participants the ability to discuss their institutions, their work, and eventually the challenges facing their respective spaces. Our interview questioning directly evoked terms like "community" and "cultural memory" but avoided definitions of archival practices. Our intent was not to delegitimize the importance of professional standards, but instead we were guided by a purposeful awareness of the overarching power theoretical best practices play in helping to emphasize institutional archives as "good" archives. We have anonymized the participants and their respective institutions in reaction to some of the topics discussed and challenges evoked, particularly those linked directly to community engagement, monetary needs, and infrastructural challenges.

While these findings remain applicable specifically to cultural institutions in the Carolinas, one could assert similar findings in other rural spaces, factoring in components like racial diversity accordingly to change demographic dynamics and community concerns and issues. More directly, there are implicit racial components to historical representation in South Carolina's rural community archives that may not manifest themselves in the same fashion were one studying a rural community archive in other parts of the United States. We acknowledge these factors in this chapter, but due to their complexity we chose to mention them only when distinctly brought forward by the interview subjects.

Finally, while this methodology emphasizes locating needs in a community-led approach, it necessitates accounting for the subsequent difficulties in ascertaining the general needs of all rural community archives without overlooking the individual needs of specific institutions. As such, discussions of specific practices and approaches should not be read as definitive, and the subsequent points raised acknowledge such nuance to resolutely avoid "best practices" rhetoric.

IV. FINDINGS

Some notable trends emerged within the data (see Fig. 1). None of the interview participants suggested their space is an archives by their own definitions, though many assured that they possessed archival holdings. In fact, of the eight county cultural institutions interviewed, only one purported

	Location	Dedicated facility for collection	Dedicated director	Staffing	Funding	Digital collections	Board or steering committee
Participant 1	Central South Carolina	Yes	Yes	2 full-time 4 part-time 4 interns	10K from County	Some	Yes
Participant 2	WSW South Carolina	No	No	Volunteer run	N/A	No	Yes
Participant 3	NE South Carolina	Yes	Yes	1 full-time 1 part-time 2 interns	20K from self-funding	No	Yes
Participant 4	Central South Carolina	Yes	Yes	3 full-time 3 part-time	200k from County	Some	Yes
Participant 5	Southern South Carolina	No	No	N/A	N/A	No	No
Participant 6	Central South Carolina	Yes	Yes	N/A	25K from self-funding	No	Yes
Participant 7	SW South Carolina	No	No	N/A	N/A	No	No
Participant 8	NW South Carolina	Yes	No	Volunteer run	10k mixed funding	No	Yes

Fig. 1. Institutional information breakdown.

to have tangible plans to build a dedicated space for archival operations, primarily as a result of negotiating with the city to obtain a section of space within a soon-to-be-built chamber of commerce. Accordingly, the collections are housed in spaces that include: three museums, two museum and cultural centers, two libraries, one library and arts center, and one historical society.

Considering our interest specifically in rural community archives, six of the eight participating institutions are located near the border of Georgia and South Carolina, the major rural pocket in the state of South Carolina. This expanse of rurality is due to the urban sprawl of cities like Charlotte and Atlanta limiting the quantifiable label of "rural" being applicable to most portions of the state, despite both existing outside of South Carolina. Furthermore, given the central location of Columbia (South Carolina's capital and largest city), much of the state remains excluded from such identity labels. Aside from the six sites located in southwestern South Carolina, the other two institutions we included were located in northern South Carolina in the small rural pocket between Charlotte and Columbia.

Institutional participants included site directors (either employed by their county or appointed by board of directors), long-time volunteers, and individuals operating as hybrid librarians and archivists. In all eight cases, the individual interviewed served the role of running the respective institution, either formally or informally. None of the sites operated on what might be called normal, full-time business hours, with each site being closed at least one or two days a week. Further, hours of operation for each institution were less than a traditional eight-hour work day. Most participants appointed to their directorial job worked the entirety of the time their institution was open and often beyond, for fundraising events and special research requests.

The reason for the presence of nine cultural institutions in this study, despite only having eight interview participants, is that one institution possesses two distinctly different museums within their location but stores archives in a joint space. All but one of the institutions had a direct presence of a board to help guide decisions and funding, though many of these boards reflected the larger board of directors for the given institutions in which the archives are held. At least four participants identified county funding as part of their economic sustainability, with ranges of funding being quite drastic. Of those receiving a direct budget line, the lowest acknowledged county funding was $10,000 per fiscal year, while another larger cultural institution had a county funding line of $200,000 per fiscal year. Most of the participants also acknowledged the crucial role that fundraising plays in their viability, with methods of fundraising ranging from traditional mail solicitation to annual galas. One participant's cultural institution hosted an annual dinner tied to local heritage items that became the themes of the meal. Conversely, another interviewee—working for one of the nonbudgeted institutions—noted a complete absence of economic viability, suggesting that their economic suste-nance came from volunteer labor working to keep the institution open.

Much like the funding landscapes of these institutions, staffing also var-ies. The aforementioned volunteer model of the underfunded institution is similar to the larger cultural institutions we explored. Most necessitated a high degree of unpaid work to operate at a minimal level of functionality. However, even within these volunteer-driven workflows, many institutions possessed some degree of paid staff and managerial positions. Three sub-jects identified their institutions as possessing full-time directors as well as at least one additional full-time employee. Three organizations also include part-time employees, while another two specifically had student employees and volunteers. Further, of the two that employed students, one did so as part of a summer internship program in which a youth training program paid for the student labor. Of the managerial and directorial staff, only one identified as having training related to historic preservation, whereas another possessed managerial experience prior to taking on their leadership role. In at least one case, an interview subject admitted to taking their present position after their mother stepped down from the role.

In terms of physical space and technology needs, the sites we examined possess varying levels of technological infrastructure, which we define as dis-tinct from outward-facing mechanisms such as online or social media pres-ences. The latter is provided as a suggested issue to be addressed for rural community archives. "Technology" here refers to items used in the function of maintaining and working with archival materials. Of the 8 participants who provided information, only 2 had more than 10 computers in their spaces for staff and researchers, whereas at least 2 possessed no computers outside of those tied to staff use. Two sites had microfilm readers, though one admitted to theirs being broken. Two also noted having scanners and copiers. Two sites possessed databases tied to reference computers, one of which emerged directly from an IMLS grant. Finally, one site noted posses-sion of a television and VCR for reference work. Like microfilm readers, we argue that VHS-based reference services reflect considerable, albeit acknowl-edged, technological limitations.[4] Finally, only two of the eight institutions acknowledged adherence to the standards for access set by the Americans with Disabilities Act (ADA). One subject felt their space provided adequate services and had direct ramp entrances referred to as "The Loop," while another acknowledged their inability to adhere to basic ADA standards as a "major issue."

Materials within the collections of the eight cultural institutions appear to be the only area of general overlap, with many housing letters, photographs, and personal materials of local families. Along the lines of many of the collections growing from museums, interviewees noted antiques as part of archival holdings, with items like school desks, farming implements, apothecary supplies, and at least one Model-T automobile. Further, a handful of the collections included oral histories, implying a concern for community history, to be explored later in this chapter. Of course, given the regional nature of these cultural institutions, it is no surprise that collections include Civil War relic rooms, cotton production tools, and Christian religious paraphernalia. Again, acknowledging that a discussion of race relations within South Carolina is beyond the scope of this chapter, an astute reader can glean implications from the fact that none of the institutions interviewed laid claim to histories of civil rights or slavery within their collections.

A. Variations of Community Archives

Many community-led rural archives began as historical or genealogical societies associated with local public libraries. These community groups share an interest in the history of people, places, or events within the local community and collect memorabilia from and about members of the community, many of whom libraries serve. Flinn (2007) notes that there was a wave of growth in local community history beginning in the 1980s as communities "felt deprived" of historical narratives and "established their own local collections" in response (Flinn, 2007, p. 155). Two community archives represented in this study directly evoked Flinn's sentiment. One historical society and another genealogical society began in the back room of their community libraries. Each depended on their local library for assistance in making the materials available to patrons. Yet, eventually both organizations accumulated more materials than their respective libraries were capable of handling, thus warranting a need for their own spaces. One heritage agency moved from the rear of the library to an old, abandoned factory within two years of its founding, while the other moved to a local historic site. Each shift emphasizes the desire to entrench community history into the locale, rooting collections within the town's most iconic space. More importantly, it speaks to the needs of defining spaces as archives, which can develop reactively to what is often an unanticipated growth at an exponential rate.

Consequently, as venues change, so does the nature of the archives itself. What began as extensions of library collections grew into distinct archival collections, even if the name does not suggest such an identity, such as a relic room within a town's museum. Further, in most cases, what began as a simple means to demarcate the history of specific communities grew into larger and more expansive attempts at defining a cultural memory perceived as yet unchronicled.

Although the collections of mainstream archives and heritage groups grow from donated materials—and on rare occasions, purchased items—the nature of the collections deviates considerably between locales and different rural environs. Often, the nature of any rural community archive's collection correlates to patrons' desires to access their histories in either local libraries or more mainstream archives. As such, a concept of community evolves, creating a "shared sense of place, with this 'sense of place' involving relationships with the people, cultures, and environments (both natural and built) associated with a particular area" (Flora, 2015 p. 41). So, while the rural archives studied in this endeavor may have similar types of items that chronicle similar moments in the history of the American South, the figures and persons represented within the collections remain fixed to the folks living in the area in and around the respective county.

Unsurprisingly, in this process less attention is applied to the collections' overall curatorial management, instead prioritizing how these materials narratively define the histories of the community. In multiple instances, the archives within the cultural institutions we examined placed priority on displaying important community artifacts for all to see, as opposed to placing them in archival safekeeping, only discoverable through a finding aid or database. The reasons for this remain twofold. First, as the definitions of cultural memory imply, it is about affirming a localized history through which to create community camaraderie. Second, this suggests an alternative way of thinking about access in a rural setting. It is not simply that patrons and staff cannot use or afford technology, but that a full line item description of materials (one normalized by database-driven description) is simply not how these communities share their collections. In the minds of these groups, materials are not hidden behind physical lock and key. For rural South Carolina community archives, it is exactly the opposite; they highlight what they find valuable, presuming deep description to be a cost-ineffective disservice to their larger institutional narrative. In some ways, it asks other practitioners to radically reimagine the purposes and uses of deep collection description.

If one teases apart history and memory, so as not to make history the enemy of memory, then memory becomes "the shifting record of the sense we make of things" (Jimerson, 2010, p. 193). Memory is edited, forgotten, and sometimes buried. Only through the history of the record can memories become reconstructed to reveal worlds "once held only in memory" (Jimerson, 2010, p. 194). Theoretical constructs of memory aside, archives serve as evidence of both memory and history—intricately entwined, similar and different in both name and function. Rural archives, but more specifically the rural archives we studied, promote community memory above standardized curatorial practices and work within this understanding of memory as community driven. For rural community archives, memory practices help us understand the relationship between any given town and its storied history. The information stored within such collections only functions if it is available for all to see, presuming that one's desire to see includes a willingness to visit the community in question.

In this way, the emerging themes of the rural community archives are complex relationships between the tangible archival contents of a space and their inextricable ties to the intangible memories embedded in that space of the community. This enigmatic connection guides how patrons seek information, informally, within their historical repositories. As one interviewee astutely observed, "unless we had an archives here and people brought them here, those records would be gone." To this end, many of the participants acknowledged the importance of accruing materials and making materials available as immediately as possible, often knowingly sidestepping more traditional processing practices with a prioritized concern for a proactive curation of history. Thus, when engaging with rural community archives, it becomes important that persons know their community archives are access points for information about the rural township's community memory, even if this practice is not engaged within any regular manner. The rural community archive must be there, not for consistent repeated use, but because it is the location for all that indicates the past of community. Indeed, when later exploring the major hurdle of digitization as it pertains to rural community archives, this chapter considers the ethical considerations latent in choosing to make such items available virtually, especially in light of multiple acknowledgements of the potentially detrimental effects such distanced access might have on a rural institution's economic viability and, more importantly, the cultural vibrancy of a small community.

The rural communities we studied are neither isolated nor insulated from the dynamics of change, which proved both beneficial and destructive to their archival livelihood. To dispel pervasive myths of "rural as backwards" and, further, to avoid the complications involved in presuming economic disadvantages in rural locales, the agency of these communities must be acknowledged. Indeed, if one accepts rural community archives as agentic in their decisions, even when mired in technological limitations, unpredictable funding sources, and understaffed spaces, those engaging with their archives zealously and messily remain far more vital than persons with detached clinical precision.

Indeed, the undertakings of such small archives may not appear to be what one does in "traditional archives," but it is necessary to remember that rural community archives know they are not such a space and thus develop their best practices through experience and patron needs in an ad hoc manner while also embracing the plurality of the phrase "best practices." Although very few archivists in rural communities have an MLIS degree or extensive archival experience, there is no sense of ignorance of the challenges faced in their work. Each decision to display a fragile document out of preservation containers or hesitancy to place items online is not due to lack of understanding of why the alternative would be a proper course of action, but instead an indication of a thoughtful analysis of archival issues unique to the rural landscape. To think about archival practices and needs within this world is to necessarily reject the theoretical presumptions of not why people save materials, but how that occurs and what it should look like.

V. SUGGESTIONS FOR ADDRESSING NEEDS OF RURAL COMMUNITY ARCHIVES

Rural communities design their archives, knowingly, to double as both historical repositories and informed memory spaces. It is hardly a surprise that the community archives represented in this study include spaces that function more expressly as a permanent museum exhibit than an archives proper, such as rooms adjacent to a replica of a Civil War soldier or in attics above a restored cotton mill where the crucial document needed to create extensive archival records lays. Yet, even as the importance of such rural community archives becomes increasingly apparent, little remains known about these smaller, sometimes independent archives that function as historical records keepers for geographically rural communities. Moreover, even less is known about the perseverance, resourcefulness, and reliability of these rural community archives. None of the archivists we interviewed and visited evoked what one might imagine as an institutional archive. Yet, of the individual locations looked at, each unsurprisingly brought forth the exact concerns and challenges latent in archiving in the twenty-first century. Accordingly, what follows reflects a tentative needs assessment for rural community archives via

distinct suggestions to amplify such collections while respecting the complicated contexts that allow such spaces to emerge and thrive. These suggestions
reflect a national scope for rural community archives even as they refer to
challenges faced uniquely within the context of South Carolina.

A. Digitization/Transfer Stations and State Institutional Aid

With the rise of community archiving and personal digital archiving comes
a need to intervene on the behalf of individuals and communities deemed to
possess potentially important materials. Of course, endeavors in this type of
digitization are expensive, as materials range from traditional print resources
to fragile audiovisual materials housed on obsolete formats such as U-Matic
tape and 8 mm film. It is simply not possible for each small rural archive
to possess all the hardware, software, and digital space to ingest such items.
Indeed, even when housing older formats, much remains inaccessible due to
broken machinery (e.g., the aforementioned issues facing one rural South
Carolina archive with a broken microfilm reader) or lack of access to legacy
technologies. Attempting to access these legacy materials is often not a con-
structive use of limited staffing and fiscal resources. As such, a major need for
these communities is the aid of mobile or pop-up digitization and preservation services. A project such as this might reflect the pop-up archive practices
of the University of Kentucky's "Eating Kentucky," wherein archivists enter
a space not traditionally deemed an archive and invite those occupants to
share their stories, artifacts, and materials to build its own unique archival
space, giving some degree of permanence to otherwise "temporal community
moments" (Rice & Rice, 2016, p. 250). Furthermore, this approach importantly re-centers the community history into the process, making the narrative about the cultural memory of the community and not a narrative to add
to the memory of the imposing institutional archives.

   To aid in this process of reorienting digital archival production,
StoryCorps provides basic tools to facilitate archival memory building for
the masses. As their robust mobile app suggests, StoryCorps aims to "help
create an archive of the wisdom of humanity" (StoryCorps Inc., 2017). The
nonprofit organization, known for its evocative public radio interviews, provides access to two key components of building cultural memories: a recording method and a place to store such recordings. By synchronizing both
the recording process and subsequent distribution, the mobile app provides
our participants and other similar-sized institutions a great point of entry
into digital content production. Working with this specific mobile app also

enmeshes users within a social media community with overlapping interests and draws the attention of interested parties for potential collaboration and financial support. This connectivity provides a digital presence that we argue, in the next section, remains a point of expansion for rural community archives. Although the software storage methods that house the interviews remain strictly the property of StoryCorps, the application's terms of service suggest that users maintain control over their productions so long as they do not do anything potentially illegal or in violation of preexisting copyrights (StoryCorps Inc., 2017). Accordingly, as the application provides limited use of photographs, description notes, and keywords, it is easy to imagine how smaller, rural archives might incorporate this free application into building awareness of their collections. Furthermore, with a growing user base of over 200,000 and at least 60,000 interviews saved at The Library of Congress, engaging with such an application transcends considerable barriers between well-funded, large-scale institutions and the institutions we interviewed (Annual Report 2015, 2016).[5]

The pop-up archive approach acknowledges that many spaces—especially small, rural community archives—simply do not have the institutional backing to practice long-term digitization and archival permanence. They can benefit from aid by way of quick, tutorial-heavy digital replication. Again, the goal is to capture the unique sense of historical knowledge in the community rather than attaching merit to a larger narrative of archival logic more common in large-scale institutional archives. An example of audiovisual-media-specific initiatives is that of the New York City–based XFR (Transfer) Collective. According to the organization's website, "XFR Collective is a non-profit organization that partners with artists, activists, individuals, and groups to lower the barriers to preserving at-risk audiovisual media—especially unseen, unheard, or marginalized works—by providing low-cost digitization services and fostering a community of support for archiving and access through education, research, and cultural engagement." (XFR Collective, 2015). While notably inclined toward individuals, the terminology raised by the XFR Collective shows the type of work necessary for aiding rural community archives. Specifically, this type of initiative could, like the work of XFR Collective, "lower the barriers" to digital preservation for materials at risk in such communities. While XFR Collective is unique to audiovisual materials, such an engagement within rural spaces would arguably apply to all materials, print or otherwise.

A specific example of this within the context of South Carolina is the Digitization in a Box Project, offered by the South Carolina State Library. The program offers materials to libraries in need of scanning equipment and other technology to do transfers, but crucially also offers training on managing workflows, structuring sound metadata, and engaging in quality control. This highlights the major skills learned in an MLIS program without the economic and time-based inaccessibility of returning to school to attain a degree. Currently, items for the South Carolina State Libraries' Digitization in a Box Project are leasable throughout the state. Unfortunately, the current iteration of Digitization in a Box only applies to institutions defined expressly as public libraries, so while the initiative could prove fruitful for some of the rural community archives interviewed, it would not suffice for institutions such as small-scale historical societies, church archives, or volunteer-led community spaces that fall outside of such a restrictive definition (Stone, 2016). If the XFR Collective and Digitization in a Box stand as opposing poles with regard to the options on how to engage with rural community archives, one can imagine a version of this approach where a mobile scanning station is sent throughout rural communities that identifies not only rural libraries, but potentially all rural information centers offering methods to digitize archival holdings, however loosely they may be defined. Although such endeavors cost money, it would be easy to make the case that such work falls under the Common Heritage work of the National Endowment of the Humanities (NEH) or warrant consideration for funding from the Council on Library and Information Resources (CLIR) Hidden Collections project.[6] As detailed in suggestion 3, entities like medium-sized institutions could approach granting agencies with a proposal to create such a unit that would serve their smaller peers, thus spreading digital preservation practices to rural community archives while also funding employees within their own organizations. This solution would be mutually beneficial and could potentially inform future practices of emerging archivists, in addition to establishing the aforementioned archives (and all rural community archives) as information holders beyond simply repositories for localized historical knowledge. An additional significant advantage of expanding this model would be that it allows digitization and digital preservation efforts to be dispersed in a way that achieves economies of scale.

Of course, this idyllic approach fails to address the implications of passivity on the part of rural community cultural institutions. Does the emergence of a digitization mobile unit merely replicate the problem of institutional co-opting of cultural memory? Further, are clear conversations about the needs of the rural community and their archival collections had before such work begins? As should be apparent, just because a community has holdings of rich historical value and they make such value known, does not mean one should equate this with consent to provide digital access. Many of the archivists we interviewed purposefully rejected the idea of having a digital repository because it might result in their losing what few in-person patron visits they had each year. As one interviewee emphatically argued, "If you get the information online, why do you need to come see us? You are not getting a memory, you are getting a date ... it doesn't become the whole experience." Following this sentiment, the choice not to digitize collections results in a radically self-aware stance on the part of the rural community archives, which offers itself up not as a repository for quantitative fact checking, but a space wherein the historical memory must always be tied to the physicality of the space itself. Indeed, when thinking about the emphasis on the haptic nature of archives rather than the rising desire or anticipated need for digitized materials, one can understand collection stewards' resistance to meet broad public demands that everything be put online.

Latham (2010, 2011) provides clear arguments for a reclamation of physicality within archives. Tracing the misplaced hopes thrust upon a digital revolution within archives, Latham warns that much of the knowledge latent in the context of materials stands to disappear when cleaved from a physical space. It is not merely the document in any form that matters. As our many participants noted, the history of their archival holdings is inextricable from their respective location. Further, Latham notes that "each new user of archival materials brings varied experiences and knowledge with them to their encounter," and this knowledge iteratively builds during each new interaction between an archivist and their patrons (2011, p. 14). While it is plausible that some relief may come through an increased use of crowdsourcing for digital archival content, an object's place still matters. As Latham argues, and our participants so clearly agree, an item in an archive is "more than just a file," it is an "expression of human communication and behavior" (2001, p. 14).

B. Harnessing a Digital Presence

With an increasing demand for digital literacy comes the expectation for a digital presence. As discussed, many archives, even those in rural communities, expressed anxiety over how and what to do with regard to entering such a digital landscape. The anxiety is well founded, as a digital identity is essential to any functioning archival space, particularly in a moment of technologically driven research. While it may not yield high use in historical writings and small-scale community use, a digital identity asserts that collections exist and are potentially of inquiry. What is less clear in the rise of digital presences for archives is how exactly such spaces are supposed to look. We argue that a digital presence need not be elaborate nor necessarily reflect the cutting-edge work of highly funded digital humanities projects. In fact, a digital presence merely means that the collection or archives is searchable through basic information retrieval processes. Examples of useful digital presences for such smaller archives include but are certainly not limited to an archival Facebook page, an information WordPress site, a collection uploaded to Archive.org, and other ebbing and flowing social media spaces. However, for any rural community archive, a clear tie to the point of contact is more crucial than the actual digital presence. An obvious example of this is the provision of a digital website, but a failure to include something as simple as the email address of the collection's curator. Fig. 2 shows the dramatic scale regarding the digital presences of our participating archives.

Alternatively, archives can work through a larger digital repository to make connections on a geographical or thematic basis. Take, for example, the work of the Washington Rural Heritage project. Implemented by Evan Robb, the project "enable[s] small and rural libraries to create digital collections of unique items that highlight institutional holdings and tell the stories of their communities" by housing the respective collections on the larger Washington State Library website (Washington Rural Heritage, 2015). The example immediately calls to mind the aforementioned Digitization in a Box project through the South Carolina State Library; however, what makes the Washington Rural Heritage project slightly more cohesive is the inclusion of a geographic information system (GIS) map that shows specifically where the collections are located within Washington. By clicking on the mapped point, an individual is then able to locate not only a further description of the collection, but in most instances a point of contact to the institution housing the respective collection. This makes the necessary

	Website	Email	Blog	Social media
Participant 1	X	X		
Participant 2	X	X	X	
Participant 3	X	X		
Participant 4	X	X		X
Participant 5	X			X
Participant 6				X
Participant 7	X			X
Participant 8	X	X		X

Fig. 2.   Breakdown of digital presence.

connection between the items, their housing location, and the contact information, should the individual desire to do extended research. In this manner, awareness about the collections is raised, while connections are simultaneously built (if only through digital linkage) between other similarly sized and presumably funded digital archives. Notably, this type of initiative relies on the graces of a larger institution that is willing to house digital content and make use of higher-end coding work, but it is a tenable solution that relieves some of the greater stresses of enacting a digital presence. Structurally, though, the presence of an institutional caregiver is not always necessary to make the connections between smaller institutions and respective collections. Sometimes a thematic connection can work to link the rural with the large-scale institution.

At the 2014 Association of Moving Image Archivists conference, Jasmyn Castro introduced a project called the African-American Home Movie Archive. Conceived in opposition to the discourse Castro was experiencing around the idea that home movies created by black communities simply did not exist, she took it upon herself to interrogate how collections were being described and how they were being sought out. Castro, adamant in her endeavor, discovered that not only did such items exist, but that a community led predominantly by white archivists was overlooking items latent in their own collections or potential acquisitions available on online platforms such as Ebay. By reconstituting what one would define as an African-American home movie, Castro built a connecting repository for collections with such footage. Furthermore, Castro approached all types of institutions, both established and small scale, a practice that the aforementioned archivists simply were not doing. Her website http://www.aahma.org shows her findings, some of which are housed at rural archives. Take, for example, the collection noted in the index, which is housed at Northeast Historic Film: 37 reels of African-American home movies that exist at a well-known archive within the moving image archival community. However, considering that Northeast Historic Film is in Bucksport, Maine, it is easy to overlook due to its location in rural New England. Here, Castro has made a connection that shows the exceptional scope of locations housing materials when a thematic identity ties repositories together. Building off this revelatory work, one can imagine a small rural archive not necessarily building its own digital repository, but seeking out larger thematic repositories and offering up their information if they have collections or items that fall within that theme. Again, it is not the digital presence that is of the utmost importance, but the provision of contact information for further exploration.

C. Refiguring Grant Writing and the Funding Landscape

Undoubtedly, any practitioner in the field of archives knows the constant struggle latent in funding. More specifically, most archivists accept the inevitable role grants play in funding all levels of archival practices. Rural community archives, however, face the amplified challenge of needing funding streamlined while also locating grant funding applicable to their unique situations. We believe an obvious starting point is the offerings of the IMLS. While their general listings lack clear ties to the work of rural communities, as a national granting agency IMLS is beholden to 20 U.S. Code § 9141 known as the Library and Services Technology Act. Aimed at equitable distribution of grant funds, one of the highlights of U.S.C. § 9141 focuses on "targeting library and information services to persons having difficulty using a library and to underserved urban and rural communities" (20 U.S.C. § 9141). While we are not legal scholars, the emphasis on direct concern for rural communities suggests a direct outlet for heightened grant appeal. Of course, such a code necessitates grant applicants being aware of this nuance and, further, possessing an employee or advisor capable of constructing a grant application that illuminates such discussions. Nonetheless, the IMLS reflects the largest and, historically, most consistent funding pool for the many cultural institutions moving within the orbit of libraries and museums, archives being one such entity. Further, multiple projects mentioned within this chapter were, or currently are, recipients of such funding, the most notable of which being StoryCorps.

The American Library Association (ALA) offers similar, albeit fewer, general grants, many directed broadly at library infrastructure. None of the grants currently evoke verbiage directly concerning rural libraries, though generalizability favors such potentials. Indeed, the only remaining award with any direct links to small and rural librarians is the seemingly defunct EBSCO Excellence in Small and/or Rural Public Library Service Award. The winner is awarded $1,000 for being a single library serving fewer than 10,000 persons that "demonstrates excellence" or provides "a special program of significant accomplishments" (EBSCO Excellence in Small and/or Rural Public Library Service Award, 2012). Although both the American Library Association and the Public Library Association (PLA) list the award as open to applications, the most recent winner listed by the ALA was in 2012. Of note, the last award recipient's project, "One-Stop-Shop," worked to create a space to display and chronicle the history of a rural Kansas community (EBSCO Excellence in Small and/or Rural Public Library Service Award, 2012). Given the consistent concerns of our participants in evoking and sharing localized history, such an award seems worth pursuing for rural community archives, especially those linked to library facilities.

Perhaps, the broadest option available to rural community archives is within the NEH grant Sustaining Cultural Heritage Collections (SCHC). Although we have already discussed the Common Heritage initiative funded by the NEH, this grant focuses specifically on long-term preservation of America's history with more regionalized nuance. The SCHC grant provides scaled funding for projects concerned with jointly conserving collections that have an aggravated need for protection from environmental threats and those collections looking to illuminate their collections despite financial insta-bility. The major requirement of this specific grant is the need to "clearly address sustainable preventative conservation strategies," though the grant accedes that such plans "can take many forms" (Sustaining Cultural Heritage Collections, 2012). Latent within this grant are potentials for scalable projects that we believe could benefit not only many of the archives we interviewed, but a majority of rural community archives nationwide. As the grants appear to receive funding from a general pool, the likelihood of a small request receiving a larger percentage of funding seem more favorable, whereas a larger institution asking for a higher amount is only likely to receive a small portion of their requested funding. Furthermore, this grant directly evokes environmental concerns such as proper storage as an issue arguably more cen-tral to rural communities than urban locales. Moreover, the potential projects proposed for such grants tie ostensibly to the other aforementioned CLIR project, Hidden Collections, which also encourages scalable projects, making clear a specific interest in "approaches to digitization that make possible new kinds of scholarship in the digital research environment" (Digitizing Hidden Special Collections and Archives, 2014). The Hidden Collections initiative highlights a concern for scalability as well, theoretically making rural com-munity archives an ideal fit for such a project. Crucially, of all the aforemen-tioned grants, online information suggests the Hidden Collections project has the funding stream with the most long-term vitality.

Admittedly, the grants discussed previously share a common national scope. Applying for IMLS grant funding means vying for resources with other institutions, many of which are much larger than small community archives and in possession of full-time staff devoted to grant writing and funding acquisition. This gap is not easily traversable. Exacerbating the anxieties within pursuing grants is the high risk of failure, making it unappealing for a practitioner whose "hard work may never be recognized by their employers or by granting agencies" (Nelson, 2009, p. 163). As many of our participants attested, with needing to oversee multiple divergent tasks, the addition of gambling on applying for grants is simply not part of their workflow. We believe that the only way to alleviate this concern on the part of smaller—and specifically rural—archives is to increase transparency in granting agencies, which aim to aid underserved and overlooked populations. While financial records must remain confidential to a certain degree, the process for applications to obtain aid should not be. Our suggested changes to the grant process include the following: (1) offer options to submit grants via methods other than online forms; (2) name individuals available to serve as reliable points of contact and answer questions regarding the application process for smaller, rural cultural institutions; (3) provide examples of successful (and unsuccessful) grants to which novice applicants can refer; and (4) dedicate time to provide meaningful feedback to unsuccessful grant applicants. Of course, many of these suggestions seem obvious, but after frustrations with repeatedly confounding (and exasperating) results, the rural community archives we interviewed found the process wholly off-putting.

Finally, one of the more complicated issues of funding relates to use of materials by users. More specifically, multiple practitioners indicated hesitancy to give too much information to researchers who were only looking to advance their own careers. At least one participant spoke to this as a concern about intellectual exploitation, stating: "Why should I give people access to stuff when I could be writing about it myself?" Clearly, this participant displays a need to possess the integrity of the information as they see fit; however, a larger narrative of economic disincentive resides beneath the sentiment. An alternative statement might read, "Why should I let somebody else make money off this collection when I could be doing the same myself?" Controversial as it may sound, we believe it necessary to reconsider the contributions of researchers and patrons using materials in particularly underfunded, understaffed, and overlooked archives. Those fortunate enough to possess funding for research must take care to share the provisions of such research. While many scholars, authors, and general content producers offer gracious forms of thanks within their respective works, these platitudes provide little to no long-term economic aid to rural community archives. Simply put, thank-you notes do not keep the lights on, and if a person plans to gain economically from collections housed in such institutions they have nothing less than a moral obligation to reimburse the institutions for their labor, even if this is through providing assistance in grant writing or advocacy for the institution. Veteran researchers and academics in particular can attest to the rich resources hidden within rural community archives, so it behooves such individuals to offer up the equally valuable service of their time.

VI. CONCLUSION

Although only one of many states within America with a considerable rural population, South Carolina reflects a state saturated with rural cultural institutions. Whether they are understaffed libraries or underfunded museums, these small institutions operate differently than their larger, more urban counterparts. As chapters in this text show, advocacy and outreach must look different for such institutions. This sentiment proves unequivocally true for rural community archives that often exist on the periphery of the aforementioned libraries and museums. Rural community archives throughout the United States are by no means traditional and cannot benefit from being forced into traditional approaches. Through the lens of community archives, we examined eight rural South Carolina institutions facing the challenges of continued budget cuts, dwindling staff, and growing invisibility in an era of rampant social media use. However, we did not meet defeated archivists or pessimistic local history advocates. In fact, we met exactly the opposite. Despite facing challenges that would derail even the most well-built institutional archives, the community practitioners interviewed showed resilience. By reconfiguring notions of digital preservation, curatorial access, and community outreach, we found folks engaging in radical work.

Unfortunately, the very same problems that hinder established archives erect barriers for rural archives twofold. Much like other archives, the community archives interviewed manifest anxiety around a world where one can Google a desired object and find some acceptable version of it, legally or otherwise. However, whereas big institutional holdings would still show up somewhere in search results, rural institutions lack the capacity to have even their name show up in a search engine results page. Accordingly, the archives we interviewed built tightly webbed connections with their communities and other similar institutions around them, and, as our use of snowball sampling shows, many of these community archives only emerged to nonrural practitioners by word of mouth.

The insularity of rural community archives is simultaneously their biggest strength and their greatest weakness. By creating small-knit communities, the archives we interviewed were able to ensure their viability for another financial year and make sure that knowledge building was retained internally, not mined and exploited. Adversely, the insularity increases exclusion and makes advocating for funding a challenge. This means that rural archives exist in a catch-22 wherein to reach out for help with access means conceding to an inevitable co-opting of holdings; however, to avoid such connections is to ensure an increasingly dangerous anonymity.

The issues raised by our interviews are hardly new, but the ideas and answers evoked by our participants are. Using this chapter as a guide, we offer potential solutions, not definitive answers. Such assured certainty only works to reinforce exploitative practices. Rural community archives in South Carolina and elsewhere manage to thrive with or without the help of outside actors. Nothing is gained by operating from a deficit model. What is needed now is a willingness to listen to how we can help their cause, as opposed to asserting how such help should look. These archives can no longer play the role of a curiosity to be fawned over. These spaces continue to mirror the work of their larger counterparts with the resources they have available. This resilience matters, as an uncertain future for funding at all levels of archiving means operations will have to do more for less. In turn, the community archives discussed here might offer not merely an alternative, but the better alternative.

NOTES

1. For an exploration of shifting definitions of what constitutes an archival collection and evolutions around archival sciences, see Eastwood (2010). For a discussion on the ethical role archives play in providing historical accounts in the vein of social justice, see Jimerson (2009). For a contestation of the purity of archives and a critique of their problematic history as agents of state suppression, see Harris (2002) and Schwartz and Cook (2002), respectively.

2. The list of rural South Carolina counties can be found in Bunch's report: http://dc.statelibrary.sc.gov/bitstream/handle/10827/15126/DOC_Analysis_of_Rural_Definition_2008-1.pdf.

3. Snowball sampling consists of beginning with a subject group identified by some characteristic and locating initial members of that group for research purposes. Upon engagement with that group, suggestions for new participants are offered by members of that group. Snowball sampling offers an ideal approach to accessing hard-to-reach populations while providing communities agency in identifying important persons or groups within their respective social spaces. An accessible, yet thorough, overview of the benefits and challenges of snowball sampling can be found in Atkinson and Flint (2001).

4. This limitation acknowledges the continued full-scale decrease in the use of magnetic media-based recording with moves toward exclusively disc-based and born digital content. Extensive histories of the use of magnetic media-based production both theatrically and otherwise can be found in Dobrow (1990), Wasser (2001), and Greenberg (2008).

5. It is also worth noting that success stories of projects rooted in StoryCorps methodologies. A specific example is seen in the *Kids of Birmingham 1963* project. According to Yaco et al. (2015), the project with its ease of access and clear use helped

to provide "societal provenance" to a group while also establishing "archival provenance" in the same wave (p. 416).

6. Information on the Common Heritage grant is available at http://www.neh.gov/grants/preservation/common-heritage.

REFERENCES

Atkinson, R., & Flint, J. (2001). Accessing hidden and hard-to-reach populations: Snowball research strategies. *Social Research Update, 33*(1), 1–4.

Buckland, M. K. (1991). Information as thing. *Journal of the American Society for Information Science (1986–1998), 42*(5), 351.

Bunch, B. (2008). Developing a rural definition: Analysis of South Carolina counties. *South Carolina State Documents Depository*.

Castro, J. (2014, October 11). *Unearthing the African-American through home movies*. Lecture presented at The Association of Moving Image Archivists 2014 Conference. Savannah: Georgia.

Dobrow, J. R. (1990). *Social & cultural aspects of VCR use*. New York: Routledge.

EBSCO Excellence in Small and/or Rural Public Library Service Award. (2012, November 5). Retrieved July 31, 2016 from http://www.ala.org/awardsgrants/ebsco-excellence-small-andor-rural-public-library-service-award

Eastwood, T. (2010). A contested realm: The nature of archives and the orientation of archival science. *Currents of Archival Thinking*, 3-21.

Flinn, A. (2007). Community Histories, Community Archives: Some Opportunities and Challenges 1. *Journal of the Society of Archivists, 28*(2), 151–176.

Flora, C.B. "Community capitals and the rural landscape" in Flora, C. B., Flora, J. L., & Gasteyer, S. (2015). *Rural communities: Legacy+ change*. Westview Press.

Greenberg, J. M. (2008). *From betamax to blockbuster: Video stores and the invention of movies on video*. Cambridge: The MIT Press.

Harris, V. (2002). The archival sliver: Power, memory, and archives in South Africa. *Archival Science, 2*(1–2), 63–86.

Jimerson, R. C. (2010, November). Archives for all: The importance of archives in society. *Congresso, 10*, 2013.

Latham, K. F. (2011). Medium rare: Exploring archives and their conversion from original to digital part two—The holistic knowledge arsenal of Paper-based archives. *LIBRES: Library & Information Science Research Electronic Journal, 21*(2), 1–21.

Latham, K. F. (2010). Medium rare: Exploring archives and their conversion from original to digital part one: Lessons from the history of print media. *LIBRES: Library & Information Science Research Electronic Journal, 20*(2), 1–14.

Nelson, B. (2009). Empty archives. *Nature, 461*(7261), 160.

Rice, J., & Rice, J. (2015). Pop-up archives. *Rhetoric and the Digital Humanities*, 245.

Robb, E. (2015, July 3). About: Washington rural heritage. Retrieved August 5, 2016, from http://www.washingtonruralheritage.org/cdm/about.

Schwartz, J. M., & Cook, T. (2002). Archives, records, and power: The making of modern memory. *Archival Science, 2*(1–2), 1–19.

Stone, A. (2016, July 29). Digital collections: Digitization in a Box project. Retrieved July 31, 2016, from http://statelibrary.sc.libguides.com/digital-collections/diab

StoryCorps Inc. (2015). Annual Report 2015. Retrieved from: https://storycorpsorg-staging.
    s3.amazonaws.com/uploads/AR2015_FINAL_-Web-Publication-1.pdf
StoryCorps Inc. (2017). StoryCorps (Version 2.5.2) [Mobile application software]. Retrieved
    from http://itunes.apple.com.
Swan, D. W., Grimes, J., & Owens, T. (2013). *The state of small and rural libraries in the United
    States.* Institute of Museum and Library Services.
Sustaining Cultural Heritage Collections. (2012). Retrieved July 27, 2016 from https://www.neh.
    gov/grants/preservation/sustaining-cultural-heritage-collections.
Wasser, F. (2001). *Veni, vidi, video: The Hollywood Empire and the VCR.* Austin, TX: The University
    of Texas Press.
What is an archives? (2007, October). Retrieved July 21, 2016, from http://www.archivists.org/
    archivesmonth/WhatIsAnArchives.pdf.
What are archives? (2015, September 5). Retrieved July 21, 2016, from http://www.nationalarchives.
    gov.uk/help-with-your-research/start-here/what-are-archives/.
XFR Collective. (2015, January 25). Retrieved July 31, 2016, from https://xfrcollective.wordpress.
    com/.
Yaco, S., Jimerson, A., Anderson, L. C., & Temple, C. (2015). A web-based community-building
    archives project: A case study of Kids in Birmingham 1963. *Archival Science, 15*(4), 399–427.

EXHIBITING AMERICA: MOVING IMAGE ARCHIVES AND RURAL OR SMALL LIBRARIES

Jennifer L. Jenkins

ABSTRACT

This chapter presents a historical analysis of how rural and small libraries have traditionally used nontheatrical film, including a discussion of how bookmobiles presented these materials to persons in broader service areas. After establishing the entertainment and educational benefits patrons historically received from the screening of these materials, the author transitions to discuss how recently established regional film archives and other organizations have made significant strides in recent years in preserving motion pictures that document local and regional culture. The chapter concludes with an analysis of how rural and small libraries can work with regional motion picture archives to design screenings and other programs that fulfill traditional roles of entertaining and educating patrons while also reaffirming local cultural identity.

Summative research and archival sources provide the foundations for the discussion of the role and purpose of film in rural and small libraries. Specific libraries and collections serve as case studies.

Rural and Small Public Libraries: Challenges and Opportunities
Advances in Librarianship, Volume 43, 181–201
ISSN: 0065-2830/doi:10.1108/S0065-283020170000043008

- *Small-gauge motion pictures were popular with rural library and book-mobile patrons during the first three-quarters of the twentieth century, bringing entertainment and information to persons who normally had limited options in these areas due to geographic barriers.*
- *Regional film archives and nontheatrical film advocacy organizations have emerged during recent decades, collecting previously overlooked materials that can help reaffirm local and regional culture.*
- *Several regional film archives have already collaborated with rural and small libraries as well as other local institutions, providing a road-map for libraries that wish to expand their cultural-heritage-oriented programming.*

Numerous scholars have published studies on regional and local nontheatrical film in recent decades, but relatively little has been written to connect these films with their value to rural public libraries and their constituents. By beginning with a historical analysis of how films have traditionally been of value to these audiences, the author is able to transition to presenting ideas on how nontheatrical works can continue to be of value in rural contexts. This has practical applications for rural libraries and other rural cultural organizations throughout the United States.

Keywords: Nontheatrical film; orphan films; home movies; bookmobiles; rural libraries

Movie night has long been a draw for rural and small public libraries as a way to get people in the door and to bring communities together in a shared experience. Before the proliferation of digital video and personal viewing devices, small and rural libraries—like their urban cousins—served as venues for educational, industrial, and sometimes even feature film exhibition on 16 mm. In the twenty-first century, small libraries have continued to be sites of exhibition, although the content has changed to young adult (YA) adaptations, retro-oldies film series, youth and community media projects, and Home Movie Day celebrations. Regional film archives have shared and supported small libraries' community-based mission by preserving and promoting local culture on audiovisual media. Indeed, dedicated regional film archives, historical societies, and state archives have become trusted repositories for local moving image history. As most small and rural libraries have no resources dedicated to the preservation of special materials, these regional archives serve a critical function. This chapter will examine the history of film use in rural libraries, followed by an exploration of a variety of regional film archives and their changing outreach, support, and inter-action with rural libraries in relation to the regional audiovisual historical record.

I. MOTION PICTURES BECOME PUBLIC LIBRARY MATERIALS

In her landmark 2005 essay, Elena Rossi-Snook charts the development of film collections in U.S. public libraries as loosely parallel to the growth of the motion picture industry in America. Some larger libraries actually installed 35 mm projectors when that was the dominant gauge in the first two decades of the twentieth century. The debut of the 16 mm format in 1923 popularized and made smaller-gauge film affordable as an educational and instructional resource. Up sprang an entire industry of nontheatrical moviemakers aimed at educational, industrial, church, school, and hobbyist audiences. Many such audiences in rural areas had their first exposure to small-gauge nontheatrical film at the local library. As Rossi-Snook explains,

> Public librarians were intrigued by the potential for using film as a means of expanding patronage and more efficiently developing literacy. If not promoting their own services, libraries worked with local movie theaters to advertise the use of books in conjunction with screenings. Encouraged by the body of work being produced during the documentary movement of the 1930s, librarians began using films within their own buildings to accompany discussion groups, and by the 1940s, film programming within the public library was used to present information on contemporary public issues (Rossi-Snook, 2005, p. 3).

Progressive librarians soon came to see film as simply another format of information equal to print: "It is just as much our obligation to provide these materials as the books, periodicals, maps and pictures we have included in our budgets for years. We must also use them with the same intelligence and respect" (Stevenson, 1956). Setting a high tone and a premium on inquiry, some librarians welcomed film into the library as an enhancement to collections. During the postwar period, urban libraries began to hire dedicated film librarians, and the professional literature debated the proper balance of film training to library science needed for such positions. As late as 1970, Paul Spehr, then the motion picture specialist at the Library of Congress, advocated for cross-training librarians and film scholars:

> Only students with individual initiative can obtain training in both fields and almost no
> effort is made to relate the two. Furthermore, should the library science student prepare
> himself for work with films, there is almost no possibility that there are jobs waiting for
> him. It seems axiomatic that if any program to provide the film scholar with library ser-
> vice is developed, it must be done by well trained professionals who have a background
> in the history, aesthetics, and some of the technology of the motion picture field (Spehr,
> 1970).[1]

People with knowledge of film history, aesthetics, and technology often
developed that training informally through clubs and hobbyist organizations. Film societies and cine clubs emerged very early in the lifespan of the
medium, usually in urban centers and among educated and privileged classes.
As Ben Davis describes, New York was the real epicenter of the 1930s film
societies, be their ethos aesthetic or agitprop:

> Over a decade after the first ciné-club appeared in Paris, both the Film Forum and the
> Film Society were founded [in New York] during January, 1933. The Film Society, whose
> first screening (at the Essex House on Central Park South) reflected its elitism... [while]
> the moving force behind the Forum was Tom Brandon, a founding member of the left-
> leaning Workers' Film and Photo League" (Davis, 1994).

However, such activity only flourished in urban centers during this time,
where the population was high enough to support it.

Rural constituencies, by their very geographic, economic, and demographic conditions, were often excluded from or denied access to such
activity. Yet rural librarians perceived early on the value of film screenings as the basis for education, discussion groups, and practical training.
Both the YMCA and 4-H distributed films to rural library networks, and
librarians in the 1930s and 1940s were developing programming around
demonstration films, "cine-tours," and film lectures presented by a doc-
umentarian narrating his or her own work (Czach, 2014; Rossi-Snook,
2005). In the first half of the twentieth century, urban and rural film exposure differed significantly in content and exhibition practice, the former
replicating salon culture of the eighteenth and nineteenth centuries and
the latter aligning with the grange hall and church groups. Rural libraries in some ways bridged the gap between cosmopolis and countryside by
offering Hollywood films as well as industrial and educational titles, all
in 16 mm formats that were easy to ship, handle, and project and called
for a relatively small initial investment in a projector, bulbs, and a screen
(Rossi-Snook, 2005).[2] Clearly, there was much overlap with rural schools,
as libraries and school districts pooled resources. But rural libraries offered
reference services to materials outside the local collection and sought films
other than classroom titles.

Libraries were a boon to rural amateur cinema enthusiasts. The hobbyist club was dedicated as much to making as to viewing motion pictures. For the hobbyist with access to a library, location was no deterrent. The rural cameraman could order equipment, film stock, and developing chemicals by mail. Advice from peers and experts came in the form of periodicals such as *Movie Makers*, the journal of the Amateur Cinema League from 1926 to 1954; *Better Home Movie Making*; and *Home Movies* (1934–1959). Most rural libraries offered some form of interlibrary loan, and specialist journals for local clubs were a priority. Even if rural and small libraries could not present their own film programs, they could support amateur filmmakers by locating information and providing space for club meetings and screenings. While the abovementioned periodicals were initially directed in tone to the gentleman cinematographer with his own film library and resources to spend on equipment, after World War II the tenor and content shifted to the citizen hobbyist of more limited means but equal creativity and tenacity.

II. STICKS NIX HICK PIX

Rural constituencies have long been more sophisticated than urban centers credit. In July 1935, *Variety* ran the now-iconic headline, "Sticks Nix Hick Pix," indicating pushback from rural audiences being fed corn-pone fare at their local movie houses. While most rural libraries did not present first-run Hollywood features, film librarians and librarians in general knew to program material with social value rather than condescending content. Advice to librarians in professional journals suggested programs that served American libraries' agenda of democratized access to information in its many forms. In a 1956 article in the *ALA Bulletin*, Grace T. Stephenson discussed "The Library Use of Films" as a unique adult niche apart from educational, sponsored, and children's programs: "They can provide factual information in many fields; they can portray and interpret all aspects of life and the world we live in; they are, themselves, one of the arts of our time" (Stevenson, 1956, pp. 213–214). Clearly, "hick pix" held no appeal in rural public libraries, where the mission was—and is—access and education with a civic purpose. In the following year, the *ALA Bulletin* reported that "films can serve small and out-of-the-way places—if the public library is part of a modern, cooperative film program" (Ellis, 1957, p. 713). The Missouri Libraries Film Cooperative, established in 1948, provided annual fee-based access to a catalog of "packets" of films on a variety of topics in different genres. Film packets were distributed in a "round-robin" method through the library system, like a cinematic chain letter, thus ensuring content availability and circulation throughout the region (Ellis, 1957). This kind of circuit, paralleling or presaging in some ways the function of the bookmobile or traveling exhibit, afforded patrons of rural and small libraries access to film programs similar to what their city cousins enjoyed.

Such was the state of film in rural and small libraries at midcentury. As Rossi-Snook (2005) details, the postwar period enjoyed a proliferation of 16 mm production and an influx of inexpensive military surplus projectors that fed the growth of film collections and programs in urban public libraries. Despite brief cultural lag, rural and small libraries benefitted as well. By the Kennedy era, library film collections were a reasonable expectation of many public library patrons in the United States, regardless of whether they lived in the country or the city. The progressivism of the 1960s also supported new filmmaking practices, thereby expanding the catalog of 16 mm offerings to include social justice, sociology, animation, experimental, and documentary films and representing a broader swath of society than previously documented. Nixon-era budget cuts curtailed library film expansion, but the rapid growth preceding the recession meant that most libraries or library systems had respectable film collections already in place by the mid-1970s.

III. RURAL LIBRARIES AND HOW THEY GREW

It is instructive to look at new rural libraries and their relationship to film at start-up. A 1959 report on the creation of a rural library system in central Washington state provides a good index of the mid-century professional understanding of library service priorities and rural user bases (Cutler, 1959). The five north-central counties served by the Columbia River Regional Library—Chelan, Douglas, Ferry, Grant, and Okanagan—experienced rapid growth in agriculture as a result of the Grand Coulee and four other dams on the Columbia River. In an area of 15,000 square miles on the dry side of the state east of the Cascades, only one county had any rural library access prior to the implementation of the project to expand services. Washington's State Library Commission tied this project—paid for by matching funds from the federal Library Services Act—to a popular and progressive public works program: the damming of the Columbia River for hydroelectric power and high desert irrigation of agriculture. Providing library service to the populations attached to this infrastructure project was a definable and achievable goal. Soon the new regional library system had "3 bookmobiles, 56,000 books, 900 record albums, and a staff of 8 librarians and 13 clerks" (Cutler, 1959, p. 669).

Notable within all this data is the fact that film gets its own callout: "Film service to the region is also operated through the regional centers. The demonstration [project] has joined a film circuit of twelve Washington libraries through which monthly packets of films are available to all the communities and citizens within the vicinity of each [subregional] center. Additional funds have been budgeted so that special films may be rented for specific needs" (Cutler, 1959, p. 670). Firm in their commitment that "all materials are available to all citizens of the area wherever they may live," the Columbia River Regional Library loaded up loaner films and projectors in the bookmobiles as often as they did bestsellers, general interest books, and special requests. Twenty-two years later, *Wilson Library Bulletin* reported on another small rural library in Washington state: the community-based creation in 1973 of a "rural area volunteer library" in unincorporated Wahkiakum County. On the mouth of the Columbia River, with a county population of 3,600, the Skamokawa (Washington) library by 1981 had a dedicated building, a book collection, paperbacks, interlibrary loan, reference services, volunteer tutoring in reading and French—and a "film borrowing service" (Martin, 1981, p. 440). Not much had changed from 1959 to 1981 in these rural Washington libraries in terms of collections, diversity of materials, user services, and access. Film was still a core aspect of collections.

On the other side of the country, the U.S. Department of Health, Education, and Welfare surveyed nine rural communities in Maine, Vermont, and New Hampshire in 1969 and issued a report, *Where the People Speak: The Role and Function of Rural Public Libraries in Northern New England*. This report examined many aspects of the role of libraries in rural communities, including the competition with school libraries, concerns about town-based funding, the independence and complexity of boards of trustees vis-à-vis town councils, and the like. Surveyors specifically asked residents about inclusion and expansion of film in library collections. Fifty percent of respondents agreed that "The library should have films on a regular basis or have special film programs" (U.S. Department of Health, Education, and Welfare, 1969, p. 160). Audiovisual materials were ranked sixth out of nine suggestions for collection development (U.S. Department of Health, Education, and Welfare, 1969, p. 225). Seventy-four percent of the users in favor of film were "younger" people—presumably born after World War II—many of whom had familiarity with 16 mm films from classroom and training films. The report comments, pointedly, on the role of public libraries in residents' access to film:

It should be noted that in some of these rural towns, the library represents the only opportunity for the inhabitants of the area to be exposed to films. In some cases, it is

> many miles to the nearest large town, college or similar institution where such films might be available. In these cases, the library would be able to fill the need for recreational and educational films.
>
> The introduction of film programs in rural libraries would serve many purposes. Educational enrichment would be put within the range of the inhabitants. Supplemental programs could be implemented for school children (U.S. Department of Health, Education, and Welfare, 1969, p. 238).

The librarians surveyed largely concurred but lacked the equipment to show the films that were offered by the state or regional library system (U.S. Department of Health, Education, and Welfare, 1969, pp. 234–235). New England's traditions of town-council governance aside, this survey seems to indicate not just a regional but a national condition for rural libraries at the end of the 1960s. Film was viewed as desirable but nonessential material by rural constituents in general, while librarians and progressive, younger users viewed them as not just desirable but necessary.

IV. ON THE ROAD: FILM IN THE BOOKMOBILE

While numerous mid-century rural libraries participated in film cooperatives or group-rental circuit services, these efforts were mainly directed at serving the individual user's request for a specific title or implementing film-based programming in the rural library building. Bookmobiles commonly delivered films and projectors, along with other library materials, to rural patrons for home or club use. By the 1950s, however, the heyday of the bookmobile, some libraries were sending film programs out to their rural constituents in their own venues.

For example, the Warren (PA) *Times Mirror* reported in June 1950 that "The Bookmobile Committee of the Friends of the Warren County Library is getting many requests from granges to show the Bookmobile films at their meetings" ("Bookmobile film to show at Scandia," 1950, p. 5). The article notes that "the free sound motion pictures" begin at 9 p.m. in various grange halls and are open to the public. Also in 1950, the Green Bay *Press-Gazette* reported the "vital" role of bookmobiles in bringing visual materials to rural schools. "It didn't take long for the enterprising Brown County Teacher's Association to realize that here, too, was the answer to one important phase of a comprehensive visual aids program in the county system—that is distribution." The county allocated 10% of bookmobile funds to purchase film materials, and the "teachers dug down into the association pocket and donated two projectors and two screens themselves." The reporter notes that "all 34 of the schools in the southern portion of the county are taking advantage of the program. These include one-room schools, state-graded schools, and parochial schools" (Lee, 1950, p. 20). The collaboration between the library system and the rural teachers' association illustrates the forward-thinking nature of both librarians and teachers in serving the rural populations and keeping up-to-date with film materials.

Films could also help make the case for establishment of new rural libraries. In 1952, the bookmobile was being "demonstrated" by Rhinelander, Wisconsin, librarian Dorothy Whittaker to "show what it would be like to have a regional library and a permanent bookmobile in the area" of Oneida and Vilas counties. The story goes on to point out that "A regional library set up in the two counties would offer more services than just the bookmobile. Maps, films, and other items would also be handled in such a library" ("Bookmobile to be demonstrated here in October," 1952, p. 7). Clearly, moving image materials were considered part of regular library service by the time bookmobiles were available to carry them to rural constituents.

Films were viewed as complementary to "regular" book-based library services. The Fitchburg (WI) Public Library instituted a program of taking movies to children in hopes of encouraging readership (Hyatt, 1958; Ottwein, 2013). Films with book tie-ins were rear-projected from within the bookmobile and seen on a screen covering the rear window of the vehicle. The same kind of rear-projection programming was used by Denver Public Library, beginning in 1969, to meet needs of Spanish-speaking constituents. Films were shown in city parks in Spanish-speaking neighborhoods. As a program of the San Joaquin Valley (CA) Library System, La Biblioteca Ambulante showed Spanish-language films, mainly popular Spanish-dubbed Disney films, for migrant workers and Mexican communities in Fresno, California, in the 1970s. Focused on service to migrant grape-picking populations, the bilingual staff went door to door to explain the bookmobile and brought bilingual and Spanish-language books, records, and movies into the communities. Patrons could register without ID, and there were no fines or overdue notices. The bookmobile announced itself with Herb Alpert's *Spanish Flea* played on loudspeakers, as many mobile businesses do in Latin America (Ottwein, 2014). In all of these examples, library staff seems to have been motivated by a commitment to underserved populations and the professional tenet of "access for all."

V. LIFE CYCLE OF A MEDIUM: ADVENT OF VIDEO

In 1982, *American Libraries* reported on a survey of administrators of 63 public library film collections in which film use was quantified. Nearly all participants reported that their film demand was increasing, although budgets were static or decreasing and audiovisual librarian positions were being cut. Interestingly, survey participants indicated that they saw no threat to the 16 mm film collection from video: "Videocassette and film borrowers are different clienteles. Groups, often large in size, tend to use film. Video borrowers usually are individuals interested in home entertainment" (Palmer, 1982, p. 142). The distinction between information-based and documentary content on 16 mm film and entertainment-based content on emerging consumer formats such as VHS is nicely articulated here. As we all know, the flood of inexpensive VHS and Beta tapes utterly changed U.S. viewing habits, led to a surge of production for direct-to-video markets, and spawned new formats (laserdisc, DVD), which themselves ultimately fell to streaming video services and personal media access devices in the new millennium. The nonfiction content that was traditionally available on 16 mm still is so, as evidenced by the vibrant circulating 16 mm collection at the New York Public Library (NYPL) and the revival of 16 mm as a legacy format in college library collections.

This is not a discussion of the death of film. Indeed, some public libraries became de facto film archives by dint of format recession and the budgetary shift to magnetic and then digital media. Most notable is the large—and still circulating—16 mm collection in the Reserve Film and Video Collection at the NYPL. It is a living collection, not an archive, but functionally it has preserved a swath of film history: 6,000 titles on film to date (Reserve film and video, 2017). The same is true with the Enoch Pratt Free Library in Baltimore: it maintains a collection of over 2,000 films, many with content not available in other formats. Unlike NYPL, Enoch Pratt does not offer projectors for checkout, somewhat limiting usership to self-selected film aficionados (About our 16 mm film collection, 2017). Both of these urban collections operate on a passive "preserve and project" model.

Passive preservation has come to be celebrated as a boon to film history and format retention. Small and rural libraries, many constrained by local tax-based funding, have maintained their film collections, even as new(er) media joined their collections. What could have been a widespread purge by format, as happened to local newspaper collections (Baker, 2002), became passive preservation by dint of limited resources and remote locations. Locally made material can often be found within rural and small library collections. These films survive as a direct result of what is usually viewed as a problem: lack of resources. Limited library hours; limited staff time for weeding; the need to move forward with programs, outreach, and new titles—all of these considerations have kept some moving-image collections in amber, so to speak, and thereby saved from the dumpster. And from these small and rural libraries, local treasures can emerge. Discovery or rediscovery and public screening of long-unseen local material can foster community pride; create opportunities to engage with different user constituencies and sectors of the population; and forge collaborations among libraries, historical societies, historical preservation groups, and local boosters.

VI. NORTHEAST HISTORIC FILM

Film can document and preserve evidence of lives lived as well as provide communities with a dynamic link to their own history. The now-venerable film archive, Northeast Historic Film (NHF) in Bucksport, Maine, provides a well-documented example of regional film preservation and impact at a time when the public believed that film was dying or dead. The series of events that led to the founding of NHF began with David Weiss and Karan Sheldon's resuscitation in 1984 of Alfred Ames' 16 mm black and white film *From Stump to Ship* (1929–30). The rediscovery of this film sparked an early preservation initiative along with a legendarily successful outreach effort to communities across the state of Maine. The trajectory of this one film led to the founding of a regional film archive, raised regional awareness in the 1980s of the value of film as historical record, and foregrounded amateur film as a viable and important aspect of regional collection. NHF, now in its 30th year, serves as a repository and resource for community media, both film and video, across northern New England.

As Jones (2005) describes, *From Stump to Ship* served as a point of convergence for film awareness and community engagement with historic media. Shot by Alfred Ames, president of the Machias Lumber Company, the film documented the process of woodcutting, transport, milling, and shipbuilding without much mechanical intervention. The film was stored in various Ames family homes after its initial screenings during the political season of 1932. *From Stump to Ship* languished both before and after its donation in 1970 to the University of Maine at Orono. Through a series of university and regional connections, the film found its way to Karan Sheldon and David Weiss, both experienced television producers who had newly relocated from Boston to the Downeast region of Maine. Only in 1984 did the film re-emerge through the efforts of University of Maine faculty, Weiss and Sheldon, and a grassroots network of exhibition sites. The film was then—and is now—hailed as a local record of woodsmen, camp culture, and a way of life that was rapidly chang-ing in nearly millennial Maine. Jones writes that the film captured a world on the brink of change: "The woods life that Ames captured on film had changed little during the 150 years prior to the making of *From Stump to Ship* ... Ames was filming the lumber industry at a critical and transitional period in Maine's history, for the age of heavy machinery was beginning to reach the woods" (Jones, 2003, p. 195). Weiss and Sheldon researched and wrote a Maine Humanities Council grant, funded in 1985, for the preservation and restoration of the film to a format that could be exhibited. Building on Maine Humanities Council funds and a match from the university, they secured a large grant from Champion International, a paper company. This array of funding sources generated broad buy-in from Maine constituents and a sense of ownership of the film as a Maine treasure. After the final 28 minutes of film were assembled, a voiceover was recorded from Ames' original presenta-tion script by Tim Sample, a Boothbay Harbor native familiar with Maine dialects and locutions. Once the audio and visual tracks were merged, the film was ready for distribution.

The Maine Humanities Council grant required expanded access to the project and interpretation by scholars. Thus, *From Stump to Ship* went out across the state with a viewer guide containing a map, essays by the involved scholars, and historic photographs to set context for understanding the film as historical artifact as well as historic film. David Weiss remembers the intense local interest in the film during that first exhibition tour in 1985: "We showed it at least 25–30 times, getting crowds like 1,100 to the premiere in Orono, 600 in Farmington, 800 in Machias, 500 in Bethel, etc. Some crowds were smaller, usually because the screening hall was smaller. We did have library sponsors but maybe more historical societies. Sometimes [we had] multiple sponsors and then showed it in the school auditorium" (personal communication, August 18, 2016). While such projects happen with some regularity in the twenty-first century, in the late 1980s this was a groundbreaking initiative that set the standard for subsequent preservation and access projects in regional archives. As Jones explains, the effect of this reanimation was profound:

> While just its recovery is culturally significant, the critical factor in *From Stump to Ship's* widespread popularity is that the film was made deliberately accessible to the people of Maine. While some archival films are carefully protected and seen only by archivists and scholars within a controlled environment, *From Stump to Ship* broke free from the archi-val setting and went on the road. Viewed by thousands of people from various socioeco-nomic backgrounds in cities and small towns across the state of Maine, the film helped

to foster a collective memory of woods life. It also helped to publicly commemorate the
work of early twentieth century woodsmen, enhance a sense of regional identity and
increase interest in Maine history (Jones, 2003, p. 193).

The impact of this film was such that it was nominated and accepted to the
Library of Congress' National Film Registry in 2002. It continues to be
screened around Maine with some regularity and is taught as an example of
successful non-Hollywood, grassroots preservation in U.S. and U.K. college
film studies courses on nontheatrical film. It is held in libraries in small U.S.
towns such as Wrangell, AK (pop. 2,400), Carthage, TX (pop. 6,854), Clifton
Forge, VA (pop. 3,884), Port Hadlock, WA (pop. 3,476), Kirksville, MO (pop.
17,500), and a number of small college towns outside New England with
historic connections to logging, mainly in the Pacific Northwest and Rocky
Mountain states.[3]

NHF has continued to serve rural Mainers and New Englanders. A
state-of-the-art conservation center opened in 2004, and an archival storage
consortium of nonprofit film organizations began depositing collections that
same year. By preserving and streaming local film from across the region,
NHF has expanded access to these films nationally and internationally. The
"Movie Queen" films, shot in small towns in Maine in the 1930s, afford
glimpses of local businesses and town notables. These one-reel 16 mm films
rely on a fictional premise of a hometown "movie queen" who returns
for a visit to the key sites and sights of the village. Footage captures the
daily life of Depression-era Maine towns and their activities. *Movie Queen
Lubec*, for example, takes place in the easternmost point of Maine, on the
Bay of Fundy, and shows its contemporary industry: sardine fishing and
canning. Product placement is rampant, with strategic shots of signs—
"Bear-In-Mind the Lube Drug Store," "Pike's Market," "R.J. Peacock
Canning Company"—and clerks proffering wares to the camera. Sturdy
female cannery workers file past the camera, smiling or hiding their faces
in coats. These casual shots of hometown folks allow twenty-first century
descendants to see their relatives in action as they lived their lives. Similarly,
Cherryfield, 1938 captures the small Maine town's architecture, town plan,
leading merchants and citizens, church, and school. The finding aid notes
that "The Cherryfield-Narraguagus Historical Society has identified every
person in the film except one baby in a stroller" (Cherryfield, 1938, 2017).
Streaming links are accessible in small libraries throughout the state, and
indeed the world, on the NHF website. As originally launched, NHF's
outreach efforts focused on Maine K-12 education, specifically social
studies and history curricula, in collaboration with the Maine Humanities
Council (Roundtable 3, 2004). Such programs could be replicated through

and hosted at small and rural libraries, as the original screenings of *From Stump to Ship* illustrated.

VII. TEXAS ARCHIVE OF THE MOVING IMAGE

With a similarly regional focus in a wholly different part of the country, the Texas Archive of the Moving Image (TAMI) has developed a collection of over 30,000 Texas-related films through a traveling program of free digitization. TAMI accepts 16 mm, 8 mm, Super 8, VHS, VHS-C, Betacam SP, ¾"/U-Matic, and 8 mm/Hi8/Video8/Digital8 magnetic media (Texas Film Round-Up, 2010). The sole requirement of the free digitization of materials is a donor agreement to deposit a digital copy with TAMI. Original media are returned to owners. Film and video are collected in a traveling program called the Texas Film Round-Up, which sets up in local libraries or historic theatres and screens collection highlights and local material. The nonprofit, founded by Caroline Frick in 2002, operates on a "catch-and-release" model of preservation:

> The Texas Film Round-Up provides FREE digitization for Texas-related films and videos in exchange for the donation of a digital copy.... The program is open to home movies, advertisements, local television, community films, and more. ... To qualify for free digitization, participants must be willing to donate a digital copy of their materials to TAMI's archive, a digital collection at texasarchive.org (Texas Film Round-Up, 2010).

Visiting towns like Nacogdoches, Amarillo, Galveston, and Abilene as well as larger urban centers, the Texas Film Round-Up provides a spotlight on local film(ed) history and encourages awareness of film as cultural patrimony through home movies, industrial films, educational films, advertisements, local television, feature films, student films, and community video projects. An example of the local treasures found comes from Nacogdoches, a town of 33,000 in central east Texas near the Louisiana border. The Round-Up, held at the Judy B. McDonald Public Library, brought out a reel that had been saved by a local high school assistant principal during a school renovation in the early 1960s:

> "Nacogdoches 1938" is important to moving image history for several reasons. The first is that it still exists. Luckily, Mr. DuBose chose to save it from disposal in the 1960s and then acted as a protective guardian for the following decades. Because film is impermanent and requires storage in a controlled archival environment to prevent decomposition, the stable condition of this film is also remarkable. Seventy-five years after this film was made, we were able to rescue it and allow its content to be watched by new eyes.

> The other reason this film is noteworthy is the amount of community history it captures—not only its citizens, but Main Street, businesses, factories, and schools. Some of the buildings in the film still stand, and some of the descendants of the residents in the film still live in the area. This film truly captures the life in Nacogdoches in 1938 for certain parts of the community (Spotlight on Nacogdoches, 2015).

Along with educating the public about the value of those long-shelved moving images in the back of the cedar closet or storage shed, the Round-Up specifically targets Texas's moving image history across film gauges, formats, and decades. Screening such materials in their local communities instills interest in local history and pride in communities and often sends viewers and enthusiasts to the local library for further research. A 2016 Round-Up in Galveston (pop. 48,000) asked the celluloid question, "What does Waikiki Have that Galveston Doesn't?" and showcased film from the 1931 Pageant of Pulchritude, all at the Rosenberg Public Library—incidentally the oldest continuously operating library in Texas (Texas Film Round-Up comes to Galveston, 2016).

VIII. RECLAIMING FILM

Twenty-first-century interest in legacy media as historical documentation and as kitsch has led to both institutional and individual collection of small-gauge film produced by amateur filmmakers. Large collecting institutions, such as TAMI, the Pacific Film Archive, and of course the Library of Congress, hold home movie collections. The Center for Home Movies hosts small collections on their website, and the Internet Archive hosts over 1,400 home movies (Center for Home Movies, 2017; Home Movies, 2017). Rural and small libraries, or libraries attached to rural historical societies, may find local film in their collections; often, these records simply take up shelf space due to the absence of playback technology, knowledge of projector operation, and familiarity with formats. There is nothing to fear here. Older community members and retro-fixated millennials alike love to tinker with older machines and get them working. Makerspaces can host repair and operation workshops and can use 3D printers to create replacement parts for legacy machines. Local content that may only exist in legacy formats may then be brought back into public view as a matter of public pride.

It is a truism that film lasts longer than other audiovisual media if stored in relatively benign conditions. Because of its durability, film is still considered the optimal preservation medium. While digitizing can be expensive and far outside the scope of small and rural library budgets, grants are available from state humanities councils, and donors can often be found to sponsor preservation of films with historical and local significance.

Indeed, the National Film Preservation Foundation (NFPF) provides grants for historically significant films to be restored and printed to new film elements, with digital access copies. A quick perusal of the list of films preserved by NFPF since 2000 indicates that, as they say, "The National Film Preservation Foundation has supported film preservation projects at 284 organizations in all 50 states, the District of Columbia, and Puerto Rico" (Awarded Grants, 2017). Home movies have been preserved, as have local and regional films, among them Northeast Historic Film's *Maine Marine Worm Industry* (1942) and numerous home movies from New England. As these and the following examples illustrate, amateur film captured information that no other medium did. It is a window into the past.

In addition to being a preservation medium itself, film can also document and thus preserve small and rural library history. The Willie Lee Buffington amateur film collection, held at the University of South Carolina's Moving Image Research Collection, records a faith-based initiative to establish libraries in underserved, segregated, rural black communities in Georgia and South Carolina in the early 1950s. Preserved by a National Film Preservation Foundation grant in 2015, the six reels of Mr. Buffington's personal home movies of Faith Cabin Libraries show collection development through mailed donations from across the country and distribution by Jeep. They also show black children in their own rural communities of clapboard houses and dirt streets: children approach the camera with interest and comfort, read aloud, and play and stand in front of their schools in this empathic and rare footage. Lydia Pappas, assistant director and curator of the Moving Image Research Collections at South Carolina, comments, "These films show communities working together to improve the lives of others during a difficult time in American history, and provide rare moving images associated with the education and library services for African Americans in the South" (Faith Cabin Library, 2017).[4] These films provide precious images of midcentury progressive library practice as well as of an under-documented community not often shown in amateur film. In addition, the films show those citizens as readers, reinforcing the message of libraries and democracy. As documents of African-American life in the segregated South, these moving images show lived lives and culture in ways that still images can only approximate. The dynamic nature of the moving image allows us to reach across time into these communities. The discovery of such material affords the opportunity for oral history projects, community-based archiving, and further embedding of the library within the small or rural community it serves.

IX. HOME MOVIE DAY

Home Movie Day, started by a group of small-gauge film enthusiasts in 2002, now has worldwide reach and annual screening celebrations in eight countries. Billed as a celebration of amateur filmmaking and citizen moviemakers, Home Movie Day events screen "bring-your-own" films in 8 mm, 16 mm, Super 8, and, in some locations, VHS. These small-gauge moving images offer a glimpse into distant worlds: family celebrations and vacations, the first day of school, marching band performances, school plays, weddings, christenings, birthdays, soldiers on leave and on the battlefield, protests, marches, and people at work. What is common among these moving image records is their capture of real people doing real things, as in Morton Savada's film of Halloween 1958 (2017). More so than still images, these films show how people moved, laughed, gestured while talking, carried themselves and their babies, and mugged for the camera. As an example, a common shot in home moves is the mom turning away from the camera with a laughing "oh, I look awful" gesture. The commonality of these films is such that Home Movie Day offers bingo cards for people to spot license plates, tractors, wagons, rocking horses, cats, dogs, goats, cacti, beach umbrellas, and other ephemera of mid-century daily life.

Of course, some amateur filmmakers went beyond turning on the camera just to capture family events. A sector of the amateur filmmaking population also wrote and directed their own fictional films, often based loosely on the style of Hollywood productions. Even these scripted films have a do-it-yourself quality to them, as in Musgrave Hyde's 1932 mummy picture, *A Dream* (2017). As popular history, these documents are priceless. As cultural memory, they offer windows into worlds somewhat unimaginable to twenty-first century viewers, even with the media saturation we enjoy. The Center for Home Movies (CHM), a nonprofit preservation and education entity, initially produced DVDs of the "best of" submissions from Home Movie Day locations. In 2013, they decided to take the project online, and now the Home Grown Movies site posts entries from around the world (Home Grown Movies, 2013). Anyone, from public and local libraries to book clubs and local student media clubs, can sponsor a Home Movie Day. Public libraries provide natural settings for such an event, as do historical societies and local museums. A "Saturday Morning at the Movies" theme can bring people in; one Home Movie Day showed a mashup of 1970s commercials before the local material began. The CHM can also provide examples of local moving image material to alert sponsors and attendees alike about what to look for.[5]

In the United States, many Home Movie Days are held in public libraries and serve as a means of building or identifying collections of citizen media. The University of Georgia reported in 2006 that they held three Home Movie Day events, in Athens, Butler, and Columbus, Georgia. The Athens event was held at a public library rather than on the University of Georgia campus due to the good location and parking. The Butler, Georgia (pop. 1,779) event was hosted by a library board member. Ruta Abolins, director of the Media Archives & Peabody Awards Collection at the University of Georgia, reported: "The highlight of the event was listening to all the people in the audience commenting on community members in footage that was over 50 years old, especially the 2-year-old spraying his relatives with water from a hose who is currently the sheriff" (Home Movie Day News, 2017). Another library board member hosted the Home Movie Day in Columbus, paying for a theatre venue at the Columbus Museum. Abolins notes the highlight of the event: "This was also the venue where we got our first lot of African-American-taken home movies. A Mr. Thomas had seen the morning news report on TV and brought his Super 8 films from the early 1970s—a wedding, July 4th, his family, and trips to London, Acapulco, and Florida. He was there early and stayed for nearly the entire event. He also ended up donating some of his films" (Home Movie Day News, 2017). As the University of Georgia examples show, film-on-film is alive and finding audiences in rural as well as urban venues, often sponsored by libraries, library trustees, and librarians.

X. CONCLUSION

Library Journal's Best Small Library in America award, founded in 2005 and co-sponsored by the Bill and Melinda Gates Foundation, recognizes libraries serving populations below 25,000 (Berry, 2016). A survey of the decade's worth of winners and special mention sites indicates that in twenty-first century small and rural libraries media engagement persists, adapted to digital dimensions. Book groups include movies screenings; adult programs schedule documentaries and discussion groups; YA programs center on digital storytelling, filmmaking and editing. While these are not your grandparents' 16 mm educational film and cine-club experiences, the fact remains that small and rural libraries have always been—and continue to be—points of access to the moving image in its many dimensions beyond (and including) Hollywood movies.

At the very least, film programming—in whatever exhibition format—sustains and enriches rural and small library communities. Larry Grieco, director of the Gilpin County Public Library in Black Hawk, Colorado (pop. 5,000), places screenings at the top of his programming list: "Film showings can afford a shared experience to a small group of people, who, immediately after viewing, are able to talk about what they just saw. And when you can get a local film critic or film buff to facilitate the discussion, it's even better.... We have had up to three five-part film series each year for the last ten years, with a noted film critic leading a discussion about each film (funded by the Friends of the Library)" (Greico, 2016).

The life cycle of film is an existential balance of the yin and yang of content and format. Some content still only exists on 16 mm or U-Matic or Beta-cam, and many rural libraries hold local history in those formats. Unlocking that content through digital transfer is one way to reclaim local visual content. As access expands across the digital divide, small and rural libraries have become conduits for popular media delivery as well as of "analog" or "legacy" archival, local, and public domain material. Artists, book groups, youth groups, students, workforce returners, caregivers, and seniors all access media through local libraries. It behooves local libraries to meet those needs without fear of format and to embrace of the magic of the moving image in its many forms.

NOTES

1. It is worth noting that dedicated training programs for film archivists were only developed in 1996, the Jeffrey L. Selznick School at the George Eastman House (now Museum), and in 2002: the Moving Image Archiving Program (MIAP) at New York University and Moving Image Archive Studies at UCLA. Spehr's prescient recommendations are now routinely followed by graduate students with "individual initiative" in Library Science who have an interest in film, and those in Film Studies who have an interest in archives, including several authors in this volume.

2. Rossi-Snook reports the cost of 35 mm projector at $225 in the late Teens and early Twenties; by the early 1930s, with a decade of 16 mm production and reductions of 35 mm silent titles from the early days of Hollywood, new projectors cost around $200, while a purchase from the lively second-market could run one quarter of that. See, for example, ads in *Movie Makers*, Dec. 1935. https://archive.org/details/moviemakers10amat.

3. Worldcat listings may be found at: https://www.worldcat.org/title/from-stump-to-ship/oclc/14290272&referer=brief_results.

4. For more on African-American libraries and access, see Knott, C. (2015). *Not Free, and Not For All: Public Libraries in the Age of Jim Crow*. Studies in print culture and the history of the book. Amherst: University of Massachusetts Press.

5. More information about planning a Home Movie Day, along with a step-by-step guide and downloadable bingo cards, may be found at: http://www.centerforhomemovies.org/host/ and http://www.centerforhomemovies.org/documents/.

REFERENCES

About our 16 mm film collection. (2017). Retrieved from Enoch Pratt Free Library http://www.
    prattlibrary.org/locations/sightsandsounds/index.aspx?id=5627

Awarded Grants. (2017). Retrieved from National Film Preservation Foundation website https://
    www.filmpreservation.org/nfpf-grants/awarded-grants

Bookmobile film to show at Scandia. (1950, June 20). *Warren Times Mirror*, p. 5. Retrieved from
    Newspapers.com

Bookmobile to be demonstrated here in October. (1952, April 30) *The Rhinelander Daily News*,
    p. 7. Retrieved from Newspapers.com

Baker, N. (2002). *Double fold: Libraries and the assault on paper*. New York, NY: Vintage.

Center for Home Movies. (2017). Retrieved from http://www.centerforhomemovies.org/.

Cherryfield 1938. (2017). Retrieved from Northeast History Film website http://oldfilm.org/con-
    tent/cherryfield-1938-1

Cutler, D. (1959, September). Pioneering library service in Washington State. *ALA Bulletin*,
    53(8), 667–673.

Czach, E. (2014). A thrill every minute! Travel-adventure film Lectures in the Post-War Era. In G.
    Cammaer & Z. Druick (Eds.), *Cinephemera: Archives, ephemeral cinema, and new screen
    histories in Canada* (pp. 73–93). Montreal & Kingston: McGill-Queens University Press.

Davis, B. (1994). Beginnings of the film society movement in the U.S. *Film History*, *24*(3–4),
    7–26.

Ellis, S. (1957, October). The A-V circuit. *ALA Bulletin, 51*(9), 713–714.

Faith Cabin Libraries – Buffington – home movies. (2017). Retrieved from University of South
    Carolina Moving Image Research Collections website http://mirc.sc.edu/islandora/object/
    usc%3A2528

Grieco, L. (2012, July 10). The rural library as the focal point of learning and culture.
    Programming Librarian. Retrieved from http://www.programminglibrarian.org/articles/
    rural-library-focal-point-learning-and-culture

Home Grown Movies. (2013). Retrieved from Center for Home Movies website http://www.
    centerforhomemovies.org/home-grown-movies/

Home Movie Day News. (2017). Retrieved from Center for Home Movies website http://www.
    centerforhomemovies.org/category/home-movie-day-news/

Home Movies. (2017). Retrieved from Internet Archive website http://archive.org/details/home_
    movies&tab=collection

Hyatt, H. (1958, April). A unique use of the bookmobile. *Wilson Library Bulletin, 32*(8), 570–571.

Jones, J. (2003). From forgotten film to a film archive: The furious history of *From Stump to Ship*.
    Film History, *15*(2), 193–202.

Knott, C. (2015). *Not free, and not for all: Public libraries in the age of Jim Crow*. Studies in print
    culture and the history of the book. Amherst: University of Massachusetts Press.

Lee, J. P. (1950, February 17). Distribution of visual aids vital bookmobile sideline. *Green Bay
    Press-Gazette*, 20. Retrieved from Newspapers.com

Martin, I. (1981, February). Skamokawa story: Rural library service in Washington State. *Wilson
    Library Bulletin*, *55*(6), 440–442.

McCall, G. (1935, July 17). Sticks nix hick pix, *Variety, 119*(5), 1.

Morton S. H. 1958. (2017). Retrieved from Center for Home Movies website http://www.center-
    forhomemovies.org/morton-savada-halloween-1958/

Musgrave Hyde – A Dream. (2017). Retrieved from Center for Home Movies website http://www.centerforhomemovies.org/musgrave-hyde-a-dream/

Ortwein, O. (2013, August 20). Movies on the bookmobile. [Web log] Bookmobiles: A history. Retrieved from https://bookmobiles.wordpress.com/2014/02/22/el-numero-cinco-and-la-biblioteca-ambulante-taking-books-to-migrants/

Ortwein, O. (2014, February 22). El numero cinco and la biblioteca ambulante: Taking books to migrants. [Web log] Bookmobiles: A history. Retrieved from https://bookmobiles.wordpress.com/2013/08/20/movies-on-the-bookmobile/

Palmer, J. W. (1982, February). Mediatmosphere: The future of public library film service. *American Libraries, 13*(2), 140, 142.

Reserve film and video. (2017). Retrieved from New York Public Library website https://www.nypl.org/about/locations/lpa/circulating-collections/reserve-film

Rossi-Snook, E. (2005, Spring). Persistence of vision: Public library 16mm collections in America. *The Moving Image, 5*(1), 1–26.

Roundtable 3: Digital moving images in the classroom. (2004). Retrieved from Northeast Historic Film website http://oldfilm.org/content/roundtable-3-digital-moving-images-classroom

Spehr, P. (1970, April). Feature films in your library. *Wilson Library Bulletin, 44*(8), 848–851.

Stevenson, G. T. (1956, April). The library use of films. *ALA Bulletin, 50*(4), 211–214.

Spotlight on Nacogdoches! (2015). Retrieved from Texas Archive of the Moving Image website http://www.texasarchive.org/library/index.php?title=News:Spotlight_On_Nacogdoches

Texas film round-up. (2010). Retrieved from Texas Archive of the Moving Image website http://texasarchive.org/library/index.php/Texas_Film_Round-Up.

Texas film round-up comes to Galveston! (2016). Retrieved from Texas Archive of the Moving Image website http://www.texasarchive.org/library/index.php/News:Texas_Film_Round-Up_in_Galveston.

U.S. Department of Health, Education, and Welfare. (2006). *Where the people speak: The role and function of rural public libraries in northern New England.* Bedford, NH: Educational Research and Service Corporation.

RURAL AND SMALL LIBRARIES: THE TRIBAL EXPERIENCE

Jennifer L. Jenkins, Guillermo Quiroga (Yaqui), Kari Quiballo (Sioux), Herman A. Peterson (Diné), and Rhiannon Sorrell (Diné)

ABSTRACT

This chapter discusses some of the challenges faced by tribal libraries. Considering the information provided throughout the rest of this volume, it is clear that some of the core issues—such as poor broadband availability, difficulties in achieving economies of scale, and barriers to collaboration—are shared between tribal institutions and rural libraries throughout the United States.

The chapter presents a brief review of the literature on tribal libraries, establishing how they compare with rural public libraries in the United States. The remainder of the chapter is designed as a conversation piece, with responses from interviews with librarians from two tribal libraries detailing how the challenges faced by these outlets parallel those faced by America's rural libraries.

- *Tribal libraries face obstacles that are common among nontribal rural public libraries, such as poor broadband Internet availability, lack of funding, and geographic barriers that limit patron access.*

Rural and Small Public Libraries: Challenges and Opportunities
Advances in Librarianship, Volume 43, 203–218
Copyright © 2018 by Emerald Publishing Limited
All rights of reproduction in any form reserved
ISSN: 0065-2830/doi:10.1108/S0065-283020170000043009

- *Although public libraries exist in some tribal communities, other forms of libraries and cultural heritage institutions often fill the service roles that public libraries occupy in nontribal communities.*
- *Public-oriented information institutions in tribal communities commonly preserve and promote tribal heritage, often as one of their primary purposes. Considering that this is often achieved on limited budgets, further documentation of these efforts could be useful for guiding nontribal rural public libraries that wish to do more to preserve and promote their local cultural heritage.*

This study creates bridges between rural public libraries in the United States and tribal libraries, which are commonly studied as two separate phenomena. Although the authors document how these types of institutions differ from each other in significant ways, barriers of broadband access, geographic isolation, and lack of funding are common across both rural and tribal libraries. The information provided in this chapter shows that both types of institutions need solutions for similar problems.

Keywords: Tribal libraries; Native cultural heritage; rural libraries

This chapter takes the form of a conversation about tribal libraries and their roles in twenty-first century U.S. Native culture. In no way attempting to be exhaustive, it draws upon responses from Yaqui and Diné (Navajo) tribal libraries and museums. It provides a snapshot of two kinds of tribal libraries and how they developed, function, and serve their communities. The accompanying literature review provides context for the firsthand remarks.

Focused study of tribal libraries began only in the 1990s with the work of the estimable Lotsee Patterson (Comanche), founder of the American Indian Library Association (AILA). In 2014, Dr. Patterson recalled the history of tribal libraries: "Though there is no formal record of the first 'tribal library,' the Colorado River Tribal Council in Arizona established its own library in 1958. Tribal libraries serving the Mohawks of New York State and the Shoshone-Bannock of Fort Hall, Idaho, followed in the 1960s. In the 1960s, Vista volunteers placed small collections of donated books in tribal buildings" (Sampson, 2014, p. 26). While the first recognized tribal college was established as Navajo Community College in 1968, the library was a key component and is often cited as the first official tribal library. In 1991, Cheryl Duran assessed the role of libraries in the development and accreditation of tribal colleges in a longitudinal study of seven tribal colleges.

In the intervening 30 years, definition and recognition of tribal libraries and information repositories have expanded exponentially, and several university schools of information now offer a degree focus in tribal libraries.[1]

Within the context of tribal communities, a library can have many definitions and functions. Peterson (2004) describes it thus: "A tribal library can be a kind of public library for the community, an education and literacy center, as well as an archive that records and preserves the heritage of a tribe" (p. 129). This diversity of function speaks to the needs of diverse communities but can have a downside when it comes to funding: Peterson notes that tribal libraries that do not define themselves also as "public libraries" are often excluded from state or federal library funding initiatives, despite the very good reasons for knowledge keepers to protect some kinds of tribal information.

While not all tribal or Native community libraries are rural, the majority sit on Native land in Indian communities. Certainly in the western United States, libraries and information centers on tribal lands would be classified as rural and many as "small," although the supertextual and extratextual knowledge holdings are vast. As Patterson observed in 2008, the definition of "tribal library" is various and situationally specific. Some are small collections of books, others are large and plural collections of papers, material objects, and governmental and medical resources for community members. A library space is not defined by items on the shelves, but by the knowledge it shelters: "Tribal libraries serve as 'culture keepers' for tribal-specific history, culture, consortiums, and related information. They are not only expected to serve as centers of education and literacy, but also as archival hubs for the recording and preservation of tribal heritage" (Chen & Ducheneaux, 2017, p. 21). Indeed, the Alaska Division of Libraries, Archives, and Museums (2013) designates their workers as being engaged in the "culture-gathering professions."

In 1994 Patterson described the life cycle of some tribal libraries, observed for her *Directory of Native American Tribal Libraries*:

> I have witnessed more than one tribal library grow from a shelf of books in a hallway to a freestanding building specifically designed as a library. Some libraries that were in spacious facilities disappeared or faded into something else altogether. Sometimes they come back, sometimes they don't. This situation may depend on the interest or attitude of tribal administration, tribal finances, some other program needing or wanting the space, a lack of trained personnel to manage the library, or any number of other things that happen on reservations. Overall, tribal libraries have flourished since federal money, which provides a small but stable source of funding, became available to them in 1985 (Patterson, 2008, p. 8).[2]

A significant boost to tribal libraries came in 1997, with the formation of the Native American Library Services program under the Institute of

Museum and Library Services (IMLS), and in 1999, with the Bill and Melinda Gates Foundation Native American Access to Technology Program (Sirois, Gordon, & Gordon, 2001).[3] It is worth remembering, however, as Theresa Kappus of the Washington Library Association explains, "Because they serve independent sovereign nations, they are essentially national libraries and, as such, they get no funding from city, county, or state taxes" (Kappus, 2012, p. 7). Of course, tribal libraries receive grants from state and federal agencies, but they do not receive a portion of the local or federal tax base, as public libraries do, unless they are aligned or allied with the public library system. Funding remains the primary and constant challenge to tribal libraries, as Internet access demand grows and user expectations of libraries shift from a simple repository and information center to a multimodal access point to the digital world.

An accurate census of tribal libraries is nearly impossible to take at any point, as they fall under a variety of designations (library, museum, collection, archives) and entities (tribal, nation, community, band, pueblo). Data mapping is enormously complex. While the IMLS; AILA; Rural, Native, and Tribal Libraries (RNTL, through ALA); and the Association of Tribal Archives, Libraries, and Museums (ATALM) all maintain membership lists, there is no master roll of tribal-affiliated library-like institutions in the United States or North America. Yet common concerns are recognized and regular governmental reports, status reports in the professional literature, and blog posts keep the issues facing tribal libraries present and current (Jorgenson, Morris, & Feller, 2014; Khetarpal, 2016; American Library Association, 2008).[4] In 2011, a thoughtful collection of essays was published that dealt with applied practice and professional standards in concert with traditional knowledge systems: *Tribal Libraries, Archives, and Museums: Preserving Our Language, Memory, and Lifeways* (Roy, Bhasin, & Arriaga, 2011). This landmark collection of essays both serves as best-practices documentation and addresses the unique situation of managing information in a context in which language and information may be culturally sensitive or sacred. Additionally, the *Protocols for Native American Archival Materials* (2007) has become a standard part of the curricula for many Master of Library and Information Science (MLIS) programs, which have increasingly defined cultural competency as part of core graduation requirements.

Tribal libraries have also emerged as centers of cultural preservation through creative language recapture programs. The first-ever winner of the Best Small Library Award from *Library Journal* and the Bill and Melinda Gates Foundation was the Haines Borough Public Library, in Haines, Alaska.

Bordering on two Tlingit communities, the HBPL sought to partner with the Chilkoot Indian Association on the Dragonfly Project:

> The dragonfly is a Tlingit symbol for transformation. The project, funded by an Enhancement Grant for Native Americans from the U.S. Institute of Museum and Library Services (IMLS), teaches at-risk youth the skills and patience to become technology mentors and experts for the rest of the community, especially older folks not yet computer-literate. It works like a charm. Mentors, age 10 to 21, write curricula and develop classes and one-on-one sessions. They provide support for people, and HBPL lends laptops inside the building, which has wireless access. In its second phase, the project expanded to digital media and filmmaking. The DVDs and tapes produced, most about Native American culture, are now a popular part of the library's collection (Berry, 2005).

This is but one instance of the many, many ways in which tribes and libraries have partnered to preserve cultural heritage, language, and culture while bringing twenty-first century information tools to these tribal communities.

What follows is a snapshot of two different tribal libraries in Arizona. While the sample for this study cannot be said to be broad enough to represent the diverse circumstances of all tribal libraries, these discussions provide an invaluable, practical analysis of how the needs of and barriers to success for these institutions parallel and contrast with those of rural and small public libraries throughout the United States. As librarians and their supporters develop advocacy and action plans for rural and small outlets, the discussions below can help guide these stakeholders in understanding how they can include tribal libraries as part of these efforts. Likewise, as other chapters in this volume have discussed how rural public libraries and other information institutions can further engage with local cultural heritage, the efforts of tribal libraries to perform these functions with limited resources can provide valuable examples.

I. OLD PASCUA MUSEUM AND YAQUI CULTURAL CENTER, TUCSON, ARIZONA

The Old Pascua Museum and Yaqui Cultural Center sits in the (now) urban village of Old Pascua, within the original 40 acres bought by the Yaqui refugees from Mexico to establish the village (then) north of Tucson in the early 1900s. While independent of the tribal governance structure, the Old Pascua Museum and Yaqui Cultural Center functions like many tribal libraries, as a history and memory institution. Curator Guillermo Quiroga (Yaqui) shared his thoughts about the founding and nature of the Old Pascua Museum and its role as a preservation center of culture and knowledge for the community. He was interviewed by Kari Quiballo (Sioux), an archival intern from the Knowledge River program at the University of Arizona's School of Information.

II. TRAINING, EDUCATION, AND ADVOCACY: SUPPORTING PROFESSIONALISM IN RURAL LIBRARIES

Who founded your library, and when?

GQ: The San Ignacio Yaqui Council of Old Pascua Village in August of 2013. Old Pascua was the original settlement for tribal members who fled persecution in Mexico in the early 1900s. Refugees settled along the Santa Cruz River, then relocated to Old Pascua on land set aside by a benefactor. The building on the land set aside by the benefactor was used for many purposes, but transitioned into the Old Pascua Museum and Yaqui Cultural Center in August of 2013.

Is your library part of tribal government?

GQ: No, the 400-square-foot museum was originally a home built in the 1920s and willed to the San Ignacio Yaqui Council when the owner died. The San Ignacio Yaqui Council is a 501(c)(3) nonprofit and is independent from tribal governance. The museum's mission is to preserve and strengthen Yaqui culture and traditions. It is one of the earliest residences of Old Pascua and is listed on the National Register of Historic Places. Councils in the past had planned a museum but had never been able to realize this goal until 2013.

What was its original purpose or function (community, school, archive, meeting place, etc.)? Has that function changed, and how?

GQ: The original purpose was to strengthen the cultural traditions within the Yaqui community and share those with the non-Yaqui surrounding communities. The function is still the same.

What kind of training is expected in your library for the librarian, the reference desk, the aides?

GQ: This is a museum and cultural center. There is a curator, archivist(s), and different people working on multiple preservation projects. The curator has a degree in sociology and business. The archivists at the museum have MLIS and Master of Arts in Library and Information Science (MA-LIS) degrees. The preservation, decolonization, and indigenization work is through community projects involving other museums and their conservators and the University of Arizona Knowledge River archive students and graduates.

How does your library or library system support or encourage staff training?

GQ: Each person does research on new movements and professional practice in each of their professions and applies these when they are a fit to the mission of the museum and the people represented, the Yaqui of Old Pascua Village.

How does your library or library system advocate for your library, and to whom?

GQ: The curator does professional outreach, institutional outreach, and community outreach.

III. PARTNERSHIPS AND REGIONALISM: ENHANCING LIBRARY IMPACT THROUGH MEANINGFUL COLLABORATION

Does your library belong to a consortium or partnership with similar libraries? If so, which one(s)? What are the advantages/disadvantages of that?

GQ: No, but we do have museums with greater resources interested in projects meant to help us with preservation and conservation. Also, some of the archivists come from the University of Arizona's AILA-sponsored student organization. The students are also Knowledge River scholars in the School of Information at the University of Arizona, whose educational focus is advocacy for American Indian and Latino information issues in archives, libraries, and museums. Their volunteer work is a direct result of their professional focus and commitment to issues like the limited funding for much-needed projects in American Indian museums.

What is the focus of the consortium (i.e., collaborative training, group buying power, information sharing, professional development, sharing resources, other)?

GQ: Local museums are interested in the above-mentioned conservation of manuscript and photographic materials. Examples are the Angel Project from the Western Association of Art Conservation Annual Conference (WAAC), which will help bring more preservation and conservation professionals to our museum to help with ways to get donated equipment and other items necessary for preservation, and the work past and present AILA student members are doing.

What kind of activities do you collaborate on, formally or informally, with other librarians and libraries, even distant ones?

GQ: So far there is the Angel Project (WAAC), which is a photographic and multimedia preservation project. There is also a film project, where access to a 1972 National Geographic film has inspired "tribesourcing"[5] for the decolonization and indigenization of the film for the Yaqui museum's mission to strengthen and preserve Yaqui culture. This film project is also linked to the University of Arizona Information School and The Center for Education Resources in Culture, Language, and Literacy.

What kinds of activities do you collaborate on with other local institutions?

GQ: The community is linked in everything within itself for the benefit of the Old Pascua community. There are attempts to try to make sure everyone benefits from social cultural activities and grants and to include governing community members. Examples of community activities that take place at the museum are Old Pascua youth group meetings. The museum is also host to Wiko'i Ya'ura (Coyote Society) education and traditional dance practice. The director and curator, Guillermo "Bill" Quiroga, also created guidelines for handling Old Pascua's culturally sensitive material in museums that have Yaqui collections and distributed them to museums known to have Old Pascua intellectual property (Quiroga, 2016).[6]

Please describe your library's impact on the tribe or community.

GQ: The museum works toward its mission statement, and this impacts the community by strengthening and preserving the living Yaqui culture.

IV. THE RURAL INFORMATION ECOSYSTEM: BEYOND RURAL PUBLIC LIBRARIES

How would you define the "information ecosystem" in your library?

GQ: As a tribal information institution, the museum and cultural center is well known in its community. Also, Arizonans are aware of the history of the Yaqui escaping arrest and deportation by the Mexican government and joining family groups in residence in southern Arizona. There is a simple system of information flow. We are in the process of creating more access and community-created metadata and making digitized collections available to community members unable to leave their homes or living outside the community.

How do traditional knowledge systems (TKS) intersect with the library's information function?

GQ: The museum's mission is in preserving TKS for the community, and it is true to that mission.

V. SPECIFIC CHALLENGES: INNOVATION IN LIBRARIES

What is or has been the biggest challenge facing your library?

GQ: Funding and a need for materials to preserve the art, photos, and other materials of community and cultural significance.

Is change embraced or resisted by the staff? By the clients?

GQ: Growth is embraced and progress is embraced in terms of the museum, but a change in mission would be a change against the community and defy TKS and the cultural strengthening needed by the community.

What kinds of innovations do clients request?

GQ: Users want access to all of the museum's holdings.

What kinds of innovations do you want to implement?

GQ: The professionals want to and seek to create broad access for the community, especially those unable to physically travel to the museum.

VI. CHARLIE BENALLY KINYAA'ÁANI LIBRARY, DINÉ COLLEGE, NAVAJO NATION

At the start of the new millennium, Patterson (2002) reported that "the most promising trend in tribal library development is that of the emergence of tribal college libraries" (p. 23). She cites Diné College (initially Navajo Community College) as the bellwether and explains how tribal college libraries truly changed information access in Indian Country:

> In the last 25 years, tribally controlled colleges have grown from the first chartered by the Navajo Nation in 1968 to 24 in 2000. Each of them have a library and the pressure imposed by accreditation requirements assure that they receive an annual budget

sufficient to support staff, have an appropriately educated librarian and that materials adequate to support the college's curriculum be added to the collection. In 1994, the federal government granted these colleges land grant status which made them eligible for an annual appropriation from Congress. They serve the reservation as a public library. With educated personnel, stable funding and an annual acquisition budget these tribal college libraries are setting the pace for reservation libraries (Patterson, 2002, p. 23).

The following interview is with Dr. Herman A. Peterson (Diné) and Rhiannon Sorrell, MLIS (Diné), at the Benally Library at Diné College in Tsaile, Arizona.

VII. TRAINING, EDUCATION, AND ADVOCACY: SUPPORTING PROFESSIONALISM IN RURAL LIBRARIES

Who founded your library, and when?

HP: The library was founded when the college was founded, in 1968. The same people who founded the college also founded the library. The college moved to its current location in 1973, when the library building now in use was constructed.

Is your library part of tribal government?

HP: Not directly. The college has a charter from the Navajo Nation, and the members of the Board of Regents are appointed by the president of the Navajo Nation and confirmed by the Council. Otherwise, the college functions separately from tribal government.

What was its original purpose or function?

HP: Both the original and current purpose of the library is academic—we serve the students and faculty of the college. We also allow the community to use the library, but that is not our primary purpose.

What kind of training is expected in your library for the librarian, the reference desk, and the aides?

HP: We have four professional librarians who are expected to have a master's degree in library science. We also have seven paraprofessionals who are expected to have an associate's degree or at least five years of experience working in a library. Students are trained in-house according to their specific duties.

How does your library or library system support or encourage staff training?

HP: Professional librarians are allowed two conferences per year, paraprofessionals one.

How does your library or library system advocate for your library, and to whom?

HP: We advocate primarily to the administration of the college, but also through consortia such as the New Mexico Consortium of Academic Libraries and the Arizona Community College Library Consortium.

VIII. PARTNERSHIPS AND REGIONALISM: ENHANCING LIBRARY IMPACT THROUGH MEANINGFUL COLLABORATION

Does your library belong to a consortium or partnership with similar libraries? If so, which one(s)? What are the advantages/disadvantages of that?

HP: We are members of the New Mexico Consortium of Academic Libraries and the Arizona Community College Library Consortium, which is still in its infancy. The disadvantage is that we have locations in two different states, but the consortia draw lines at state borders.

RS: The advantages are that we have a greater amount of electronic resources for our students without straining our budget. Because we have a number of campuses (a total of six centers spread across the Navajo Nation), traveling to a center with a library can be an issue for our students. They have since embraced doing their research online using our electronic databases. The disadvantage stated above is also tied to the lack of broadband across the Navajo Nation. Our institution has changed service providers many times in an attempt to better our network. With this comes routine changes in IP addresses. We have to go through a lengthy process to update our IPs with the consortium vendors because our IPs are located in both Arizona and New Mexico.

What is the focus of the consortium (i.e., collaborative training, group buying power, information sharing, professional development, sharing resources, other)?

HP: Both consortia are focused on group buying power.

What kind of activities do you collaborate on, formally or informally, with other librarians and libraries, even distant ones?

HP: By far the most important collaboration for us is the Tribal College Librarians Institute, held every June at Montana State University. This event gathers all the tribal college librarians for continuing education, networking, and collaboration.

What kinds of activities do you collaborate on with other local institutions? Please describe.

HP: Our location is so remote that such collaborations are difficult. Mostly, we collaborate with other units within the college.

Please describe if you have formal measures of your library's impact on the tribe or community.

HP: In 2014, we conducted a library satisfaction survey, which gave us a base measure as a foundation for future improvement.

IX. THE RURAL INFORMATION ECOSYSTEM: BEYOND RURAL PUBLIC LIBRARIES

How would you define the "information ecosystem" in your library?

HP: Ours revolves around the Navajo culture, taking its cue from the mission of the college.

RS: The "information ecosystem" in our library still has its basis in word-of-mouth, storytelling, conversing, and preserving. Patrons (especially community users) seek information in face-to-face interactions rather than utilizing a catalog. Users usually prefer browsing rather than searching a specific question (e.g., browsing a section in the stacks rather than finding a specific book). Both the physical book and oral history (spoken) are considered the most authoritative resources.

Because of network connectivity issues, users are slow to adapt other "ecological systems" such as digital systems (with the exception of students at the nonlibrary centers who have limited physical access to the library).

How do traditional knowledge systems (TKS) intersect with the library's information function?

HP: The library collects and makes accessible all recorded traditional materials, whether they be published, manuscript, or audiovisual materials.

RS: The interaction of TKS with the library's information function is most evident in the approach to information literacy instruction. I have tried to implement the culturally relevant approach to research that was developed by Beatty (2011) in her book chapter "Empowering indigenous students in the learning library." This involves aligning the (former) Information Literacy Competency Standards of the Association of College Research Libraries (ACRL) with the Diné principles of Thinking (Nitsáhákees), Planning (Nahat'á), Living (Iiná), and Assuring (Siihasin). Given that the ACRL has recently rescinded these standards, I anticipate that I'll have to re-think the approach.

X. SPECIFIC CHALLENGES: INNOVATION IN LIBRARIES

What is or has been the biggest challenge facing your library?

HP: Access to a fast and reliable Internet connection. Deteriorating building and furniture.

RS: Definitely broadband issues. Because of this, many are reluctant to embrace computer and digital library innovations.

Is change embraced or resisted by the staff? By the clients?

HP: Resisted by paraprofessional staff and community users. Embraced by students.

What kinds of innovations do clients request?

HP: Open and free Wi-Fi access for all.

RS: A more do-it-yourself online framework. Many students are shy or have information anxiety and would prefer not to approach the helpdesk (even though we encourage them to seek help). Distance learners have also expressed interest in having more of these DIY innovations available for them.

What kinds of innovations do you want to implement?

HP: At this point, I just want to keep up-to-date.

RS: I want to follow the request put in by the distance learners and implement technologies and tools that will benefit our distance education stakeholders. I also want to encourage the use of digital indigenous resources. Most of the indigenous knowledge sought is through books and papers. I want to offer a digital space for these resources on a new webpage (which I am currently working on).

XI. CONCLUSION

Tribal libraries are a fast-growing sector of the information ecosystem and occupy an important place in the world of small and rural libraries. As we have seen, tribal libraries take many forms and serve many functions, from general library services to language and culture keeping. The perennial issue for tribal libraries is funding, with staff training and education a close second. But the vibrancy and commitment of the librarians and paraprofessionals make tribal libraries innovative, collaborative, and culturally affirming. The June 2017 issue of *American Libraries* reports on Judi Bridge (Winnebago), who returned to her hometown of Winnebago, Nebraska to be the Tribal Aide to Elders, a position co-sponsored by the Little Priest Tribal College and Winnebago Public Library (Ford & Hughes, 2017, pp. 26–27). Bridge recommends extending oral traditions through access to audiovisual materials and encouraging intergenerational interaction through storytelling and family reading programs. The authors note that circulation to older adults went from 0% to 27% in Bridge's first two years in the position. Bridge herself is quite modest: "They sure appreciate someone coming to see them." Bonnie Biggs, professor of library science at Cal State San Marcos, studies Southern California's reservation libraries, but her statement speaks a universal truth: "It wasn't until the early to mid-1970s that tribes began to develop libraries as we know them because most of their tradition was passed down orally," she said. "Tribal libraries now serve as the educational hub of the reservations. They're just absolutely critical" (Aguirre, 2004).

NOTES

1. Notably, the Tribal Libraries, Archives, and Museums Project (TLAM) at the University of Wisconsin-Madison iSchool (http://www.tlamproject.org/), and the Knowledge River program at the University of Arizona iSchool (https://ischool.arizona.edu/knowledge-river-0).

2. The information from this quote is drawn from Patterson, L. and Taylor, R. (1994). *Directory of Native American Tribal Libraries*. Norman, OK: University of Oklahoma.

3. The NAATP initiative placed computing equipment in 160 sites in the Four Corners states, Arizona, Colorado, New Mexico, and Utah, including 20 of the 21 tribes in New Mexico and all 110 Chapter Houses on the Navajo Nation.

4. Kheterpal's blog out of Alberta, Canada, "Expand Library Services for Indigenous Communities," is a vibrant and well-populated resource for anyone studying tribal and indigenous libraries.

5. This project was funded by a faculty grant from the Center for Educational Resources in Culture, Language and Literacy (CERCLL), a Title VI Language Resource Center at the University of Arizona. The term "tribesourcing" was coined by Jennifer Jenkins for an NEH-funded project to repatriate and record Native narrations of mid-century educational films about Native peoples of the Southwest.

The Yaqui National Geographic film was a pilot project of this initiative. http://cercll. arizona.edu/funding/researchgrant/recipients.

6. These guidelines are based on the Protocols for Native American Archival Materials, available at http://www2.nau.edu/libnap-p/protocols.html.

REFERENCES

Aguirre, A. A. (2004, March 2). Tribal library opens in Pauma. *San Diego Union-Tribune*. Retrieved from http://www.sandiegouniontribune.com/sdut-tribal-library-opens-in-pauma-2004mar02-story.html

Alaska Division of Libraries, Archives, and Museums. (2013). *Alaska native libraries, archives, and museums: Planning for training and education in the culture gathering professions.* Juneau, AK: Alaska Division of Libraries, Archives, and Museums. Retrieved from http://library.alaska.gov/pdf/anc/anlams/PlanReport4Web-final.pdf.

American Library Association. (2008). *Guide to building support for your tribal library.* Chicago, IL: American Library Association. Retrieved from www.ala.org/offices/sites/ala.org.offices/files/content/olos/toolkits/tribal_toolkit.pdf.

Beatty, V. (2011). Empowering indigenous students in the learning library. In Roy, L., Bhasin, A., & Arriaga, S. K. (Eds.). *Tribal libraries, archives, and museums: Preserving our language, memory, and lifeways* (pp. 131–140). Lanham, MD: Scarecrow Press, 2011.

Berry, J. N. III. (2005). Best small library in America 2005: Haines Borough Public Library, AK-The library Haines built. *Library Journal.* Retrieved from http://lj.libraryjournal.com/awards/best-small-library-in-america-2005-haines-borough-public-library-ak-the-library-haines-built/#_

Chen, M. H., & Ducheneaux, T. (2017) How are we doing in tribal libraries?: A case study of Oglala Lakota College Library using information visualization. *Library Management, 38*(1), 20–44.

Duran, C. (1991, September). The role of libraries in American Indian Tribal College development. *College and Research Libraries, 52*(5), 395–406.

Ford, A., & Hughes, C. (2017, June). Coming home, building community: Aiding elders on a Native American reservation. *American Libraries, 48*(6), 26–27.

Kappus, T. (2012, July). Sharing the stories of tribal libraries. *Washington Library Association Journal, 28*(2), 7–9.

Khetarpal, M. (2016, January 27). Current issues facing tribal college libraries. [Web log post]. Expand library services for indigenous communities. Retrieved from https://setuppubliclibrarywithfncommunity.blogspot.com/2016/01/current-issues-facing-tribal-college.html?m=0

Patterson, L. (2002). Tribal and reservation libraries. *Rural Libraries, 22*(1), 19–24.

Patterson, L. (2008). Exploring the world of American Indian libraries. *Rural Libraries, 28*(1), 7–12.

Patterson, L., & Taylor, R. (1994). *Directory of Native American tribal libraries.* Norman, OK: University of Oklahoma.

Peterson, E. (2004). Collection development in California Indian tribal libraries. *Collection Building, 23*(3), 129–132.

Protocols for Native American Archival Materials (2007, April 9). Retrieved from http://nptao.arizona.edu/sites/nptao/files/moving20image20best20practices20ltr20head-2.pdf.

Quiroga, G. (2016). Guidelines for the handling of culturally sensitive materials by or about the Yaqui / Yoeme / Hiaki. Old Pascua museum & Yaqui cultural center. Retrieved from http://nptao.arizona.edu/sites/nptao/files/moving20image20best20practices20ltr20head-2.pdf.

Roy, L., Bhasin, A., & Arriaga, S. K. (Eds.). (2011). *Tribal libraries, archives, and museums: Preserving our language, memory, and lifeways.* Lanham, MD: Scarecrow Press, 2011.

Sampson, Z. (2014). An interview with Dr. Lotsee Patterson, a founding member of AILA. *The Unabashed Librarian, 173*, 25–27.

Sirois, J. E., Gordon, M. T., & Gordon, A. C. (2001). *Native American access to technology program: progress report: A Report to the Bill & Melinda Gates Foundation Public Access to Computing Project.* Seattle, WA: University of Washington. Retrieved from https://ecfsapi.fcc.gov/file/7021706118.pdf.

INDEX

ABCD. *See* Asset-based community
    development (ABCD)
Academic
   librarians, 3
   paraprofessional, 134
Access networks, 107–8, 114
Accuracy, 24, 77–79
Action research (AR), 87, 98–99,
    118–20
ADA (Americans with Disabilities
    Act), 163
Advocacy, 8, 30, 38–39, 56–57, 156,
    176–77, 207–9, 212
Advocacy campaigns, 86
Affordability, 24, 27, 31
Affordable Care Act, 113
Aging and inadequate library
    buildings, 50–52
ALA (American Library
    Association), 20, 22, 32,
    34, 38–40, 45, 48, 58, 117,
    174, 206, 217
Alaska libraries, 85, 88, 90
American public libraries, 52
Archival databases, 159
Archival memory building, 168
Archives
   ethical role, 178
   small rural, 168, 173
Asset-based community
    development (ABCD),
    64–65

approach, 64, 67
connections, 65
descriptions, 67
framework, 63–64
goals, 67
initiatives, 62–69, 80–81, 91–93
literature, 70
paradigm, 65
perspective, 63, 85, 88, 90
research problem/questions,
    63–64
rural public libraries, 68–91
Assets
   cultural, 66
   identifying, 65
   monetary, 68
   potential, 6
   socia, 62, 68, 93
   tangible physical, 68
Assets, 65–68
Assets libraries, 6

Basic technology skills, 43–44
Bookmobiles, 3, 7, 69–70, 72, 75–76,
    181–82, 186–89, 200–201
Broadband
   access, 18–19, 48, 86, 204
   access plans, 17
   adoption, 35, 110, 118, 131
   adoption rate, 27
   availability, 131
   capacity, 43, 110

Printed in the United States
By Bookmasters